ABE QCF Study Manuals

MANAGING PEOPLE

Diploma Level 4
Human Resource Management

In this December 2011 first edition:

- Full and comprehensive coverage of the key topics within the subject

- Activities, examples and quizzes

- Discussion points

- Practical illustrations and case studies

- Index

- Fully up to date as at December 2011

BPP

LEARNING MEDIA

First edition December 2011

Published ISBN 9781 4453 7940 1

British Library Cataloguing-in-Publication Data
A catalogue record for this book is available from the
British Library

Published by
BPP Learning Media Ltd
BPP House, Aldine Place
London W12 8AA

www.bpp.com/learningmedia

Printed in the United Kingdom

Your learning materials, published by BPP Learning
Media Ltd, are printed on paper sourced from
sustainable, managed forests.

We are grateful to the Association of Business
Executives for permission to reproduce the Learning
Outcomes.

Contents

Introduction

Welcome to the first edition of the BPP Learning Media Study Manual for the ABE HRM Level 4 Diploma unit Managing People.

Business qualifications are traditionally very demanding. Students therefore need learning resources which go to the heart of the topics involved, yet are user-friendly and sufficiently interactive to retain the student's attention and interest. This book achieves exactly that.

This book has been specifically designed to cover the syllabus content and learning outcomes issued by the ABE for this unit, and has been reviewed and approved by the ABE.

Features include:

- An introduction to each chapter and a list of specific study objectives
- Concise yet comprehensive coverage of syllabus topics
- Activities and discussion topics to ensure student participation and ensure progress
- Chapter round ups and quizzes to consolidate knowledge

Features in this Study Manual

Definitions of important concepts. You really need to know and understand these before the exam.

Ideas and topics which are designed to be thought-provoking, or possibly controversial. If you are attending a college, you will be able to discuss the topics with your lecturer and classmates. If you are studying alone, you can use the discussion topics as a stimulus for thought and brainstorming of ideas, or raise the issues with a friend or workmate and see what perspective they can add.

Where you may find it helpful or interesting to carry out further research, we include references to websites that you may like to visit.

ACTIVITY

Activities give you a chance to test the knowledge that you have acquired and think more widely around the subject. In some cases suggested answers are supplied, and you should refer to these once you have had a good attempt at the activity. In other cases, the activity involves you considering your own experience, so there may not be a formal answer supplied.

An illustration of a particular technique or concept, generally with a solution or outcome that demonstrates a particular point.

A practical example or illustration, usually involving a real world scenario, intended to stimulate thought.

Chapter Roundup   Reviews the key areas covered in the chapter

Quick Quiz   A set of short, sharp questions testing your knowledge of the topics in the chapter.

Syllabus and Learning outcomes

Learning Outcome 1

The learner will: Understand the fundamental principles of people leadership and management applied by organisations wishing to get the best out of their people.

Assessment criteria	Indicative content	Chapter where covered
The learner can:		
1.1 Explain why, for many organisations, employees are now regarded as added-value 'assets' rather than as mere 'workers'.	1.1.1 The role of people in organisations: as employees, as workers, as contributors. 1.1.2 People as costs **or** as assets, and the implications of the alternative approaches to the management of people.	1
1.2 Justify the benefits of viewing people as positive contributors to high-level corporate purposes.	1.2.1 The components of a 'contributor culture', and its benefits for organisations, for managers, and for employees. 1.2.2 Applications of a 'contributor culture' model to specific corporate scenarios.	1
1.3 Propose people-management and people-leadership practices which promote high levels of employee performance and commitment.	1.3.1 People-management and people-leadership practices which promote high levels of employee performance and commitment.	2

Learning Outcome 2

The learner will: Understand the importance of external environmental and social contingencies as factors which influence the practice of people management and the psychological contract between employer and employee.

Assessment criteria	Indicative content	Chapter where covered
The learner can:		
2.1 Classify the environmental factors that influence organisations both competitively and also so far as their people management practices are concerned.	2.1.1 The external ('PESTLE') factors which impact on organisations and on their approaches to people management.	3
2.2 Identify the significance of major social factors upon the practice of people management.	2.2.1 The significance of major social factors upon the practice of people management, especially such elements as population change, the status of women, issues of ethnicity, and so forth – all understood in relation to their relevance for organisations.	3

Assessment criteria	Indicative content	Chapter where covered
2.3 Describe the evolving development of the 'psychological contract' between employer and employee, with particular reference to trust and the business case for flexible working.	2.3.1 The shift from lifetime employment to personal employability, and the changing nature of the employment/psychological contract between an organisation and its workforce.	3
	2.3.2 The commercial justification for flexible working and the methods through which flexible working can be implemented.	

Learning Outcome 3

The learner will: Understand the changing attitudes and expectations of people in the world of work.

Assessment criteria	Indicative content	Chapter where covered
The learner can:		
3.1 Describe the concept of the 'work ethic' and its relevance in the modern world.	3.1.1 The 'work ethic' and its significance in the modern world of organisations and work.	4
3.2 Outline the major theories of motivation applicable to people at work.	3.2.1 The meaning of 'motivation' when applied to people in organisations.	4
	3.2.2 The major theories of motivation applicable to people at work (especially those developed by McGregor, Maslow, Herzberg, McClelland and Alderfer).	1, 4
	3.2.3 The significance of money and financial reward as a motivator, both in general and also for specific occupational groups.	5, 7
	3.2.4 The concept of job satisfaction and the features of a job which generate intrinsic satisfaction for the job-holder.	5
3.3 Define the change in people's expectations about work, towards a desire for self-development, self-actualisation, self-determination, involvement and participation.	3.3.1 People's evolving expectations about work: desires for self-development, self-actualisation, self-determination, involvement and participation.	5

Learning Outcome 4

The learner will: Understand the changing expectations of employers so far as the attitudes, behaviour and performance of their people are concerned.

Assessment criteria	Indicative content	Chapter where covered
The learner can:		
4.1 Describe the development of employer expectations, from scientific management (Taylorism) through human relations (Mayo) to the age of empowerment, role autonomy, and discretionary behaviour.	4.1.1 Fundamentals of scientific management, human relations theory and modern thinking about the ways to optimise people performance and contribution.	6
4.2 Explain the reasons for these changes in employer expectations.	4.2.1 The factors which promote continuous development in the effective techniques for managing and leading people, including globalisation, the nature of the labour market, customer aspirations, and increased understanding of the employer/employee relationship.	6
4.3 Apply knowledge about changing employer expectations to situational scenarios featuring successful or unsuccessful organisations.	4.3 Applications of learning about changing employer expectations to 'real-world' situational scenarios involving the need for diagnostic skills and the development of defensible recommendations for action.	6

Learning Outcome 5

The learner will: Understand the basic framework ('hygiene') factors and the differentiator ('motivator') factors which structure the performance of people in organisations.

Assessment criteria	Indicative content	Chapter where covered
The learner can:		
5.1 Describe the distinction between the basic framework ('hygiene') factors and the differentiator ('motivator') factors as elements influencing people's attitudes and behaviour at work.	5.1.1 An analytical approach to studying the factors which encourage employee commitment and performance. 5.1.2 How the basic framework and differentiator elements fit together to encourage employee commitment and performance. 5.1.3 Applications of this basic framework and differentiator model in job design, autonomy, empowerment, discretionary behaviour and organisational citizenship.	7, 8
5.2 Explain the components of the basic framework ('hygiene') elements in the people-management equation.	5.2.1 The basic framework ('hygiene') factors explained: financial reward, working conditions, job security, quality of supervision and culture.	5, 7, 8

abe Association of Business Executives

BPP LEARNING MEDIA

Assessment criteria	Indicative content	Chapter where covered
5.3 Explain the components of the differentiator ('motivator') elements in the people-management equation.	5.3.1 The differentiator ('motivator') factors explained: responsibility, recognition, advancement, the work itself, and self-actualisation.	8

Learning Outcome 6

The learner will: Understand the specific role of managerial leadership in organisations as a means of inspiring exceptional levels of achievement.

Assessment criteria	Indicative content	Chapter where covered
The learner can:		
6.1 Outline the requirement in today's organisations for managers to become (and be accepted as) leaders.	6.1.1 The nature of 'leadership' and how it differs from 'management'. 6.1.2 The reasons why, in today's employment scenarios, managers must seek to become (and be perceived as) leaders.	9
6.2 Describe some key models of leadership and leadership styles.	6.2.1 The major analytical models of leadership: • The qualities or traits approach • The functional or group approach • The leadership styles approach • The situational/contingency approach • Transformational leadership • Inspirational leadership	10
6.3 Indicate how levels of 'engagement' in a workforce can be raised, with resultant benefits for both organisations and employees.	6.3.1 The concept of employee 'engagement' and its importance for today's organisations. 6.3.2 The factors that promote high levels of employee engagement.	11

Learning Outcome 7

The learner will: Understand the features of High Performance Working (HPW) organisations and also the principal characteristics of poor-performing organisations.

Assessment criteria	Indicative content	Chapter where covered
The learner can:		
7.1 Describe what is meant by High Performance Working and explain why HPW is an important goal for organisations.	7.1.1 High Performance Working (HPW) defined and explained. 7.1.2 The reasons why HPW practices should be adopted by organisations.	12

Assessment criteria	Indicative content	Chapter where covered
7.2 Describe the crucial components typically found in an HPW enterprise.	7.2.1 The components of HPW, analysed through the practices found in HPW organisations and also through research (Pfeffer, Guest, Johnston and others).	12
7.3 Identify the principal characteristics (and causes) of poor-performing organisations.	7.3.1 Factors associated with poor-performing organisations, and the typical causes for poor performance.	12

Assessment

- Assessment method: written examination (unless otherwise stated).
- Written examinations are of three hours' duration.
- All learning outcomes will be assessed.

Recommended reading

Please refer to the Tuition Resources section of the Members Area of the ABE website (www.abeuk.com) for the recommended reading for this subject.

Chapter 1

Fundamental principles

In this chapter we will introduce some basic ideas about people management and the economic and organisational setting in which it takes place.

First of all we will establish what organisations are and what they are for. Then we will examine some important economic considerations affecting organisations that provide goods and services in return for payment i.e. all organisations other than the simplest common interest groups. The important lesson here is that costs and revenues must be carefully managed, including those relating to the employment of people. People, in fact, are essential for the creation of value but employing them creates cost.

The overall management of the costs and benefits of employing people may be undertaken in a wide range of styles: we will look first at the traditional style of strict control. This has advantages and is still in use in some contexts, but is increasingly being replaced by a more subtle approach that emphasises motivation and empowerment.

We will conclude the chapter with a brief discussion of McGregor's Theory X and Theory Y, which provide a useful summing up of important management attitudes.

1   Some basic assumptions for the 'Managing People' unit

If you have never studied this kind of subject before, it should rapidly become apparent that it is not a subject like Accountancy or Quantitative Methods in Business. These are subjects which have two characteristics that set them apart from Managing People.

(1)   For the most part, financial and quantitative problems have definite and definitive answers which are clearly either 'right' or 'wrong'. There are no half-measures.

(2)   Also for the most part, financial and quantitative problems have the same answers all over the world, because the principles of money management and organisational operations are the same everywhere.

Neither of these assumptions is valid for Managing People. First of all, many of the problems of people management that confront managers every day are problems for which there are no absolute solutions. Much depends on how the problem is perceived (and indeed whether it is perceived to be a problem at all – for example, a given amount of labour turnover can be viewed as a problem which needs to be resolved, or as a matter of indifference, or even as an opportunity because it encourages 'new blood' to come into the business), what 'facts' are considered when evaluating the problem, and the importance attached to each of these 'facts'. As you move into the real world of organisations, you will become aware that different managers can view the world quite differently, and it is this which leads to a good deal of discussion, argument and even bitterness whenever, say, an issue like labour turnover is being investigated. Often, for instance, those managers whose departments suffer a particularly high level of turnover will be defensive about the situation and will be motivated to supply 'reasons' (frequently these are nothing more than excuses) to justify what might otherwise be a criticism of their performance.

Secondly, the 'solutions' applied to issues of managing and leading people are (so far) not the same all over the world. This is because different countries have differing cultural beliefs about the 'proper' approach to people management, and may even entertain different views about the importance of people as contributors to organisational achievement. To take one illustration of these differences and their impact, the labour market in India is quite different from the labour market in the UK. Generally speaking, India has very large numbers of relatively poorly-educated and unskilled people, so Indian employers have had to adapt their manufacturing and service operations to cater for this scenario, whereas the UK (again, generally speaking) has a growing shortage of unskilled people, so its employers have had to resort to other devices to enable them to overcome such shortages, eg by flexible working, the use of immigrants, and automation. I should emphasise here that these comments reflect a very broad overview of the differences between India and the UK, and there are always exceptions, but the differences described here remain valid.

That said, it would be wrong to conclude that because there do not appear to be very many universalistic answers to the issues surrounding people management and leadership, then any answers will be acceptable because they are all as good as any others. The objections to this point of view can be briefly summarised as follows.

(1)   There are some parts of the Managing People syllabus where the relevant knowledge, understanding and practical applications are all very clear-cut and relevant to any part of the world. This applies, for instance, to content about the handling of disciplinary issues and the systematic approach to recruitment and selection.

(2)   The truth (as you shall see when you dig deeper into this Study Manual) is that the best-performing companies and organisations all over the world are those which treat their employees as valuable assets to be nurtured rather than as unpleasant costs which have to be minimised.

(3)   As you will find in a later chapter getting the best out of people requires the creative application of a mix of 'infrastructure' (or 'hygiene') factors and 'differentiators'. Effective people management processes and systems relevant to today's highly competitive world are theoretically available to every employer: so once these processes and systems are established, then theoretically no employer could claim an advantage in the labour market merely by applying these processes and systems, because every other employer would be doing the same. In reality, of course, this never happens – if only because some employers continue to function as if they were managing people 200 years ago, though there are lots of other reasons as well. For a business to get ahead, to attract, retain and motivate people, it must develop some differentiators. These could be based on what Purcell and his colleagues call a 'Big Idea'; they could begin to recruit people on the basis of their attitudes rather than their specific and immediately job-related skills; they could clearly encourage empowerment and discretionary behaviour; they could support self-managed learning and development. In truth, so much research has been conducted about the 'secret' of creating a contributor culture that it is no longer a secret at all: **we now know the difference between those organisations that manage their people systematically and in accordance with the dictates of 'best practice', and those organisations which lead their people inspirationally in line with their view of 'next practice'.**

THE IMPORTANCE OF THE STAPLER

If you're not sure what we mean when we talk about 'infrastructure' and 'differentiator' factors as contributors to the commitment of employees, reflect on the implications of the following story.

When a consultant's research team was investigating staff attitudes and morale at the B&Q store in Huddersfield, Yorkshire, they found that for checkout employees the absence of staplers was a significant factor. To a girl working only 16 hours a week, the absence of a stapler could be a huge source of frustration, because she feels embarrassed when a customer asks to have the credit-card slip stapled to the invoice and she has to say, 'Sorry, actually I can't do it. I don't have a stapler; there is a stapler three checkout counters away, but there are no staples in it.'

So this one little tool – the humble stapler and the even more humble staples – assumes a significance well beyond its actual cost and size, merely because it isn't there. The stapler, then, is an 'infrastructure' or 'hygiene' element in the work environment: if there were a stapler, and it was equipped with staples, then nobody would give it a second thought – but once there is no stapler and no staples (though staples are not much good without a stapler), then the stapler becomes a magnificent symbol and the embodiment of managerial failure.

For these reasons, the approach to Managing People reflected in this Study Manual is one in which people working for organisations are viewed as follows:

* As human beings who deserve to be treated with dignity, consideration and sensitivity from the moment they first apply for a job to the moment when they finally leave the organisation.

* As actual or potential sources of 'added value' for their employers [see Section 7 for an explanation about what it means to add value].

* As individuals with capabilities that can be developed and utilised for the benefit of the business.

* As employees who have a right to derive satisfaction from their work and rewards commensurate with their contributions.

Moreover, this Study Manual does not set out to be an academically detached review of the strategies, processes and practices associated with people management and leadership. The ABE is a professional body, not a university, and its graduates will conventionally enter managerial and professional careers, which means that they want to know 'how to' manage and lead people to achieve optimal results: they seek practical advice and help, not merely a disinterested analysis of the methods which companies and organisations can use when mobilising the talents of their employees. They want to know about 'next practice' and 'good practice', not just about 'best practice', which is often nothing more than a euphemism to describe the methods used by the majority of employers, whether they actually work or not. ABE students, as prospective practitioners of people management and leadership, want to know about employee 'engagement' and High Performance Working and about the techniques like empowerment which help to transform the attitudes and behaviour of people in organisations beyond the merely instrumental – beyond, in other words, the belief that work is merely an unpleasant necessity undertaken for purely monetary reasons, and instead the recognition that work, properly designed, and people, properly led, can be sources of both personal achievement and also competitive advantage.

With all the above in mind, let us start.

2   People in organisations

Organisations exist in order to achieve results that individuals cannot achieve by themselves. They enable people to be more **productive**.

(a)   They overcome **individual limitations**, whether physical or intellectual.

(b)   They enable people to pool their **expertise** and to **specialise** in what they do best.

(c)   They **save time**, because people can work together or do two different aspects of a task at the same time.

(d)   They **accumulate and share knowledge**.

Organisations are, in essence, groups of people working together for a common purpose. Other resources such as finance and equipment of various kinds will also be necessary, but the basic nature of an organisation is that it contains a group of people. Similarly, many aspects of management must be undertaken in organisations, but the various activities we call human resource management (HRM) might be considered to be the most fundamental, since they bring the people concerned together and sustain them.

3   People, costs and revenues

As we have said, organisations are groups of people and, apart from those that have neither costs nor revenues, they are economic entities. It is inevitable, therefore, that the **costs and benefits of employing people** will be carefully examined by the senior management of any organisation: the organisation cannot exist without people, but they have to be paid and administered and taxes on employment, such as the UK's National Insurance employer's contribution, have to be paid. It is therefore vital that the human resource is managed in a way that will ensure a favourable balance between costs and benefits.

3.1   Manufacturing industry

One approach to achieving this emphasises **control of costs** and consists, essentially, of keeping pay as low as possible while controlling work force output at a standard level. This approach was widely used in many of the larger industries in the developed world and was normal in manufacturing.

(a)   Industrial engineering techniques such as time study and motion study were used to define **work practices** and required **output levels**.

(b)   Complex **piecework** schemes were used, partly to ensure that labour cost was related to output.

(c)   Wage rates were set by an **adversarial process** of collective bargaining, with the sanctions of strike or lockout held in reserve as final coercive arguments.

It was possible for good will, and a degree of trust and co-operation to exist under this system, particularly among skilled workers, but its basic premise was based on engineering efficiency: labour was seen as an **expensive resource** to be used for specific, well defined applications and in the smallest quantities that could be contrived. The success of the organisation depended on meeting strict specifications for cost, volume, quality, delivery and so on, all of which were decided in advance by a system of expert planning. Organisations that used this approach were typically based on a **pyramidal hierarchy** of command positions with the heaviest applications of control and cost pressure applied to people at the lower levels. Workers were employed on the basis that they would do as they were told.

The effect of this kind of management strategy on most of the people concerned was, typically, a reluctant acquiescence, a lack of interest in the work and an expectation of regular increases in pay.

> http://www.thestar.com/business/article/224917--auto-giants-seek-labour-cost-cuts
> accessed 15 May 2011

3.2 Service industries

So far we have only discussed the manufacturing industry. In fact, the general approach of cost control has been widely used in **service industries**. Many such industries depend on the efficient processing of information rather than physical material, but the basic elements of careful planning and control of standardised work are very similar. Good examples are the retail banking and insurance industries, where very large numbers of transactions of many kinds must be processed rapidly and accurately. Such work is easily analysed and improved by techniques similar to those used in factories.

Before the widespread adoption of sophisticated information technology (IT) systems, all of this processing was done manually; speed and precision were promoted by the use of **work procedures** entirely analogous to the manufacturing system outlined above. People formed the elements of a carefully designed system that was specified in detail in documents such as job descriptions, procedures manuals and quality standards.

From the point of view of people management, the main difference from manufacturing was that the relationship between management and worker was less adversarial because the work force had a different self-image: staff were usually paid at a weekly or monthly rate rather than by piecework; the work was clean and demanded intellectual rather than manual skills; and office jobs were generally perceived as being more secure than those on the shop floor.

Burns and Stalker (1961) called this approach a **mechanistic** system of management and described its characteristics in detail. Here is a summary.

Mechanistic organisations

- Tasks are specialised and broken down into subtasks.
- There are precise job descriptions and delineations of responsibility.
- People are concerned with task efficiency rather than overall organisational effectiveness.
- Knowledge of the organisation's procedures is more highly valued than wider business knowledge.
- There is a hierarchic structure of control, with insistence on loyalty to the concern and obedience to superiors.
- Operations and working behaviour are governed by instructions issued by superiors.
- Decisions are taken at the top, where knowledge is supposed to reside.
- Managers are responsible for co-ordinating tasks.
- Interaction is mainly vertical, up and down the hierarchy and takes the form of commands and reports.

4   A more positive view

4.1   A note of caution

The cost control approach to labour is still in use where procedural accuracy is very important and in parts of the developing world where competitive advantage consists mostly of low manufacturing cost. Also, the basic principle that revenues must exceed costs in the long run applies to all organisations: even where a very different approach to the work force is used, **costs must still be controlled**.

4.2   A different approach

Much manufacturing employment has disappeared from the developed world as a result of automation and the expansion of low-cost manufacturing in developing countries. Similarly, much of the work that was typically done under mechanistic systems is now done by advanced IT systems, while improved communications make it possible for quite complex but essentially routine work that requires human input, such as typesetting and call-centre operations, to be contracted out to lower-cost countries.

Employment in the developed world has shifted to the provision of **more complex services**, frequently involving requirements to solve problems. At the same time, advanced IT systems have replaced much of the information filtering, distribution and reporting work of middle management, allowing cost savings in management salaries to be achieved through the process of **delayering**. These developments have been accompanied by an accelerating pace of **change** and increasing **uncertainty** about the business environment. Commercial organisations in particular have had to become more agile and creative in their strategic responses, while continuing to operate efficiently.

The result of these developments has been the emergence of a different kind of service worker and a different kind of management. In business, the struggle for **competitive advantage** has accelerated and intensified. Businesses have emphasised customer service, innovation, high quality, attractive brand values and improved efficiency of processes.

The emphasis in people management has been on the nurturing of a motivated, empowered workforce that is capable of working largely unsupervised in order to achieve high levels of customer service. This has been referred to as a 'contributor culture', which is to say, a managerial culture that views employees a not as commodities to be used, but as important contributors to organisational success. Managers are much fewer in number and their role is to coach rather than to supervise in detail. The importance of innovation in a rapidly developing world has led to the encouragement of suggestions for improvement from the workforce, recognising their intimate familiarity with how work is currently done.

4.3   Motivating staff = Added value = Motivated staff: The Virtuous Circle

In 2002 the Talent Foundation published a report, *Seven Factors for Business Success*, based on a survey of almost 400 companies. This research gives a striking picture of how top performers – those that have been growing, developing and increasing their performance over the previous five years – motivate their people and how this impacts on their sustained success. In essence, the study found that top-performing companies employ two main strategies to motivate their employees at an individual level:

(1)   **Individual employees are valued as contributors and not as mere commodities.** For example, in a top-performing company managers are 70% more likely to take an individual's preferences into account when assigning work and jobs. In these organisations, managers try to fit the job to the employee rather than the employee to the job. Employees recognise and respond to this.

abe Association of Business Executives

(2)   **Top performers are quick to recognise individual and team contributions with immediate and personal thanks. They** are 30% more likely to do so than poor performing organisations, i.e., companies that have failed to grow or gone out of business altogether. At the same time, top performing organisations are much less likely to dismiss hard work as 'just part of the job'.

Staff treated as individuals will feel valued and therefore motivated. They know that when they put in time and effort their contributions will be noticed and appreciated. Thus the Talent Foundation research also showed up significantly higher levels of staff loyalty and fulfilment within top performing firms.

A motivational attitude to employees helps to create other factors in a business's performance, which in turn motivates its employees even more because they can feel pride in belonging to a successful organisation. It is then much more likely that these employees will recommend their organisation as an employer to their friends, relatives and others seeking employment; they will also recommend the organisation as a supplier of goods and services. At Tesco, for instance, nearly 90 per cent of Tesco workers speak well of the company as a source of employment and as a company worth trading with. In this way the company benefits from the effects of a virtuous circle: motivating staff leads to improved results and reputation which in turn leads to motivated staff. And so it goes on.

Good motivators are good knowledge managers. This is because organisations that are good at motivating also tend to have strong workplace relationships. As a result they make more use of informal meetings to share information and encourage creative ideas. They also make sure that IT systems play a supporting rather than a dominating role, which may not sound like a major point but in reality is very important in making employees feel as if they truly matter: nothing is more demoralising for employees to believe that they are slaves to an impersonal IT-based method of working.

As implied in the previous paragraph, top performing businesses are particularly good at harvesting creativity and turning it into sustained business success, and they always find it substantially quicker and easier to reinvent themselves when they have to do so because of some competitor's invasion. Interestingly, these top performing businesses tend to find inspiration from their own people – the people who know their business best – whereas low performing companies make much more use of external consultants. When the time is right for change, top-performing organisations are already primed. They are 50% more likely to have a flexible organisational structure in place and 70% more likely to have a change-friendly culture of continuous improvement.

The importance of leadership in top-performing companies cannot be overstated. In such firms, leaders strive to cultivate relationships with their peers; they don't believe in a 'them and us' mentality; they walk the floor, talk with staff at all levels and listen. Leaders in top-performing companies are 70% more likely to allow ambiguity, 50% more likely to allow mistakes (and thus encourage risk-taking), and 30% more likely to listen before responding. Overall, therefore, these leaders are much more likely to show faith and trust in their staff than their peers in low-performing firms.

For those concerned that the Talent Foundation's research might have been biased in any way, it's worth noting that similar results have been produced by other studies. The Best Companies organisation, for example, has found that companies which look after their staff on average out-perform the stock market by two or three times: there is thus no moral dilemma in either choosing to make money or look after people.

4.4   Burns and Stalker again

The approach described above is not new. Burns and Stalker (1961) described a similar organisational philosophy that they named **organismic** (this term has now largely been replaced by the simpler and more familiar word 'organic'). Many of the characteristics they identified are typical of modern practice, despite having been first described over half a century ago.

Organic organisations

- Communication consists of information and advice rather than instructions and decisions.

- Interaction is as much lateral as vertical and communication between people of different rank represents consultation, rather than command.

- Job performance and conduct derive from commitment to the organisation and to colleagues.

- Job descriptions are less precise: it is harder to 'pass the buck'.

- Each task is understood to relate to the total situation of the firm: people are concerned more with organisational effectiveness than with obeying the rules.

- Each task is adjusted and redefined through interaction with others.

- Relevant technical and commercial knowledge is utilised wherever it is found; it can be located anywhere, not just among senior management.

- Commitment to the concern's task is more highly valued than loyalty as such.

ACTIVITY 2   10 mins

Once again, think about organisations you are familiar with. Do you recognise any of the characteristics listed above? Have you ever seen characteristics such as these in the same organisation as more mechanistic characteristics of the type discussed earlier?

5 Theory X and Theory Y

Much of this chapter has been taken up with explaining two contrasting organisational approaches to the management of people. These approaches have co-existed for many years: in their study, Burns and Stalker observed mechanistic and organic organisations operating at the same time and in the same regional economy (Scotland). There has been something of a movement away from one and towards the other in recent decades, but this change has not been universal: as we have pointed out, the more rigid approach is still in use in some organisations today.

Our discussion has been largely in terms of organisational characteristics, such as reward systems and management structures. A slightly different analysis of the same overall phenomena in terms of management attitudes was presented by Douglas McGregor. He suggested (McGregor, 1960) that managers in the USA tended to behave as though they subscribed to one of **two sets of assumptions about people** at work: Theory X and Theory Y.

(a)   **Theory X** suggests that most people dislike work and responsibility and will avoid both if possible. Because of this, most people must be coerced, controlled, directed and threatened with punishment to get them to make an adequate effort. Managers who operate according to these assumptions will tend to supervise closely, apply detailed rules and controls, and use 'carrot and stick' motivators.

(b)   **Theory Y** suggests that physical and mental effort in work is as natural as play or rest. The ordinary person does not inherently dislike work: according to the conditions it may be a source of satisfaction or dissatisfaction. The potentialities of the average person are rarely fully used at work. People can be motivated to seek challenge and responsibility in the job, if their goals can be integrated with those of the organisation. A manager with this sort of attitude to his staff is likely to be a consultative, facilitating leader, using positive feedback, challenge and responsibility as motivators.

Each theory is intended to illustrate an extreme case rather than describing actual groups of managers. It is important for you to understand that **McGregor never said there were 'Theory X people' or 'Theory Y people': his argument is that 'Theory X' describes a set of managerial assumptions about people at work. If managers then manage in accordance with these assumptions, then indeed many workers will act in ways which encapsulate these 'Theory X' beliefs – and managers will say, 'we told you so', little realising that it is their actions which have caused such behaviour.**

Theory X and Theory Y have been very influential in management training over the years, though McGregor himself never intended that they should be regarded as illustrating desirable and undesirable management practice. As you will see when we consider motivation and leadership, there is no simple theory of management style that works in all circumstances.

'THE WORST CAR FACTORY IN THE WORLD'

On 31 March 2001, The Economist published an article about Halewood, the Ford car factory on Merseyside, near Liverpool. What follows is adapted from that article.

In the 1970s, the Halewood factory epitomised the ills of manufacturing in Britain at that time. The quality of the cars made there was poor, the workers were rebellious and the place was a battleground for class warfare. So bad was the factory's reputation and performance that Ford was planning to close it, and was only persuaded to try a different approach after being given £40m of government aid.

In the 1970s, the aisles at Halewood were narrow and crowded; visitors tripped over piles of carelessly stacked components and bits of rusty metal. Managers used to hide in their offices poring over printouts and emerge on the factory floor only to shout at workers to get them to do their job better and faster, or even to do it at all, since work tended to interfere with smoking, sleeping, betting or discussing football. It was not quite as bad as the Fiat factory in Turin, where they actually had brothels in the plant, but it was very bad indeed.

Today everything is different. The walls of the refreshment and meeting rooms are festooned with charts detailing progress on everything from quality to production volumes. Line workers, grouped in small teams, begin the day with briefing meetings and work according to a meticulous manual showing how to do each job with minimal effort.

But the biggest difference is the people. To change the culture, the then factory director drew up what he called the 'Halewood Charter', a kind of psychological contract promising that management would treat the workers with respect and making it clear that in return workers should co-operate with management to make good cars. Each employee had to sign an individual contract detailing the new philosophy and way of working. Some 600 out of 3000 Ford workers refused to go along with this. They left, making the job of transforming the company easier. Jaguar has subsequently recruited hundreds of local, mainly young employees, and under the ownership of the Indian company Tata has brought about a massive shift in values, attitudes and behaviours.

6   Yesterday's organisations and the transition to today

What follows is a list of the typical features for organisations of the past. Of course, they never applied to every organisation, and it would be foolish to argue that none of these features is present in the organisations of today, but by and large these characteristics have been replaced by cultures that are more forward-looking, more customer-focused and more entrepreneurial.

6.1 The organisations of the past

Yesterday's organisations were characterised by:

- A belief that there are universal laws of management and business – generally expressed through the so-called 'principles' of management (Planning, Organising, Controlling, Directing, Co-ordinating, Reporting and Budgeting). Note the absence of any reference to leadership and people skills.

- A command-and-control, hierarchical system of managing. Though such organisations could be concerned about the welfare of their workforces, such concerns would typically be paternalistic and would not extend to genuine participation.

- Disciplines (for work organisation and employee supervision) that were management-imposed, management-run and management-monitored.

- Reactive, mechanistic problem-solving. Problems would be addressed as they emerged, but seldom would potential problems be tackled proactively.

- Single-function specialisms operating mainly in self-contained and independent silos. Note the absence of any reference to team working.

- A culture of individualism reflected principally in the design of the reward systems. It was generally assumed that employees were self-centred and, if anything, were in competition with each other.

- Task-based job descriptions. Employees were thought to be 'good' workers if they fulfilled all the elements of their job descriptions; there was no question of people exceeding their authority or using their initiative: any attempts along these lines would often lead to severe reprimands or even dismissal.

- Rigid adherence to procedures, 'rules and regulations', and a bureaucratic culture. The organisations of the past had many hierarchical levels, so each level was tightly constrained in terms of the decisions they were permitted to take.

- A relative lack of competitive pressure – sometimes no competitive pressure at all. The world of the past contained many monopolies or quasi-monopolies which did not particularly need to be customer-centric because in effect their customers had no choice. This was an economic system dominated by large-scale, traditional organisations that were more concerned with surviving in parallel with their competitors than with competition itself.

- All of these factors combined to produce a context in which the quality of goods and services was always problematic – so organisations spent a good deal of time, money and people resources on dealing with customer complaints.

- A broad mass of consumers (or customers) who tolerated this state of affairs, if only because there were no obvious alternatives. In the UK, anyone of modest means purchasing a car had to approach one of a limited number of (largely) UK manufacturers, all with questionable reputations for product reliability. Anyone wanting a telephone had to become one of the Post Office's 'subscribers' (the term 'customer' was not yet in use) and wait quietly until it was seen fit to complete the installation.

6.2 What has changed?

In brief, most of us now live in a world which (whether we like it or not) displays these priorities:

- New channels of communication – principally the media and the Internet, available worldwide to populations with much increased levels of literacy. For the first time, it is now possible for customers to purchase products and services from a worldwide framework of suppliers, and it is equally possible for customers to switch their loyalties from one supplier to another at the 'click of a mouse'.

- A significant shift of power in favour of customers and consumers – as customers and consumers become more aware of the quality of products and services in other parts of the world, and so become more demanding and aspirational themselves.

- Globalisation, global competition and privatisation – creating opportunities for previously tied customers to switch suppliers, therefore causing service levels to improve and prices to fall. In the UK, for example, globalisation has led to the virtual disappearance of the UK car manufacturing industry and its replacement by foreign companies (Toyota, Honda and Nissan).

- An increasing level of incremental development and transformational, disruptive change, especially resulting from technological innovation – making some organisations and products obsolete virtually overnight.

- Enterprises which now extend themselves in every direction – like Tesco, available everywhere and expanding its operations into car sales, legal services and medicine.

- A requirement for people to 'add value' rather than simply perform tasks – symbolised through a move to 'discretionary behaviour' and 'organizational citizenship'.

- Recognition that knowledge is a strategic asset – especially for organisations that depend on the advancement of knowledge for their competitive strength.

- From the 1980s onwards there has been a major ideological shift towards privatisation, one argument being that in pursuit of profit, organisations would have to become more customer-focused. Also, the loosening of anti-competitive controls has allowed ambitious new entrants to appear in many marketplaces.

6.3 The demand for new companies

All of these developments (and the list above is not exhaustive) create opportunities for

- Companies that can act quickly
- Companies with slim overheads
- Companies that can move responsibilities closer to the customer
- Companies that can manage change
- Companies that can do more with less

FIRST DIRECT – AN ORGANISATION DRIVEN BY CUSTOMERS

First Direct is a telephone and Internet bank which has only been operational since 1994 but which has established an enviable reputation as a 'world-class' company whose ability to differentiate itself has been helped by the bureaucratic inertia of its large-company competitors. The bank is run from two call (contact) centres which receive about 12 million inbound telephone and Internet calls each year; it is proud to claim a round-the-clock availability of customer-service representatives, even on Christmas Day (some customers even make phone calls to First Direct on 25 December principally to enable them to test the company's promises and not really because they want a loan or an up-to-date statement).

Most inbound telephone calls are dealt with by the member of staff that receives them, and a hand-off to colleagues is only allowed in circumstances where the nature of the query justifies the involvement of specialist employees who deal with more complicated issues like debt counselling and matrimonial conflict. It is First Direct's philosophy that customers should be dealt with by human beings, and so it has set its face against introducing any form of Interactive Voice Response (IVR) system.

When recruiting employees, a good telephone manner is a key capability, but successful candidates still undergo five weeks' intensive training focused on the First Direct culture and values, product knowledge, and competent understanding of the bank's systems. What is particularly interesting is that First Direct generally refuses to accept job applications from anyone who has previously worked in a bank – because the company does not want staff who have been conditioned to accept the methods of working associated with very large financial institutions.

First Direct's workforce enjoy high-quality amenities, including a restaurant and a well-organised nursery for the employees' young children. Great efforts are made to retain high-performing staff, and the management style is predominantly focused on encouragement, praise, recognition and 'engagement'.

For a variety of reasons, First Direct has been phenomenally successful, and how has a base of well over a million accounts, and it regularly leads the industry in terms of customer satisfaction. First Direct seldom undertakes any advertising, and much of its new business comes from recommendations made by existing customers to their friends, colleagues and relatives.

6.4   'Contributor Culture' businesses

And in turn this has led to the emergence of more organisations with what we can call a 'Contributor Culture' in which every employee is valued as a potential contributor to the organisation's overall success, progress and performance. These 'Contributor Culture' businesses typically exhibit the following features:

- A unifying 'big idea' or organisational mission.

- A range of core values that are embedded throughout the company.

- Top-down role modelling and leadership by example.

- The replacement of task-based job descriptions by output-based accountability profiles.

- The replacement of person specifications by an organisation-wide competency framework.

- Constant concern for employees – their welfare, their job satisfaction, their work-life balance, their well-being.

- Recognition that people work for managers, not for the organisation. As Marcus Buckingham and Curt Coffman say, 'The main determinant of an effective employer is not its reward structure, pension scheme or working conditions: it is the quality of people's individual relationships with their line managers.' (Buckingham and Coffman, 1991)

- Recruitment and selection based on psychological fit, not just technical skill.

- Measures of organisational success that rely heavily on what customers value.

- Synergy between systems, rewards and leadership.

- Constant restlessness and dissatisfaction, featuring the questions 'Why do we ...?' and 'Why don't we ...?'

- Facing outwards – learning from the best, copying with pride, inventing ahead of customer needs.

- Reward, recognition, celebration – management by appreciation.

- People are free to scare themselves – a belief in empowerment and 'discretionary behaviour'.

- A culture of continuous improvement and transformational change.

6.5 The importance of 'employability'

As an example of this new kind of regime in action, read the following message which has been taken from a document issued to every employee in the Philips Electronics company several years ago. This document made it quite clear that the old idea of a 'job for life' had now disappeared, as you can see:

- You are not guaranteed life-long, and perhaps not even long-term employment.

- If the business is at risk, you are at risk.

- If you are not improving, you are at risk.

- You must add value to the business and to those with whom you work – your value must exceed your cost.

- Keep yourself employable ...

7 What does it mean to 'add value'?

You may have noticed that there's now a lot of talk in the management literature about 'adding value', and this has largely replaced the previous view that all employees had to do was fulfil the duties outlined in their job descriptions. A much more popular school of thought nowadays believes (as in the example from Philips Electronics) that as an employee you are a 'cost' to the business, but your employment is justified if the 'value' you supply exceeds your 'cost'. [You should remember that the 'cost' of an employee doesn't just mean the employee's wages or salary, but also embraces all the relevant overheads, like the cost of machinery, equipment, parking spaces, and so on.]

A simple way of understanding the concept of 'added value' when applied to people in the organisation is to recognise that everyone's job involves four different dimensions – and only two of these 'add value'.

Dimension 1: 'MAINTENANCE'

Crudely put, 'maintenance' means 'keeping the show on the road' – in other words, ensuring that the situation at the end of the working day is no worse than it was at the outset. If you work in a fast-food outlet, 'maintenance' means serving customers with burgers and other food items all day long.

Dimension 2: 'CRISIS PREVENTION'

'Crisis prevention' means making sure that things don't go wrong, or that if they do then the situation can be contained. In the fast-food outlet 'crisis prevention' covers the handling of customer complaints, offering refunds and restitution as part of a customer service recovery exercise. It may also mean re-adjusting machinery so that a production problem is solved.

Contrary to popular belief, 'crisis prevention' does not add value because it simply restores the process to a position of functional efficiency.

Dimension 3: 'CONTINUOUS IMPROVEMENT'

'Continuous improvement' means performing current tasks better (to a higher standard of quality), faster (within quicker response times) or cheaper (at lower cost), preferably in ways which are important to customers. 'Continuous improvement' is where people begin to add value.

Thus the team leaders in the customer service department at Prudential Assurance expect their employees to ask this question of themselves at the end of their shifts: 'What have you done today to make a difference?'

Dimension 4: 'CHANGE MANAGEMENT'

Employees who can propose, persuade and implement change are 'adding value' all the time. 'Change management' does not simply refer to large-scale changes; it can also mean tiny innovations like the removal of an unnecessary column in a page of cost calculations.

And let us be clear: it is within the scope of every employee to manage change. As John Seddon, a well-known management consultant and business guru, has written: 'People need to think: WHY DO I DO THIS or HOW COULD WE DO THIS DIFFERENTLY OR BETTER? People need to be unreasonable. They need to question the assumptions that govern today's practices. It is not just the leader's job to think unreasonably.'

INTRODUCING A 'THINKING PERFORMER' CULTURE AT ZURICH FINANCIAL SERVICES

The world of financial services is highly unpredictable and competitive. Zurich Financial Services, like others in its sectors (and most businesses in every sector) must move with agility. It must respond to rapidly-changing customer needs and provide what they want before competitors do. Staff have to be able to make decisions without reporting up through a traditional command-and-control structure.

Not long ago, Zurich employees had to wait to be told what to do. And when they finished one task they had to wait again. In some way this system resembled the way the US Army used to operate, because as recently as the Vietnam war, every rank-and-file soldier had to get permission to fire his weapon. By contrast, when US troops went to Bosnia as part of a peace-keeping force, the rules of engagement specified that if any soldier felt threatened, he or she could use deadly force immediately and without reference to higher authority – because the US Army can now rely on that person thinking about the problem in the same way as the people in the Pentagon. In other words, the people closest to the front line could be trusted to make their own decisions.

None of this is rocket science – but for some organisations it is a philosophy for people performance which remains a long way off.

BUILDING A CULTURE OF COLLABORATION

Building collaborative enterprises can bring real rewards. A collaborative business is one in which people are encouraged to apply their talents continually to group projects and to become motivated by a collective mission rather than just be personal gain or the intrinsic pleasures of autonomous creativity.

Collaboration is the future model for organisations, especially for knowledge-intensive work, and there are four keys to creating a culture of trust and teamwork – what is, in effect, a 'contributor culture'.

(1)   **'Shared purpose'.** This defines how the organisation can position itself in relation to its competitors and helps employees to drive their unique contributions. Like the notion of the 'Big Idea' (of which we shall hear more), the shared purpose describes what everyone in the organisation is trying to do.

(2)   **'Ethic of contribution'.** People look beyond their own specific roles, tasks and accountabilities in order to make a difference ('add value') and advance the shared purpose. This has a collective focus, based on the needs of the business, its strategic direction, the aspirations of its employees and the needs of its customers.

(3)   **'Processes that allow people to work flexibly with discipline'.** Unless people have their contributions linked together, collaboration will fail. Infrastructures that prevent collaboration between business units, or allow differing structures for rewarding output, are examples. The business has to be properly aligned both vertically (the co-ordination of traditional bureaucracies) and horizontally (so that differing functions are united by the same priorities and values). Interdependent process management is crucial so that the processes used in one department (say, Production) are readily consistent with the processes used in another (say, HR).

(4)   **'Creating a collaborative infrastructure'.** The watchword here is 'participative centralisation', a framework in which collaboration is valued and rewarded, whereas a 'silo mentality ' (i.e., a pattern in which parts of the organisation operate as self-contained 'empires') is punished.

[Source: Paul Adler et al, 'Building a collaborative enterprise', *Harvard Business Review*, July-August 2011]

Chapter Roundup

↳ Problems in managing people rarely have easily defined correct answers and effective solutions may vary in different parts of the world.

↳ The best-performing companies and organisations all over the world are those which treat their employees as valuable assets to be nurtured rather than as unpleasant costs which have to be minimised.

↳ Getting the best out of people requires the creative application of a mix of 'infrastructure' (or 'hygiene') factors and 'differentiators'.

↳ **Organisations** exist to achieve results that individuals cannot achieve by themselves. They enable people to be more productive.

↳ All organisations must strike a balance between **costs** and **revenues**.

↳ Commercial organisations must incur cost in order to create the value that their customers want and are prepared to pay for but the costs and benefits involved must be properly managed. This includes those relating to the employment of people.

↳ This can be achieved in manufacturing by strict control of pay and work practices using a command-oriented pyramidal hierarchy. This approach produces alienation in the workforce, whose motivation is related only to pay. A similar approach in service industries, with emphasis on procedure and control leads to a **mechanistic** organisation.

↳ Such methods are still in use where routine and procedure are important, but a different approach has been developed in the developed world. This has been a response to increasing uncertainty and accelerating change in the business environment; and increased emphasis on innovation, customer service, brand values, quality and process efficiency in order to create competitive advantage. This approach promotes motivation, empowerment and initiative, all of which are important aspects of the **organismic** (or organic) organisation.

↳ Douglas McGregor suggested that managers in the USA tended to behave as though they held one of two alternative sets of assumptions about people at work. **Theory X** managers believe that most people dislike work and responsibility and will avoid both if possible. Because of this, most people must be coerced and controlled to get them to make an adequate effort.

↳ **Theory Y** managers believe that work is as natural as play or rest; according to the conditions it may be a source of satisfaction or dissatisfaction. People can be motivated to seek challenge and responsibility in the job, if their goals can be integrated with those of the organisation.

↳ **Yesterday's organisations** display characteristics such as robust hierarchy, reactive problem-solving, adherence to procedures and market power. **Contributor culture organisations** getting the best out of people requires a the creative application of a mix of 'infrastructure' (or 'hygiene') factors and 'differentiators', by contrast, display leadership by example, an organisation-wide competency framework, constant concern for employees, concern for customer satisfaction and continuous improvement.

Quick Quiz

1   Why do organisations exist?

2   How are industrial engineering techniques such as time study and motion study used?

3   How is work organised in a mechanistic organisation?

4   How are rules regarded in an organic organisation?.

5   What is meant when we say that an employee has an instrumental attitude to work?

6   What were the two sets of assumptions described by McGregor?

Answers to Quick Quiz

1   Organisations exist in order to achieve results that individuals cannot achieve by themselves. They enable people to be more **productive**.

2   To define work practices and required output levels.

3   By means of rules, decisions and instructions passed down a hierarchy of control.

4   As subordinate to the need to achieve organisational effectiveness

5   Work is seen exclusively as a means of obtaining income; no other satisfaction exists.

6   Theory X, which says that most people dislike work and responsibility and will avoid both if possible, and Theory Y, which says that physical and mental effort in work is as natural as play or rest.

Answers to Activities

Activities 1 and 2

Activities 1 and 2 both require your own reflections on your experience and your answers will thus be unique to yourself. However, it is worth remarking in connection with the second part of Activity 2 that it is not unusual to encounter organisations that display both mechanistic and organic features. Burns and Stalker's research did not discover two clearly defined categories of organisation, merely a tendency for organisations to display one group of categories or the other. It is entirely possible that environmental conditions or merely a process of slow change might lead an organisation to display characteristics from both groups.

Chapter 2

Performance and commitment

This chapter is intended to provide a very brief introduction to the kind of modern management practices that support the view of people as a source of competitive advantage. The emphasis is away from control and towards support, and commitment.

1   Background considerations

Throughout the 20th century, new models and theories of **organisation and management** emerged to reflect the accelerating pace of change in the business environment; the diversity and expectations of workers and consumers; and the increasing understanding of the behaviour of people at work. The commitment, involvement and flexibility of the workforce were increasingly recognised as a key to organisational survival.

In the **social environment**, advances in education, technological skills and general affluence had raised employees' expectations of the quality of working life and awareness of their rights within the employment relationship. The need to compete in innovative, technology-based and quality-sensitive markets put a premium on skilled **knowledge workers**, altering the balance of power in the employment relationship. Coercive and controlling approaches to management are less usual (other than in very stable markets and/or areas of high unemployment): employees expect to have access to influence, responsibility and information related to their work. There has been a shift from **compliance** to **commitment** as the core of the employment relationship.

Politically, the UK government of the 1980s encouraged a shift away from trade union power, instead emphasising entrepreneurialism, individualism and a philosophy that management and employees shared a common interest in the success of the enterprise. It seemed possible that industrial conflict could be pre-empted – and ultimately replaced – by pro-active, people-focused personnel strategies such as participation and information-sharing and empowerment.

TAKING FLEXIBILITY TO THE CUSTOMER

Solaglas is a UK subsidiary of French multinational glassmaker Saint-Gobain employing glaziers and installation workers. Its 'Moving Forward' agreement on annualised hours with the GMB and AEEU is designed to focus its business on customer service, through flexibility in working hours. Features of the agreement include: single-status employment; annual salaries; flexible start times (between 7 am and 11 am, Monday to Saturday); and computerised working for home-based glaziers using palm-tops for job allocation, progress reports and factory contact.

The benefits for the company are increased productivity, a single pay scheme, flexibility, profitability and significant reinvestment by the French parent company. Benefits for staff include enhanced terms and conditions, permanent status and greater choice in working time (of particular benefit for two men who were caring for wives with long-term illnesses). The work is also carried out at the customer's convenience.

(Bond, 2003)

2   Empowerment and excellence

Empowerment means making workers (and particularly work teams) responsible for achieving, and even setting, work targets, with the freedom to make decisions about how they are to be achieved.

Empowerment goes in hand in hand with:

(a)   **Delayering** or a cut in the number of levels (and managers) in the chain of command, since responsibility previously held by middle managers is, in effect, being given to operational workers.

(b)   Flexibility, since giving responsibility to the people closest to the products and customers encourages responsiveness – and cutting out layers of communication, decision-making and reporting speeds up the process.

(c)   New technology, since there are more 'knowledge workers'. Such people need less supervision, being better able to identify and control the means to clearly understood ends. Better information systems also remove the mystique and power of managers as possessors of knowledge and information in the organisation.

The main reason for empowerment is the people lower down the organisation possess the knowledge of what is going wrong with a process but lack the authority to make changes. Those further up the structure have the authority to make changes, but lack the profound knowledge required to identify the right solutions. The only solution is to change the culture of the organisation so that everyone can become involved in the process of improvement and work together to make the changes.

SUCCESS OF EMPOWERMENT

The validity of this view and its relevance to modern trends appears to be borne out by the approach to empowerment adopted by *Harvester Restaurants*, as described in *People Management*. *Harvester Restaurants* is a long-established, medium-sized chain of restaurants serving traditional food in the UK. The management structure for each restaurant comprises a branch manager and a 'coach', while everyone else is a team member. Everyone within a team has one or more 'accountabilities' (these include recruitment, drawing up rotas, keeping track of sales targets and so on) which are shared out by the team members at their weekly team meetings. All the team members at different times act as 'coordinator' to the person responsible for taking the snap decisions that are frequently necessary in a busy restaurant. Apparently all of the staff involved agree that empowerment has made their jobs more interesting and has hugely increased their motivation and sense of involvement.

Unfortunately, programmes of strategic change introducing these features are usually perceived merely as exercises in cutting costs by reducing staff numbers.

Meanwhile, the popularity of the American anecdotal literature focusing on 'excellence' (for example, *In Search of Excellence* by Peters and Waterman) associated the success of high-performing companies with enlightened, people-focused management practices e.g. 'All the **value** of this company is in its people. If you burnt down all of our plants and we just kept our people and information files, we would soon be as strong as ever. Take away our people and we might never recover.' (Tom Watson, former president of IBM, quoted in Peters and Waterman, 2004)

This represented a conceptual shift away from regarding employees as a cost to be managed and controlled, and towards regarding them as an **asset** (or 'human capital') to be nurtured and developed. A former IBM President, Barry Curnow, further noted in the late 1990s that:

'We've moved through periods when money has been in short supply and when technology has been in short supply. Now it's the people who are in short supply. So personnel directors are better placed than ever before to make a real difference – a bottom line difference. The **scarce resource**, which is the people resource, is the one that makes an impact at the margin, that makes one firm competitive over another.'

PERFORMANCE AND COMMITMENT AT TESCO

Tesco is now virtually a worldwide business with stores in all major countries except Australia. It is an extremely well-managed company which measures its success through the four 'spokes' of its corporate 'steering wheel', these 'spokes' being:

- PEOPLE – their commitment, retention, development and 'engagement'.

- FINANCE – profitability and cash flow

- CUSTOMERS – their acquisition, retention and loyalty

- OPERATIONS – the company's overall efficiencies in distribution, etc

In some respects Tesco is both a highly centralised organisation whilst also being very localised and devolved. Its corporate branding is very tightly controlled, as one would expect from a business which has a strong marketing thrust, and the Tesco name has now acquired a brand value in its own right. Store managers are governed by comprehensive rulebooks which even specify where their office waste-bins are to be positioned and on which office walls they may hang pictures. On the other hand, the company recognises that the strength of their reputation is heavily dependent on the amount of autonomy given to team leaders and supervisors on the shop floor, and so they are expected to exercise initiative and act discretionally when dealing with customers.

In a celebrated study of four matched Tesco supermarkets in the UK, Professor John Purcell and his colleagues found that one of the stores ('Store C') was characterised by low levels of employee commitment – and it was also by far the worst performing of the four stores when evaluated against the four Tesco 'steering wheel' measures. This study is very important in demonstrating the clear links between employee 'engagement' and organisational outcomes.

[Source: Hutchinson and Purcell, *Bringing Policies to Life: The Vital Role of Front-Line Managers in People Management*, CIPD, 2003]

A variety of research studies has attempted to support the anecdotal evidence with hard data. Although the link to **business performance** is not always clear cut, there is broad agreement that a greater focus on securing employee skills, motivation, commitment and flexible working is associated with positive employee attitudes, higher levels of productivity and higher quality of service.

---

3   A model for corporate excellence and leadership

Let us start this final part of Chapter 2 with a rhetorical question: **What organisation would not want to be 'world-class'?** Of course, there may not be any universally agreed definition of what it means to be 'world-class', though common sense would suggest that the description 'world-class' should be confined to organisations that are genuinely 'out in front', as it were, when compared with their competitors either in the same business sector or even across the whole business arena. We must be talking about organisations which consistently achieve higher levels of profitability (not merely high profitability now and again), which are innovative with their products and services, which create superb levels of customer loyalty, which continually attract new customers, and which have reputations for exceptional levels of ethicality with their stakeholders (suppliers, community neighbours, and above all, their employees). We are also likely to be talking about organisations that have become 'talent magnets', attracting high-quality recruits without the necessity for a lot of expensive recruitment advertising; they possess 'employer brand' status as an employer of choice, with lots of people queuing up to become employees – so the business can pick and choose to ensure that only the best candidates are accepted. So let us expand our starting question: **What organisation would not want to be a 'world-class' performer, with high levels of profitability, customer loyalty, employees who are committed, enthusiastic and engaged, and with the status of an 'employer brand'?**

ACTIVITY   15 mins

A serious question has been presented above. Certainly research has established that fewer than 10% of organisations are genuinely 'world-class', even though many more claim that status – so think about the factors that prevent the majority of organisations from seeking, let alone attaining, 'world-class' status. What are they?

It almost goes without saying that 'world-class' status cannot be attained without the contribution of the organisational workforce *as a whole*: merely capturing the commitment of senior executives and middle managers will not be enough. Moreover, 'world-class' status is dependent on top-down leadership, the presence of a strategic vision, the whole-hearted support of managers through strong leadership, and underpinning processes (such as HR policies, financial controls, production systems, quality assurance, and so forth) . So all the evidence shows that a 'world-class' organisation, characterised by High Performance Working (see Chapter 12), is an organisation which demonstrates positive 'bundling' between three essential components of corporate achievement:

(1)   **Strategy and culture that is aspirational** - a set of high-level goals embraced within a unifying 'Big Idea' (perhaps a corporate mission statement) and a framework of ethical values intended to permeate every part of the business.

(2)   **People commitment, engagement and contribution** – a strong orientation towards positive leadership and encouragement for risk-taking, coupled with empowerment and expectations about discretionary behaviour at all levels, ie, the willingness of the employees to go beyond the constraints of their job descriptions and use their initiative in the interests of the business.

(3)   **Processes that support the organisation's ambitions** – 'rules and regulations' which are supportive rather than punitive and which encourage a collaborative relationship with all stakeholders, especially customers.

Crucial to your understanding of this model is acceptance of the fact that *none of these will work on its own*.

- If the organisation has an appropriate **strategy and culture**, but ignores its **people** and its **processes**, widespread cynicism will be inevitable throughout the hierarchy as managers and workers see the gap between what the strategy/culture 'recipe' dictates and the behaviours which are actually condoned or rewarded. Processes in particular are likely to be insular, constructed around the supposed needs of each business function rather than around the business as a whole. Departments are likely to operate as self-contained entities – so, for example, the Human Resources practitioners are more concerned about the niceties of employment law than with the importance of attending to commercial priorities.

- If the organisation concentrates its efforts on its **people** but gives a low priority to developing its **strategy and culture** and to the creation of effective business **processes**, then the absence of strategic leadership will leave people rudderless, perhaps 'doing the best' yet without any clearly co-ordinated idea about what is meant by 'best' in the circumstances. Does 'best' mean that every effort must be made to keep costs down, or does it mean that their customers must be kept happy at all times – or does it mean both?

- If the organisation has created some excellent **processes** but ignores **strategy and culture**, and pays little attention to the **people** who inevitably act as an interface between the organisation and its outside world, then the organisation may acquire a reputation for being incredibly *efficient* yet without simultaneously being equally *effective*. Compliance with organisational 'rules and regulations' may sound important (indeed it is, especially if these 'rules and regulations' are inspired by legislation like health and safety), but sometimes it can be counter-productive and may even inhibit creativity, because innovation is crucially dependent on some 'rules and regulations' being challenged or even broken. For many organisations, in fact, the people who design 'rules and regulations' pay little attention to corporate priorities but spend more time in devising ever more elaborate procedures which are intended to cater for every conceivable scenario, but which break down whenever some entirely unexpected situation occurs.

- Of course, **efficient processes** nowadays depend a good deal on the use of information technology (IT) and certainly without IT many organisational practices and customer experiences could not exist at all. Credit cards would not exist; hotels could not accept reservations worldwide; customers could not order books or anything online; organisations would not so easily create and store personnel and product-quality information. On the other hand, technology isn't everything, and its effective deployment still depends ultimately on people – the people who design the IT systems, the people who use the systems, and the people who decide what to do with the information which the systems generate.

So it is vital that any effective organisation, and especially any organisation seeking 'world-class' status, should adopt an integrated approach to its **strategy and culture**, its **people management and leadership**, and its **process infrastructure** of procedures, 'rules and regulations' and systems. Not only do all these three 'arms' of the business need to be integrated in the first place, but also they have to be kept under constant review to ensure that they continue to meet the needs of the organisation, its stakeholders, its customers and its competitive environment. This is why no business can afford to stand still or assume that just because it has a healthily motivated workforce today, loyal and enthusiastic customers today, strong strategic leadership today, and a superbly functioning operational infrastructure today, then these will all continue indefinitely. If the three elements are perfectly aligned with each other (a state of affairs that is more difficult to accomplish than you might imagine), then a sort of multiplier effect comes into existence with the organisational results being greater than the sum of its component parts. When the three elements are not perfectly aligned (a depressingly common state of affairs), then the opposite of a multiplier effect is virtually certain – perhaps a 'divider' effect, with investment in any single ingredient yielded a much lower return than could have been expected.

Despite the fact that positive or even perfect alignment between high-level **strategy and culture, people management/leadership**, and **processes** may be hard to achieve, there is widespread evidence that it is achievable.

CLARIDGE'S HOTEL, LONDON

Claridge's is a luxury hotel in central London employing some 450 staff. When Sara Edwards became HR Director in 1998, Claridge's was battling to maintain its place in the market. Room occupancy was down and still declining, complaints were high and staff turnover was running at 73 per cent. As Sara Edwards recalls, 'People just weren't enjoying the environment in which they were working – and if the staff weren't, then neither were the guests.'

The company's turnaround began with recognition of the fact that **employees come first**: 'We strongly believe that if you don't get it right with the employees, you won't get it right with the guests,' says Sara Edwards. The process of change was built around seven newly-developed core values:

(a)   Communication

(b)   Passion

(c)   Team spirit

(d)   Interpersonal relations

(e)   Service perfection

(f)   Maximising resources and

(g)   Responsibility for actions

The staff appraisal scheme is now linked entirely to these seven values, and this, together with many other changes, has ensured that there is now a much greater level of staff continuity in the hotel.

Undoubtedly some organisations, characterised by relentless and restless leadership, have secured an impressive degree of alignment over a continuous period of years. When this happens, the following outcomes – all of them benign – indicate that the effort has been worthwhile:

- *Sustained positive bottom line results* (for organisations in profit-seeking sectors)

- *Impressive levels of resource utilisation and 'customer' satisfaction* (for non-profit-seeking sectors like charities, government departments, public agencies and municipal authorities)

- *Improved figures for customer retention, loyalty and trust*

- *Reduced costs per customer*

- *A significantly larger proportion of customers who speak very favourably about the organisation and in effect provide an unpaid marketing platform*

- *More job satisfaction among the organisation's own employees, leading in turn to reduced turnover, higher productivity and a greater willingness to engage in 'discretionary behaviour' which 'goes the extra mile'*

- *An enhanced reputation – leading to other indirect benefits, such as lower interest rates from banks, better co-operation with suppliers and an 'employer of choice' status.*

So, once again, with these advantages in mind, let us pose the question: **What organisation would not deliberately seek to attain 'world-class' status?**

4 A Model for 'World-Class' Excellence and People Commitment

Now let us look at the details of a framework which will deliver high levels of organisational performance and people commitment. In what follows we will draw heavily on research into Singapore Airlines, led by Professor Robert Johnston (Warwick Business School) and his equally pioneering studies featuring 'world-class' enterprises such as Tesco and First Direct (the UK-based telephone and Internet bank).

In this framework there are eight pillars within the three principal components of Strategy and Culture, People Performance, and Process Management. In what follows we outline what is involved with each of these pillars, why each is so important, and how each works in practice – illustrated principally with examples from Singapore Airlines but also using other organisations.

Important note: Please do not believe that because you are currently studying an ABE module called 'Managing People' then you do not need to read the following sections concerned with Strategy and Culture and Process Management. In reality each of these topics is very important to the effective management and leadership of people, and is crucial in structuring the degree of commitment and engagement which employees bring to the organisation. You must not ignore them – especially as you may be asked questions about such matters in the ABE examination.

Dimension 1: STRATEGY AND CULTURE

COMMITMENT: People performance in the business is a key scorecard measure, with high-level accountabilities and a constant focus on continuous improvement.

Companies that are authentically 'world-class' are noted for the fact that they are always restless, turbulent and dissatisfied with the status quo. Singapore Airlines certainly fits this description, because its management, from the top down, pushes for all the company's strategies and management practices to be subjected to incremental improvements all the time, plus periodic major transformations. According to Mr Yap Kim Wah (Senior Vice President, Product and Service):

> 'all our departmental heads, including myself, try to encourage our managers to be centres for discontentment! They have to be continuously unhappy with some things, not with people. You don't want to cause a morale problem. No! I don't mean that! I mean that you just have to have the sense to continually assess everything, and preferably before your boss asks you.'

Not only that, but Singapore Airlines is always looking ahead to ways in which it can continue to exceed its customers' expectations in the future. According to Mr Sim Kay Wee (Senior Vice President, Cabin Crew):

> 'In the 20th century, our cabin crew were docile, compliant, smiling, but not very vocal. I think the 21st century crew member will be more vibrant, more interactive, more outspoken. The challenge is to encourage and harness that energy to present a different kind of service image, but at the same time be very positive towards the passenger.'

A few years ago one of the authors of this Study Manual was engaged to undertake some consultancy for a well-known dairy foods business in the UK employing then about 1500 people, in an effort to improve their reputation for customer service. Thinking that the company probably had a designated customer service department or unit, the author asked the Chief Executive how many people in his organisation were concerned with customers. The response surprised him: 'All of them,' the Chief Executive confidently claimed – his point being that even if there is a customer service department, nonetheless all the company's employees depend upon the continued existence of paying customers as the ultimate source for their income. Similarly, the CEO of Singapore Airlines has drilled into the company workforce that 'whether you are a hangar assistant or a payroll clerk or an accountant, you are there because there's a customer who's willing to pay.'

Top-down leadership is especially crucial in a 'world-class' enterprise. Henry Kissinger once defined leadership as 'the art of taking people where they would not have gone by themselves', and it's a good definition to follow. Effective leaders take people beyond their comfort zones, stretching people's capabilities whilst also making them feel confident and enthusiastic about the new challenge, whatever it may be. Because effective leaders in 'world-class' companies constantly strive to go beyond the current boundaries of achievement, they can be described as unreasonable. Without stretch, 'reasonable' managers land up in the quiet backwaters of under-achievement, whereas managers who are selectively unreasonable (they are not unreasonable all the time, because they know when not to ask for the impossible) are always ambitious, always asking 'Why do we ...?' about some existing practices, and 'Why don't we ...?' about some apparently ridiculous innovation. These 'unreasonable' managers and leaders are short on theory and long on practice; they typically:

- Set stretching but not breaking targets;

- Regard obstacles as challenges to be overcome, not excuses to be accepted;

- View ambiguity as an opportunity not as a risk;

- Can be flexible about methods but inflexible about goals;

- Manage politically as well as rationally; and

- Work hard to win hearts as well as minds in order to build support.

HARMAN INTERNATIONAL – A WORLD CLASS COMPANY IN ACTION

Harman International makes some of the finest (and most expensive) home entertainment and professional hi-fi systems in the world. Its owner is Sidney Harman, whose approach to management and leadership originated in the 1960s when he was running both his company and also a Quaker college that encouraged students to take responsibility for their own education and learning. A dispute between labour and management at a factory in Tennessee over – of all things – a buzzer that sounded the coffee break opened his eyes to the factory's ridiculous, top-down management style, and from there have flowed all sorts of changes intended to encourage responsibility and improve the welfare of Harman's 10,000 employees. Thus the Harman factory in Suzhou, China, provides air conditioning, showers, English tuition and monthly parties at which workers can mingle with managers. When he has been forced to cut costs, Mr Harman has always conducted himself compassionately: for example, programmes at his California plants in the mid-1990s placed surplus workers in spun-off businesses, including one that made clocks from waste wood. Mr Harman's basic philosophy is that workers 'should have a serious emotional connection to their company.'

The Economist has noted that 'In a knowledge-intensive world, a company's most valuable assets are its workers ... if what is good for employees is also good for the company', says Mr Harman, 'how can anybody quarrel with you?'

CREDIBILITY: Your employees trust you, your customers trust you, and you work hard to justify their trust.

It is no accident that companies which enjoy well above-average levels of success – in terms of profitability and customer satisfaction – also score well for internal measures like employee loyalty. Yet 'trust' is a very delicate instrument, and organisations which understand the value of their reputation know they cannot relax their guard for an instant. Charles Handy once likened 'reputation' to a pane of glass, because once it is broken it can never be repaired, and Professor Robert Johnston makes a similar point:

'Like a bubble, reputations are fragile. Existing within a turbulent and often hostile environment they may easily be punctured. They may also be destroyed from within. It may only take one act, one decision, to undo all the effort that has been made over a period of time into creating a positive reputation. There is a need for constant vigilance and effort to develop and sustain a reputation – it is created and sustained by every single action and driven by the values that underpin the organisation.'

Yet because no organisation can monitor the actions of its employees all the time (especially if some of them are working remotely, e.g., as cabin crew on an aircraft), it must trust its people to act responsibly – and this will only work if those same people trust the company that employs them.

CONCENTRATION: *Everything the organisation does is dependent on the desire for profitability*

Being better than the competition doesn't just mean throwing more money at the problem, but it does mean constant effort to improve each of the little bits which together make up the customer (and the employee) experience. In the case of Singapore Airlines, it does not have to be spectacularly better than its competitors in everything: all it has to do is to be a little bit better than them, and this kind of incremental innovation can be undertaken without pricing each journey out of the market. It might be nice to serve lobster on short-haul flights between Singapore and Bangkok, for example, but this could easily be the first step down a slippery slope towards bankruptcy. Equally, no employer has a bottomless pit of money which can enable him simply to supply employees with endless pay increases, bonuses and non-financial benefits. **It is very important for you to understand this when considering how best to motivate people at work, because students answering examination questions in the Managing People module are apt to believe that motivational problems can be 'solved' simply by awarding pay increases, bonuses, and other costly 'incentives' like 'free' housing.**

In reality, research has established that the psychology of pay increases is much more complicated than it might at first appear.

- If employees receive a pay increase in response to their dissatisfaction with current levels of pay, whether they will feel any satisfaction or not must depend not on the actual amount of the increase but whether it is as much as they expected to receive. If it is, all well and good; if not, then they may even be more dissatisfied than before, or their feelings of dissatisfaction may only be reduced a little. This is why management, prior to the announcement of any pay increase, may work hard to reduce workforce expectations about the likely amount.

- Assuming that there is a good deal of satisfaction with the increase, how long will this last? Again, there is research evidence to show that feelings of satisfaction typically last for no longer than two to three weeks, during which time the motivation, performance and commitment of the employees may increase. However, after that short period these positive sentiments of satisfaction disappear, to be replaced by a kind of indifference until the desire for another pay rise begins to emerge.

- And here's the curious thing: for any further feelings of satisfaction with pay to be experienced, the next pay rise has to be larger than the one before. In other words, there is a kind of familiarity effect. If individuals are given an increase (or a performance bonus) of, say, £100, and they received an identical payment six months ago, their reaction is likely to be 'Is this all?'

- So if every pay (or bonus) amount has to be larger than the one before if it is to be greeted with any acceptable degree of satisfaction, there comes a point when no organisation can afford the level of payments that are being expected. This is why, ultimately, all employers must seek to motivate their people with a judicious mixture of financial rewards plus other approaches like involvement in decision-making, people-centred and supportive leadership from managers, and careful performance feedback.

At Singapore Airlines all this is well understood. To quote Mr Yap again:

> 'We are very cost conscious. It's drilled into us from the day we start working for SIA that if we don't make money, we'll be closed down. Singapore doesn't **need** a national airline. Second, the company has made a very important visionary statement that 'We don't want to be the largest company. We want to be the most profitable'.'

So the company only pays bonuses in proportion to its profitability – quite rightly, because if there is no profit there is in principle no money to reward employees for their contribution, and indeed there is no justification for doing so.

Dimension 2: PEOPLE PERFORMANCE

CAPABILITY: People are recruited, selected and trained against the organisation's high-level values and philosophies of employee commitment

Because of Singapore Airline's brand reputation as an employer, it can take its pick of the talented people who regularly forward unsolicited applications to the company's HR department. In the words of Ms Lim Suu Kuan, SIA's Commercial Training Manager, 'We have good industrial relations, good HR management, and we look after our staff well. Because when we look after our staff well, our staff will look after our customers well. It is a very simple statement, but also a very powerful one.'

The belief that people actually do make a difference is not merely a lip-service platitude in SIA but is genuine and sincere. All the HR systems for Singapore Airlines – learning and development, reward and recognition, performance management and appraisal, employee relations and involvement – are holistic, integrated and fully 'bundled' into the corporate goals so that the resulting impact is greater than the sum of its parts. As an example, one of the company's recent service improvement initiatives was called 'Transforming Customer Service' or TCS, and involved staff from five key operational areas working together: cabin crew, engineering, ground services, flight operations, and sales support. The TCS process, furthermore, uses the 40-30-30 rule, with 40% of the project resources being devoted to the training and revitalising of the employees, 30% on the review of process and procedures, and the final 30% on creating new product and service ideas.

More generally, too, Singapore Airlines believes in good communication: company-wide business briefings take place regularly to keep staff informed of the latest developments, and these are supplemented by newsletters and circulars which promote information sharing.

CONTINUITY: The business works hard to keep the people who are worth retaining, and uses a 'tough love' model for those who require remedial help

A key feature of the employee retention strategy at Singapore Airlines is its focus on training. This is reflected in a message from the company's Chief Executive, Dr Cheong – a message that might be reprinted for many other companies which may not exhibit the same commitment. In the words of Dr Cheong,

> 'Training is a necessity, not an option. It is not to be dispensed with when times are bad. We do not stint on training. Because we take a long-term view of training, our investments in staff development are not subject to the vagaries of the economy. Training is forever. No-one is too young to be trained, or too old.'

A constant struggle for any service-based business like Singapore Airlines is the necessity to offer standardised service (i.e., delivering the brand promise consistently, across the board, to all customers) yet at the same time making the 'product' personalised for each customer. Why is this important? Well, customer 'satisfaction' depends on the customer perceiving that the 'product' works (it does what it is supposed to do) and that the accompanying infrastructure (the product packaging, the product instructions, and the purchase transaction) has been carried out efficiently. Customer satisfaction is important, but in today's highly competitive world it typically isn't enough: customers want to feel special and unique, and if this happens they may then experience what is known as customer 'delight', which is much more memorable than customer satisfaction. If an organisation can generate sentiments of 'delight' among its customers, it truly does have a competitive advantage and an enviable source of competitive differentiation which will give it an edge over companies which can only produce 'satisfied' customers. What's more, it is usually the organisation's people who are the agents through which customer 'delight' can be achieved, for it is they who can 'go the extra mile', as the phrase has it, it is they who can make the customer feel important, and it is they who can make the purchase transaction positively memorable. If we go back to our original three dimensions of organisational performance – strategy and culture, people performance and processes – it is rare for customers to be thrilled by an organisation's strategy, culture or processes, because these are all too abstract (from the customer's standpoint) and, what's more, they comprise the business's infrastructure – those underpinning elements which permit its people to perform.

So, if we return to our discussion of Singapore Airlines, the company encounters a constant trade-off challenge between 'empowerment' (encouraging employees to use their initiative, make spontaneous decisions when confronted by non-routine customer requests, and establish warm interpersonal relationships towards customers) and 'industrialised' service processes which are laid down in the organisation's rules and regulations. According to SIA's Mr Sim Kay Wee, Senior Vice President responsible for cabin crew, there is a clear difference between the 'hygiene' and 'enhancing' factors in organisational performance – between the elements that customers expect as a matter of routine, and those which make the customer experience truly memorable:

> 'We have a long list of the things that passengers expect when it comes to good service: flight schedules, punctuality, seat comfort, and functional and technical skills such as safety, or just pouring a cup of coffee without spilling it all over the place. But these are just technical and I think a lot of airlines can master them. They are all hygiene factors – you must have them. The enhancing factors, on the other hand, are the softer skills, such as warmth, care and anticipation of needs.'

FLEXIBILITY: The organisation encourages ideas for innovation and improvement

Like many organisations, Singapore Airlines seeks both consistency and flexibility, which appear to be principles which pull people in opposite directions. As Mr Sim [see above] expresses it, 'the worst thing about service delivery is when everybody just follows the book, and of course this is equally true about people management and leadership in a wider context.' Of course, organisations must have procedures (to deal with standard activities like recruitment, selection, compassionate leave, absence control and so forth), but they must also have the flexibility to know when to apply these procedures and when common sense dictates that it might be more sensible to take each situation as it comes.

> 'In Singapore,' says Mr Sim, 'there is a tendency for people to be too regimented in their thinking. If a passenger asks for his vegetarian meal and we do not have it on board, for example, we want the member of staff to go back to the galley, think on the spot and create a solution, such as putting together a plate from all the fruits and vegetables, rather than annoy the customer by telling him it was not catered for so he can't have it.'

Back in 1996, Andy Grove, then the Chief Executive of Intel, published Only the Paranoid Survive. Arguing that organisations don't consult their own employees enough, he warned that 'snow melts first at the periphery'. In other words, if something is going wrong in a business, those who deal closely with its customers are frequently the first to know about it (even if they don't necessarily understand the significance of what is going on). Ignoring front-line employees is not a charge that can be levelled against Singapore Airlines, however. In the words of Mr Yap:

> 'Our crew are very important people because they are very intimately in contact with our customers. So for every flight that we operate, we listen sincerely to our crew. They know that the management takes their feedback very seriously. If they gave us feedback and we didn't do anything about it, they'd be disheartened.'

One of the other distinctive features about people management in Singapore Airlines concerns the extent to which the company works hard to create 'esprit de corps' among its cabin crew, despite the difficulties caused by the fact that the crew members are scattered around the world, in different planes going to different locations. SIA's answer is the 'team concept'. Mr Choo Poh Leong, Senior Manager for Cabin Crew Performance, outlines what this involves:

> 'In order to effectively manage our 6,600 crew, we divide them into teams, small units, with a team leader in charge of about 13 people. We will roster them to fly together as much as we can. Flying together, as a unit, allows them to build camaraderie. The team leader will get to know their strengths and weaknesses well, and will become their mentor and their counsel, and someone to whom they can turn if they need help or advice.'

One of the roles for the firm's trainers is to oversee 12 or 13 teams and fly with them whenever possible, not principally to inspect their performance but rather to help the teams develop.

Dimension 3: THE ORGANISATION'S SUPPORTING PROCESSES

In May 2003, Nicholas Carr published an important article in the *Harvard Business Review* titled 'IT doesn't matter', a suggestion which was greeted with horror by the leaders of software businesses and large companies which had invested millions in computer systems. Yet Carr's thesis was compelling. He did not deny that IT has the potential to transform entire societies, but what he claimed was that IT has now (to all intents and purposes) become part of our taken-for-granted background, like railways, telecommunications, electricity, highways and all the other technologies which were thought to be revolutionary in the past. Indeed, many of them were – IT has revolutionised the way all organisations operate – but ultimately we now *take them for granted* and don't even think about them all that much. We only do so, in fact, when the trains stop, the phones don't work, there's a power cut and there's gridlock on the roads – and then we suddenly realise how much we depend on these taken-for-granted facilities.

So Carr's argument, in essence, is that *if something exists more or less universally, then no business can secure a competitive advantage from it*. IT has nearly reached that point, where it is available everywhere; if any organisation introduces a technical breakthrough (like an exceptional speed of response on its website), then it will only be a matter of weeks or months before all other organisations have achieved the same breakthrough – indeed, some will have leap-frogged over it to boast about even faster response times. In reality, all such 'advantages' are very transient and most are illusory (all corporate claims about a competitive advantage should be taken with a pinch of salt, since many organisations are guilty of wishful thinking), certainly when contrasted with the competitive advantages reflected in a company's *people* – who offer long-term opportunities for unique competitive advantages that other organisations find virtually impossible to imitate. It's quite easy for a business to claim, for example, that it now has a strong customer-centric strategy: it's far more difficult to translate that aspiration into everyday people practices and behaviours.

None of this is meant to convey the impression that an organisation's processes are unimportant. On the contrary: they are essential, not just for legal and administrative reasons; they are essential because they are responsible for delivering the kinds of infrastructure efficiencies which customers (whether internal or external) now expect as a matter of routine.

In the UK, for instance, the mail-order firm Next Directory now promises that if a customer orders something by 4 p.m., then the item will be delivered on the following day. This is now the norm, the 'standard', to which all competitors must aspire; once they have done so (and most already have), then next-day delivery is no longer a competitive differentiator. In parts of central London, during the run-up to Christmas 2011, the same company was offering to deliver goods 90 minutes after the placing of the original order: it is difficult to imagine how such a promise could ever be beaten, unless it undertook to deliver products even before they had been ordered! And of course something like a 90-minute promise could only be applied in highly urbanised environments like central London: in more geographically diverse countries it wouldn't make sense at all. What is important for you to recognise, however, is that a standard of performance can begin by being a benchmark, at which point it is a genuine source of competitive differentiation, but once everyone becomes used to it then everyone's doing it and it's not a competitive advantage any more. At one time cars with power steering were rare and power steering was highly valued; now it is more or less ubiquitous, and therefore taken-for-granted; when buying a car, you'd be more likely to notice if it lacks power steering.

CONSISTENCY: Processes are consistently delivered

Following the beliefs associated with Scientific Management (you can read more about Scientific Management later in this Study Manual), organisations often pursue policies of standardisation because the application of comprehensive 'rules and regulations' appears to make the business environment more predictable and therefore more controllable. Standardisation also reduces the HR budget because fewer people are required and the people themselves require fewer skills and capabilities, especially if the work is programmed around a framework of tightly-structured routines. Such people, because highly-developed skills are not needed, may be performing efficiently within a day or so of their recruitment; they are low paid and more easily replaceable, almost to the point where they can be treated as if they were no more than a commodity.

This is not a people-management approach that we advocate in this Study Manual, because it has many disadvantages. First, it produces employees who are poorly motivated and so seldom 'go the extra mile' on behalf of their employer; second, these employees will typically demonstrate non-existent levels of 'engagement' with the organisation, so will do just enough to enable them to claim that they are complying with the requirements of their job descriptions; third, they may even devote some time to devising surreptitious ways of sabotaging the company's operations, e.g., by communicating negatively with customers, by refusing to co-operate with their colleagues, or by 'adjusting' machinery so that quality standards are compromised. It is surely far better to have employees – people – who are motivated, 'engaged' and supportive: it is these characteristics which a more constructive approach to organisational processes can engender.

The ability to integrate consistency with 'customisation' (that is, the ability to tailor a product or service to meet the individual customer's requirements) is well illustrated by the UK Royal Automobile Club (RAC), an organisation which, among other things, offers roadside assistance to its members if their cars break down. Nigel Paget, the RAC's Customer Service Director, has been quoted as saying that 'Our focus has always been on consistency of delivery **and** [our emphasis] treating the customer as an individual.' A more detailed study of service delivery experiences among directly customer-facing employees of the RAC includes these observations:

- 'I can do ten flat batteries a day. A flat battery is a flat battery, a car is a car, but the people you speak to are so different.'
- 'I thought my key skill was as a mechanic. I have learned that the key skill is actually dealing with people.'

In a wide-ranging comment about such experiences, Professor Robert Johnston has written: 'RAC patrol officers turn out in all weather and work in very dangerous situations, dealing with 10-16 breakdowns a day, which are often small and repetitive problems. Yet they saw every job as being distinct and a challenge, not because of the repair but because of the person they were dealing with.'

Particularly interesting, too, is this observation from Tim Mason, recently Marketing Director for Tesco:

> 'What a lot of businesses do is to design their operations to deal with exceptional customers. This means that the 99.5% of customers who behave in a perfectly normal and civilised way have to suffer because of the 0.5% who try and steal money from them. We have tried to turn this on its head and get rid of the rules.'

Clearly Mr Mason was talking about the company's customers, but one could as easily make the same point about the company's employees, because some companies design their people-management processes as if their entire workforce were composed of rogues and vagabonds. Naturally, in such circumstances, otherwise honest workers can become disillusioned.

CREATIVITY: Continuous improvement and innovation are nurtured and encouraged to flourish

In truth, not many organisations really welcome creativity or any disturbance to the current state of affairs, particularly if that state of affairs is quite comfortable. Yet the trouble is that in today's world no business can afford to be complacent. Even those that have all the answers today cannot assume that they even know what tomorrow's questions will be, let alone tomorrow's answers. The corporate history books are littered with examples of organisations that mistakenly believed there was nothing more to learn.

Because the world continues to change – politically, economically and socially – organisations must continually adapt. Better still, world-class organisations will anticipate change before it happens so that they are ready for it (even if they sometimes get it wrong) and have a head start over the others that didn't see the future coming and let it take them by surprise. In these world-class organisations, therefore, permanent change, transformation and continuous improvement are the norm.

An improvement culture is a learning organisation characterised by open-minded thinking, the constant search for new competitive differentiators, and the willingness to absorb lessons from any source, however unlikely. Creativity in organisations can originate from several sources: from the top, from the middle, the bottom, from customers (or other external stakeholders), or it may be provoked by some very threatening competitive action, the need to respond to some new legislation and pressure from regulators. Either way, for creative thinking truly to flourish, it requires a ***culture*** in which ideas are welcomed rather than ridiculed, denigrated or, even worse, ignored, where thinking is valued and where innovation is shared. Further, it has to be accepted that the capacity to think creatively is widely, not narrowly, distributed among the organisation's employees. Yet these are difficult beliefs to entertain, and it is quite common for original ideas to be received with scepticism, ridicule and resistance to change, with all kinds of spurious 'reasons' such as the claim that 'we can't afford it', either because there is no money (and it is sometimes assumed that innovations automatically cost money when in reality many of them don't), or people are already very busy doing other things. As the management guru Gary Hamel once said (speaking at the CIPD Annual Conference): 'Get people to believe that resources aren't the problem. Challenge them every time they say otherwise. I don't come across many companies that are resource-constrained; I find lots that are imagination-constrained.'

Conclusion

There are several absolutely crucial messages which you should take away from reading here about Singapore Airlines and some of the other companies which have attained 'world-class' reputations for people-management and people-leadership.

(1)   **Exceptional people performance requires a *total approach* in which all the ingredients are mixed together positively and harmoniously.**

(2)   **The *strategy and culture* dimension requires the continuous communication of aspirational and visionary messages to every part of the organisation.**

(3)   **The *people performance* dimension requires careful attention to every aspect of human resource management: recruitment, selection, training/learning and development, recognition, reward, employee relations and appraisal.**

(4)   **The *processes* dimension requires a balance between the need for top-down 'rules and regulations' and the need for bottom-up flexibility and empowerment.** Singapore Airlines has achieved this balance with remarkable skill, so that it presents a single face to the customer but simultaneously offers a very personalised service (e.g. through the simple device of calling each customer by their name).

(5)   **Singapore Airlines, like other 'world-class' businesses, has created a culture which expects all staff to add value – to think about the company's processes, systems and routines all the time, to search for incremental improvements, and even to develop radically different ways of functioning.** In the evocative words of Jochen Wirtz (National University of Singapore), 'SIA seems to improve just a little bit, but all the time and in everything. What it ultimately means is that Singapore Airlines has become that most rare of corporate phenomena, a "learning organisation".'

(6)   **Not only does Singapore Airlines concentrate on operational efficiency, people performance and bottom-line profitability, it has also pushed this focus down to every level in the organisation.**

In truth, employee commitment is a complicated concept – much more complex than it may at first appear. A 2004 article for the *American Behavioural Scientist* journal, by Todd Pittinsky and Margaret Shih, shows for example that it can be dangerous simply to believe that employee retention is a meaningful measure for employee commitment. Of course, people may remain as employees in a single organisation for lots of reasons which have nothing to do with conscious commitment – they may suffer from sheer inertia, for example, or have found it impossible to secure job offers elsewhere, so they stay for purely negative reasons.

Equally, it could be mistaken to suggest that people who hop from job to job are less committed. Pittinsky and Shih found that there is a group of highly mobile knowledge workers – described as 'knowledge nomads' – who undoubtedly form attachments and commitments in whatever organisation that employs them, even if they only stay for a short time. In other words, employee commitment is wholly separate from employee mobility, and one cannot be used as a measure for the other. What appears to be the case are that there are different forms of commitment, peculiar to each employee: commitment to a career, commitment to the work, commitment to one's family, commitment to co-workers, and commitment to personal goals. Thus the challenge for managers and a company is to have an employee's multiple commitments reinforcing each other through commitment to the company. Research suggests there are two instruments which are significant in bringing about this alignment:

(1)   **The presence of opportunities for formal and informal learning**; and

(2)   **The creation and nurturing of small work groups** – because employees are more attached to their companies when they feel attached to their team.

So the challenge for organisations is to find the precise levers which can generate and sustain the commitment of their employees. This is not a simple, straightforward issue because there is no one management lever or management practice which will work everywhere all the time. It is not a one size fits all' problem.

SELFRIDGES

'The **Selfridges** story is one of reinvention and growth, in which people management has played a vital role in creating a highly successful retail chain... One of the [new management] team's first critical choices was to decide what sort of retailer it should be – and how its people management should support that identity.

Selfridges now markets itself as the "House of Brands", with its own strong image based on that presumption. In transforming its employment culture to complement the change, it adopted a series of new HR initiatives. It conducted culture surveys, organised focus groups and replaced its old Hay job evaluation scheme with a broadbanding pay arrangement. The Trafford Park store in Manchester... put great emphasis on communication, training and development.

Behind all these innovations, Selfridges made an explicit effort to model the underlying stakeholder values required in its dealings with customers, employees, the local community, suppliers and other stakeholders. These values were expressed under four goals: to be "aspirational, friendly, accessible and bold...

Staff at Selfridges displayed one of the highest levels of commitment out of the 12 organisations in our research. The factors they particularly linked to job satisfaction, motivation and commitment were challenging work; job security; teamwork; career opportunities; appraisal; and, most of all, communication, involvement and the way their managers managed.'

(Purcell *et al*, 2003)

Chapter Roundup

↳ Workforce knowledge, commitment, involvement and flexibility are increasingly seen as vital to gaining competitive advantage. At the same time, employees' expectations of satisfaction in working life have risen.

↳ Empowerment means making workers responsible for setting and achieving work targets, with the freedom to make decisions about how they are to be achieved. Empowerment makes the best use of the knowledge of those intimately experienced with organisational processes.

There is broad agreement that a greater focus on securing employee skills, motivation, commitment and flexible working is associated with positive employee attitudes, higher levels of productivity and higher quality of service.

↳ **World class organisations** display three essential components of corporate achievement

– Aspirational **strategy** and **culture**

– People **commitment**, **engagement** and **contribution**

– **Processes** that support organisational objectives and collaborative relationships

These components must all be present and work together if they are to be effective.

↳ The **strategy** and **culture** component has the following elements:

– **Commitment** from all staff

– **Credibility** with employees and customers

– **Concentration** on the need for profitability

↳ The **people performance** component has the following elements:

– **Capability**: people are selected and trained so as to support the organisations strategy and culture.

– **Continuity**: the organisation strives to retain high-performing staff, supports those who could do better, but does not tolerate long-term failure.

– **Flexibility**: The organisation encourages ideas for innovation and improvement.

↳ The organisation's **processes** must, as a minimum, ensure that it achieves the **industry standard** of customer service: only exceeding this standard can create **competitive advantage**. Processes must be **consistently delivered** and subject to **creativity** in order to achieve continuous improvement.

Quick Quiz

1   What has been the effect upon people management of the need to compete in innovative, technology-based and quality-sensitive markets?

2   What is meant by delayering?

3   What are the three components of corporate achievement displayed by world class organisations?

4   Can any of the three components of corporate achievement components be identified as most significant?

5   What is meant by commitment in the strategy and culture component?

6   Can process excellence be a source of competitive advantage?

Answers to Quick Quiz

1   An increased requirement for skilled knowledge workers, which has reduced the scope for strict control of information and work processes.

2   A cut in the number of levels (and managers) in the chain of command.

3   Aspirational **strategy** and **culture**; people **commitment**, **engagement** and **contribution**; **processes** that support organisational objectives and collaborative relationships

4   No, they must all be present and work together in an integrated fashion.

5   Everyone in the organisation is committed to the achievement of high levels of performance.

6   Only if the degree of excellence exceeds the industry standard.

Answer to Activity

Activity

- They are in a comfortable position competitively and therefore don't see the need to embark upon all the changes that would be involved.

- They are monopolies, providing goods and services which customers have to buy and for which no alternatives exist (e.g., the Passport Office in the UK).

- They are not aware of the benefits to be gained from acquiring 'world-class' status.

- They are aware of these benefits, but don't think these benefits would in their case be attainable.

- They don't believe in the 'evidence' about these benefits – though their lack of belief may be nothing more than straightforward resistance to change, suitably disguised as if it were a purely rational reaction.

- Their competitive sector is sluggish, characterised by other organisations which are undistinguished, so there is no overwhelming pressure to change.

- Their customers do not have very high expectations, do not often complain, and do not migrate to other organisations – so again there is no pressure to change.

- They are a family-managed business which does not conspicuously seek to be the best but is content to remain 'average' or 'acceptable', on the grounds that this enables the top manager to maintain a balance between corporate commitment and personal lifestyle preferences.

- They believe that the kind of culture transformation needed to become 'world-class' would be, for them, impossible, and it is a challenge that they would prefer not to have to confront.

- Their current industrial relations climate is adversarial and lacking in the level of trust which would permit a 'world-class' programme even to get off the ground.

- They think (mistakenly) that they are already 'world-class' and so the 'world-class' change agenda doesn't apply to them.

Chapter 3

The business environment

Business activity, including those aspects we know as HRM, is guided by the organisation's overall strategic plan, which is developed within the context of the wider environment in which the organisation operates. It is from the macro-environment that major pressures emerge; these have the potential to overwhelm an organisation or to provide it with major new opportunities.

The emergence of large scale trends and regulatory changes are particularly important for the organisation's HRM function. In this chapter we will first examine a simple approach to the analysis of the environment, going on to consider in more detail the impact of a range of important developments in the social environment. The final section is concerned with the psychological contract and the way in which it seems to have developed in response to environmental pressures.

1   The organisation and its environment

Organisations do not exist in a vacuum. They are part of the society in which they operate, and as such are subject to the various factors which shape that society and affect the way in which we all live. They are also part of the societies in which they buy and sell their goods and services – their markets – and again are subject to the various factors which affect those markets, wherever they might be. This is the environment of the organisation and, in order to continue to operate and trade, all organisations must take account of the environmental factors which affect it.

The environment of an organisation is **everything outside its boundaries**. It is composed of a large number of factors as may be seen from the following diagram.

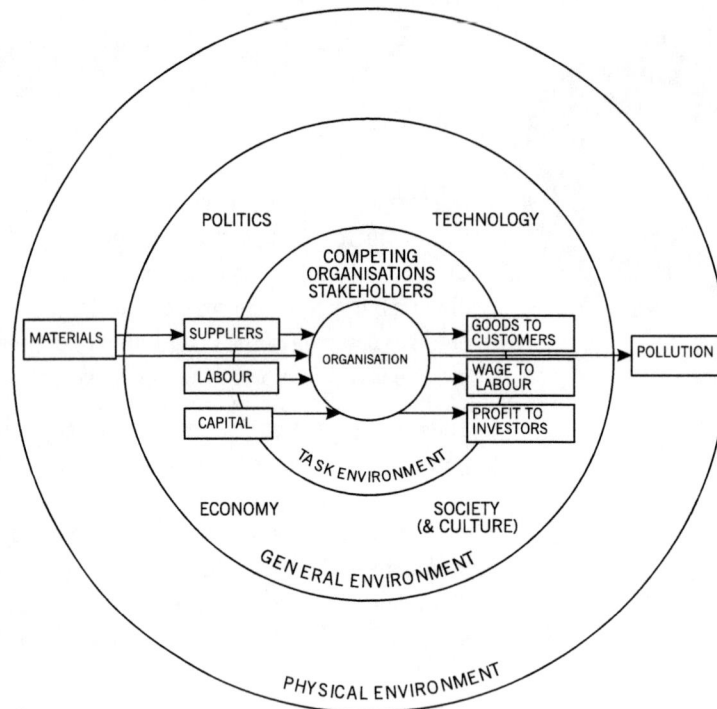

Figure 3.1: The environment of an organisation

We have distinguished here between three aspects:

(a)   The **task environment** (or micro-environment), which is made up of factors of particular relevance to the individual organisation, such as its competitors, customers and suppliers of resources.

(b)   The **general environment** (or macro-environment), which is the organisation's wider setting and includes political, legal, economic, social and technological influences.

(c)   The **physical environment**, which includes the effects that the organisation's activities have on the planet, both at a local level and the wider regional or even global levels.

In most of the rest of this chapter we will be concerned with the general environment, but we shall also touch on the other aspects as they affect the organisation's methods of conducting its business.

1.1   Analysing the environment

All the environmental factors – task, general and physical – can have a significant impact on the organisation. Environmental analysis is concerned with identifying how the various factors interact with an organisation. There are two key characteristics which need to be considered.

(a)   Its **dynamics** – in other words, how rapidly the environment is changing. Where changes are predictable or relatively slow, the environment is said to be stable, whilst uncertainty or rapid change would suggest that the environment is unstable or dynamic.

(b)   Its **complexity** – which arises from three factors:

- The amount of knowledge necessary for the business to operate. For example, all businesses would have to know about the regulatory environment relating to the employment of people, whereas only a business in chemical manufacturing would require specialist knowledge relating to the control, storage and safety matters of the chemicals it manufactures.

- The way in which environmental factors interrelate. For example, a holiday company will be affected by the price of aviation fuel, which itself will be affected by exchange rates, which are affected by interest rates.

- The variety of influences faced by an organisation. The greater the number of influences, the more complex the environment.

1.2   A framework for analysis

There are a number of ways of setting about analysing the organisation's environment, but the most common is that characterised by the mnemonic **PEST**. This stands for the following four factors:

Political

Economic

Social

Technical

Under this method, legal matters are considered under general heading of political factors, but it is now increasingly common to examine these as a separate element, adding 'L' for law to the mnemonic. Further, increasing public concern for the natural environment and corporate sensitivity about the way in which business is conducted has led in recent years to the inclusion of a second 'E' to stand for ecology and ethics.

Thus, we have a more developed series of factors to consider, given by the mnemonic **PESTLE**.

This approach provides a useful checklist for general environmental factors, but it is important to remember that these groups of factors are not sealed off from one another. In the real world, they are often interlinked and any given development in the outside world is likely to impact under two or more of the various headings. So, for example, social concern about pollution influences political thinking, which leads to legislation. Existing technology may then be affected by the banning or restriction of activities and new solutions have to be found which satisfy ecological criteria. We can illustrate this with an example from a number of years ago.

BPP LEARNING MEDIA

UNDERSTANDING THE DANGERS OF CFCS

In the 1970s concern about the effects on the ozone layer of CFC gases used in refrigeration led governments internationally to adopt targets for replacing the harmful substance and individual nations passed laws banning the use of CFCs by a certain date. New materials had to be developed and tested to ensure that they did not cause ecological damage and new technological processes were necessary for manufacturing. Many individual organisations were affected by this – all refrigeration plants had to ensure that they complied with the new regulations, manufacturers had to develop new materials, public sector laboratories and pollution inspectorates had to develop systems for testing and measuring, banks which had lent money to polluting firms had to ensure compliance with the new rules, in case they became owners of defaulting debtor companies and thus responsible for illegal equipment.

As you can see from this example, some organisations are directly affected and some indirectly. It is vital, then, for all organisations to know what is going on in their environment.

2 PESTLE factors and the business environment

How does each factor affect the organisation? We can look at them in turn and see their importance.

2.1 The political environment

The political environment is concerned with the way in which the government of a particular country affects organisations operating within that country. It may also be taken to apply to the effects of international bodies which are able to exercise power across national boundaries, such as the operation of the European Union.

In a country like the UK, that environment may be summed up as democratic/market orientation. The government is accountable to the electorate and sets out to create a framework in which market forces operate, controlled by legislation which protects employees and consumers from exploitation. Governments exercise power through administrative policy and decisions and more generally through legislation.

This last point is often taken to be the key element of political influence (and we shall examine its implications in a later section looking at the legal environment), but governments have a wider impact on the business world in general, and the way in which individual organisations operate in particular, through:

- The conduct of its economic policy – including, for example, levels and targeting of taxation and spending (including grants and other forms of support for businesses), actions taken which affect interest and exchange rates, and encouragement (or otherwise) given to stimulate economic growth. Note that governments (through public sector organisations) are one of the major consumers of goods and services from the private sector and their level of spending is a major determinant of the level of business activity in many areas of the economy.

- Its attitudes towards the role of the public sector – including, for example, the way in which education, health and other social services are provided and the priorities which they may be given.

- The stance taken on specific issues of direct relevance to particular businesses or industries – for example, on the regulation of trade (especially across national borders), types of energy sources or the development of the communications infrastructure of the country.

In the UK, and the other major democratic countries around the world, there is a strong degree of political stability. Despite differences between the political groups which compete for power within those countries, there is a general consensus about the way in which they are organised and run, with major change not being a significant feature. However, that has not always been the case, nor is it true throughout the world at the present time – it was not so long ago that the communist countries of Eastern Europe went through a huge upheaval with the fall of the centralist regimes and the move from command to market economies. That process has been mirrored to some extent by the emergence of China from relative isolation to the becoming a major world economic power. In other countries, the political environment is still characterised by wars, political chaos and regime change, social unrest, corruption and nationalism. The political stability or otherwise of a country can be measured by what is known as political risk – the degree to which such factors might affect a business's operations there and which may limit its investment or production strategies.

Business is not just the passive recipient of government policy, but plays a major part in helping to shape the political environment. Both general sectors of the business community and individual organisations attempt to influence the political decision making process in ways which will benefit their own objectives. To this end, they make contributions to political parties, or specific politicians (in, for example, the USA), to enhance those parties/politicians chances of success. They also employ "lobbyists" and public relations specialists to try to get their messages and interests across to decision makers and influence the outcome of political debates, both within government and in the wider field of public opinion (where other pressure groups may be operating to put across contrary views).

2.2   The economic environment

The state of the economy

The particular conditions existing in an economy have very significant effects on business organisations. In terms of market economics, the crucial factors are demand and supply – what the level of demand is for the goods and services an organisation can supply at a particular price and how this is affected by the cost of the resources needed to produce those goods and services. (These are generally referred to as the factors of production and include land, labour and capital, with capital being both the raw materials required and the money needed to buy them). The way in which the demand and supply equation operates is central to the future plans of businesses and we have seen, in the recessions of the 1980s, 1990s and late 2000s, that many firms will go out of business because of the economic conditions, rather than any particular failings of their own.

In general terms, most economies exhibit a trade cycle of growth and perhaps boom followed by a slow down and possibly recession. This will affect the level of demand for a firm's products. In a recession the general level of demand falls which will limit the ability of the firm to sell its goods at their full price. In the UK, the recession of the early 1990s resulted in around 62,000 firms closing in a single year. In a period of recovery or boom the general level of demand rises, which will increase the ability of the firm to sell its goods at profitable prices. It will also provide the opportunity for new firms to emerge.

Within these economic cycles, there are a number of factors which play a key role in influencing businesses.

2.2.1   Inflation

Inflation can be defined as a rise in the general price level of an economy over a period of time and is expressed as a percentage. It represents a loss in the purchasing power of money.

Inflation is usually associated with excessive growth in demand within an economy. Two types of inflationary effect can be seen:

- **Cost push inflation** – caused by businesses needing to pay higher prices for factors of production (land, labour and capital) which are increasingly scarce. As the prices of scarce resources rise, the economy may begin to overheat, as the competition to purchase the remaining supplies gets stronger. The result is that firms are forced to increase their prices, thereby, creating inflation.

- **Demand pull inflation** – caused where there is excess demand for the available goods and services in the economy and firms are unable to satisfy the current level of demand. As a result, they increase prices to ration off this excess demand.

A further problem arises when workers seek higher wages to maintain their purchasing power in the face of rising prices generally in the economy. This process is referred to as a wage-price inflationary spiral.

Inflation creates instability in an economy and monetary authorities often respond to it by increasing interest rates (and, as we have seen, this may have a negative impact on business profits).

The problem of inflation to a business is that it creates uncertainty and makes it more difficult to make predictions about costs, revenues and therefore, profits. If prices are continually changing due to inflation, then it also makes it more difficult for a business to maintain an accurate picture of its rival's performance.

2.2.2   Credit and interest rates

Credit is a key element of modern market economies. It is the facility to obtain the funds necessary to purchase the goods and services needed when the purchaser does not currently have the necessary resources to buy them outright at the time. Virtually all firms – and, indeed, governments as well as very many individual consumers – borrow money in this way and take on debts which they are then required to pay off over a period of time.

Interest is the charge made by the lender and is usually expressed as a percentage rate (applied to the loan), making the sum repaid over time larger than the initial loan itself.

Two factors are important here:

- **The availability of credit facilities** – that is the willingness of lenders to advance funds to firms (and governments and individuals); and

- **The interest rate** – the cost of borrowing and hence the level of debt, which will influence the ability of the borrower to take on and repay the loan. The level of debt carried by borrowers also influences their ability to spend on other things, so for example, if interest rates rise and the cost of repaying a mortgage increases, a household will have less money to spend on, say, buying furniture. (Conversely, if interest rates fall, borrowers have more money to spend.)

What influences these factors and what effect do they have?

The availability of credit is a function of both the level of funds that lenders have available to loan to borrowers and their confidence that, in lending it out to a particular borrower at a particular level of interest, they will be able to get their money back. Clearly, the higher the level of interest, the higher the level of risk that the borrower may not be able to meet repayments and may default on the loan. Thus, lenders invariably seek some form of guarantee that the borrower will be able to meet the repayments in full and, if they fail to do so, that the lender will be able to take possession of some asset which will offset the outstanding debt. Thus, usually, borrowers will be liable to lose the asset which they have purchased with the loan is they fail to make the necessary repayments.

This system worked quite efficiently for very many years until the credit crunch of 2007-2008 and afterwards, when lenders (principally the banks) found that they had made too many loans, mainly to individuals for house purchases, which could not be repaid when there was a downturn in the economy and that the assets against which the loans were secured would not cover the losses. The whole system very nearly collapsed and governments had to pump public money into the lending institutions to enable them to continue operations. However, that came at a price to governments which effectively took on the debts themselves, increasing the proportion of public spending required simply to meet the debt charges.

This is a very simplified summary of the events in recent years, but the effect of all this was to reduce significantly both the level of funds which lenders had available and their confidence that loans would be repaid, one consequence of which was that they looked to increase the rate of interest to compensate themselves for the risk associated with the loan. Thus, credit availability all but dried up and firms (and, indeed, some governments) found it increasingly difficult to obtain the funds they needed to continue to operate.

From the perspective of the business, the rate of interest represents an addition to total costs from borrowing to finance investment projects. When a business considers whether or not to invest on a certain project, it needs to take into account whether or not the potential returns from the project exceeds the cost of the project including the cost of borrowing.

When interest rates change, businesses are affected both from changes to their own costs of borrowing and the impact the change has upon the expenditure of the consumer. For instance, a rise in the rate of interest will not only increase the cost of borrowing to the firm, but also reduce the disposable incomes of consumers, which has a consequence for its sales. If interest rates rise, consumers are less likely to borrow money and so are likely to reduce their demand for most products. Likewise, those consumers who do not need to borrow might choose to take advantage of the increased rewards from saving and in turn, reduce their demand for certain goods and services.

Since 1997, UK interest rates have been set by the Monetary Policy Committee (MPC) of the Bank of England. This committee is charged with the responsibility of setting interest rates so that the rate of inflation achieves a government target of 2%. The objective of the move by the Labour Government of the time was to make the control of inflation independent of political issues and interference.

The theory is that, by changing interest rates, it is hoped that the rate of economic growth can be 'controlled'. When the demand for goods and services grows too quickly, the economy runs the risk of reaching full capacity. When this happens, businesses will find it difficult to recruit staff with the appropriate skills needed to expand. Therefore, those individuals with these skills will bid wages up, thereby increasing the costs of production to a firm. As a result inflation in the economy will increase, thereby, forcing the monetary authorities to seek ways to reduce consumer expenditure.

One such option available is to increase interest rates. This will make it more costly for both consumers and businesses to borrow. Consumers will spend less, businesses will invest less and so consumption and demand in the economy will fall.

One effect of the credit crunch has been that the Bank of England has reduced interest rates in order to stimulate demand and maintain economic activity and growth in the economy. However, the availability of funds to lenders remains restricted and there has been a reluctance, on their part, to make credit available at a price which is acceptable to many businesses and consumers.

2.2.3 Unemployment

In simple terms, unemployment occurs when people cannot find jobs. Of itself, this is not necessarily a problem (although it clearly can be to the persons seeking employment). It is the level of unemployment, as a percentage of the total labour force, which can be damaging if it reaches towards 10% and beyond – either nationally or regionally.

It is accepted that there will always be a certain level of unemployment in any economy. There are three main reasons for this.

- **Structural** unemployment – which is caused by changes in the type of economic activity within an economy as a whole (or particular parts, or regions). This may be seen in the shifts from a mainly agricultural economy to a manufacturing economy, and at a later stage, from manufacturing to service industries which most economies have gone through. This results in many workers losing their jobs. Although there may be growth in the new occupational areas, those jobs are often in different locations and demand different skills. Changes in technology are also a cause of structural unemployment, when businesses replace labour with machines, and also when employers look for a different range of skills.

- **Cyclical** unemployment – which is caused by businesses making staff redundant at times of recession when the demand for goods and services falls and there is less need for staff.

- **Frictional** unemployment – which is part of the natural process whereby individuals are 'in between' jobs. In effect, these are people who have left one job and are in the process of applying for another. Governments try to reduce frictional unemployment by improving the quality of information about job vacancies.

A high level of unemployment represents under-utilisation of one of the key factors of production (labour) in an economy and demonstrates that the level of economic activity is not sufficiently high enough to support the population. It also has a cost in terms of state support for unemployed persons and the loss of taxation on earnings of those people if they were employed. There can also be a significant social cost from having large numbers of people with effectively nothing to do, particularly if they are concentrated in particular areas and/or among particular age groups.

A rise in unemployment can affect demand as consumers who have lost their jobs are likely to have a reduction in their disposable income and will cut back on their expenditure. Reduced demand puts pressure on firms' abilities to sell their goods and services as planned and maintain their cash flow and profits. On the other hand, it can make it easier for firms to deal with excessive wage demands and may well be able to renegotiate both wages and costs for raw materials as the economic climate worsens.

If unemployment falls, it can mean that firms will benefit through increased sales and profits. Increased consumer disposable income feeds increased expenditure in the shops and therefore benefits businesses. However, if this growth is excessive and too fast then it could lead to wage-price inflationary spirals which in turn could create inflation and the need for interest rate increases, which would cause firms the problems already discussed.

Competition and international trade

In a market economy, businesses compete with similar businesses to sell their goods and services to customers who, in general, have a free choice about which product they wish to purchase. The decision as to which competitor to purchase from will be influenced by a number of factors – obviously price is a key consideration, but other factors such as quality, style and appearance, and availability will also play a part. Businesses therefore compete not just on price, but also on these other factors and will attempt to differentiate themselves from the competition by gaining a 'competitive advantage' in one or more of these areas. Thus, there is a business imperative to ensure that the way in which an organisation operates is efficient as possible in all these areas.

One of the most significant features of recent years has been the opening up of competition not just within individual countries, or within 'developed' regions of the world, but across the whole planet. Allied to the liberalisation of world trade associated with the foundation of the World Trade Organisation in 1995, previously less developed countries have been able to take advantage of changes in technology and use their own resources of labour to enter the international trading environment. This has led to the concept of globalisation – the whole world becoming, in effect, one (relatively) free market – a quite massive increase in competition.

One key effect of this, principally associated with the cheaper labour costs of certain countries and the efficiencies achievable by increasingly less expensive technology, has been that costs have significantly reduced. Manufactured goods have become much cheaper, to the very great benefit of consumers. However, generally speaking, consumers are also workers and the effect on them in that capacity has been less desirable. Many manufacturing and certain types of service jobs at all levels of skill have simply disappeared from western countries as production has been moved to countries with lower costs of labour, and this has caused great social and economic disruption. There is great pressure on firms to reduce their own costs in order to compete and remain in business. At the same time, in the service sector, there has been a continuing process of merger and takeover, creating global firms that inevitably seek to extract the maximum economies of scale from their operations. This has compounded the disruption.

2.3 The social environment

The concept of the social environment is particularly significant for the practice of people management and it covers both the broad make up of people in society and the attitudes and behaviours arising from culture which impact in both the workplace and the market place. As with the economic environment, there have been really large changes in the social environment in recent years as both the demographic composition of most societies has altered and cultural values have radically shifted.

We shall consider some of the effects of particular changes in the social and cultural environment on the workplace in the next section, but here we shall summarise some of the most significant trends which lie at the root of these changes.

Demography

Demography is the study of the structure of human populations and communities. It provides analysis of statistics on birth and death rates, age structures of populations, ethnic groups within communities and so on.

Demography is important for several reasons:

- Labour is a basic economic resource and a vital factor of production

- People create demand for goods, services and resources

- Government policies on such matters as health care, welfare benefits and education are heavily influenced by demographic forecasts.

2.3.1 Population growth and structure

Population growth and decline has traditionally been the result of changing birth and death rates and these factors give also rise to changes in the proportion of specific age groups within the population as people age.

The UK experienced unusually high birth rates during two relatively short time periods during the second half of the 20th century. The first, in 1946-49, was rapid but quite brief, while the second, from about 1955 to 1970, showed slower growth and decline but peaked at a higher level. Such surges in population growth ('baby booms') have considerable consequences as the larger age group works its way through society across the years. For example, there was increased demand for starter homes, in 1971-73 and in the 1980s, and subsequently for larger family homes in 1978-82 and in the late 1990s, as the 'baby boomers' formed their own families and households. The extent of the increased demand was sufficient to cause significant inflation in house prices (house prices doubled in three years in the early 1970s (Harris, 2000)), which subsequently spilled over into general inflation...

More recently, with declining or stable low birth rates in developed countries, the major effect has been that the structure of the population is aging – there has been a steady increase in the proportion of the national population over retirement age and this puts pressure on the society to enable provision to meet their needs through pensions and care services of various kinds. At the same time, an increasing proportion of the population of working age will be at the older end of the scale. This has important implications for both recruitment and the age profiles of workers in organisations. It has also given rise to legislation to prohibit discrimination on the grounds of age.

Whilst this aging population structure is characteristic of developed countries, it is important not to forget that there remain significant numbers of young people. Increasing demand for a skilled workforce puts increased demands on society for appropriate education and training, while youth unemployment is rising in economies that fail to provide an appropriate level of new jobs.

It is also important to remember that populations are not static in terms of where they live within a country and the geographical distribution of population can be economically and socially significant. Certain areas and regions may be less prosperous than others, usually for historical reasons associated with the predominant type of economic activity, and this often leads to internal migration as people move to new places in search of work. Additionally, urban areas have seen populations moving away from city centres out into suburbs.

Note that growth or decline in a national population, or in regional populations, affects total potential demand, with the potential for a knock-on effect on inflation.

2.3.2   Ethnicity and diversity

Migration on an international scale has been a major feature of demography in the last twenty years and has had some effect (although not particularly significant) on populations numbers in developed countries. This has substantially altered the ethnic mix of such countries.

There has always been some movement of peoples between different countries, often based on economic considerations as groups seek to improve their opportunities in a new country, but also based on political upheavals. In the past, host countries have actively sought immigrants to make good shortfalls in workers in particular sectors of the economy (as with Britain's health and transport industries in the 1950s and 1960s) and there remains a continued need for immigration to cover shortages in certain skills areas to this day. More recently, war, domestic unrest and improvements in communication and transport systems have combined to fuel the movement of peoples across increasingly wide areas of the world.

One result of this has been that most western countries now have very mixed populations in terms of ethnic origin. This presents a number of challenges to both society in general and the workplace in particular in absorbing the various cultural and religious differences. People management practices have been required to develop so as to manage that increasing diversity, based on the concept that organisations can benefit from accepting and recognising that individual differences should be valued and actively used in the pursuit of organisational goals (Rayner and Adam-Smith, 2009).

Culture

Culture is 'the sum total of the beliefs, knowledge, attitudes of mind and customs to which people are exposed in their social conditioning' (Kempner, 1987). Through contact with a particular culture, individuals learn a language, acquire values and learn habits of behaviour and thought.

As societies develop over the years and conditions within them change, so does the culture of that society change. We only have to think of what the major values and predominant patterns of behaviour were like, say, fifty years ago and compare them to today's values and behaviours to see this. So, culture is not static and organisations have to take note and adapt to such change if they are to prosper. This can be seen in both the style and type of goods and services they produce, as well as in their management practices.

In addition, culture is not homogenous across any particular society. Whilst it may be possible to identify certain beliefs, knowledge, attitudes of mind and customs associated with, say, the UK or France, within those societies there are likely to be quite large variations based on differences in where people live, and their age, class, ethnic background and religion. These 'subcultures' can be of great significance, both to the cohesion of the whole society itself and to businesses operating within it.

2.3.3   Family structures

The household is the basic social unit, but the composition – size, structure and cohesion – of this has varied greatly over the years, based on such factors as the number of children, whether elderly parents live at home and so on. In western countries, there has been an increase in single-person households and single parent families. Where a single parent family exists because of marriage breakdown, the lone parent is likely to be the mother. While this reflects the traditional caring role of women, it can also act as a spur to economic activity.

2.3.4   The role of women in society

A major feature in western countries has been the changing role of women.

The number of women in work in the UK has risen virtually without interruption over the past half-century, from 7 million in 1951, to 9 million in 1971, to just over 13 million in 2000, an average growth rate of 1.3 percent per year. Over 70% of women between the ages of 16 and 59 are now classified as economically active, against 56 percent in 1971 and around 40 percent in 1951. Since the number of men in the labour force has remained static, women have made up the entire net expansion of the UK workforce over this period.

This record on women's participation in paid work gives the UK an intermediate position among the advanced economies. The highest participation rates occur in the Scandinavian countries, followed by the US and Canada. The activity rate in the UK is markedly higher than in Germany or France, while rates are lowest in the southern European countries, Italy and Spain. While diversity remains, there has been a marked trend towards convergence over the past thirty years, with women's participation growing particularly strongly in those countries where it is still lowest, while remaining static, or even declining, in the Scandinavian countries, where it is already established at high levels. (Connolly & Gregory, 2005)

The growth in female employment in the countries concerned is linked to other economic and social changes.

- The decline of heavy manufacturing industries, where the physical demands meant that employees were mostly men, and the growth of the service sector with consequent demand for staff of either sex.

- Increasing divorce rates and better education for women have led to changes in assumptions about female roles. More women have found it necessary to work in order to support themselves and their families. At the same time, more women have assumed that they will have a career outside the home.

- Anti-discrimination legislation has made it more difficult to avoid recruiting women, has reduced pay differentials between men and women and has embedded maternity leave.

- Increased management awareness of the differences in strengths, weakness, concerns and culture between men and women.

Connolly & Gregory (2005) point out that there are still significant differences between men and women in employment:

- Mothers, rather than fathers, are widely regarded as the principal carers for children. Mothers are much more likely to work part-time than women without dependent children.

- Men are evenly divided between manual and non-manual work, but women tend to have non-manual jobs.

- While women working full-time do so at similar levels of responsibility to men, allowing for education and qualifications, women working part-time tend to be less well-qualified than men and to be concentrated in low-skill occupations.

- Women generally earn less than men, though the 'pay gap' has narrowed among women in full-time work.

2.3.5   Changing values and attitudes

We noted above that social attitudes have changed substantially over the last fifty years. This has been particularly noticeable with respect to notions of fairness and equality, community and the ecological environment, and has strongly affected both political thinking and business operations. For example, there is a growing belief that business should be concerned with ethical principles alongside concepts of honesty and fair dealing, and we shall consider this in the next section. And there has been a great deal of legislation to ensure fair and equal treatment of all members of society – in the workplace as well as in other social situations – again as we shall consider in a later section.

Businesses are also expected to contribute to the local community and this is seen in sponsorship of local events and sports teams and in links with local education institutions. Companies now take part in many school activities and provide work experience placements for thousands of students from schools and colleges.

CANTERBURY FOODS

In January 2006, **Canterbury Foods**, a manufacturer of food products such as pastries, sausages and hamburgers, collapsed into insolvency with debts of £15m. The Chief Executive, Paul Ainsworth, had said in September 2005 that the TV campaign by celebrity chef Jamie Oliver to drive up the quality of school meals had helped to undermine the company's position, though commentators noted that it had been heavily indebted and trading at a loss for some time. Britain's largest catering firm, *Compass*, said that sales of several food companies had been hit by the school meals campaign: 'there has been a move away from Turkey Twizzlers'.

ACTIVITY 1   15 mins

Club Fun is a UK company that sells packaged holidays. It offers a standard 'cheap and cheerful' package to resorts in Spain and the Greek islands. It was particularly successful at providing holidays for the 18-30 age group.

What do you think the implications are for Club Fun of the following developments?

- A fall in the number of school leavers

- The fact that young people are increasingly likely to go into higher education

- Holiday programmes on TV which feature a much greater variety of locations

- Greater disposable income among the 18-30 age group

- Increasing levels of Internet access

2.4   The technological environment

Technological change has gone on ever since the age of the caveman and has profound effects on products, production facilities and the organisation of work. The modern age is the age of the computer and its effects are spreading way beyond its initial impact as a commonplace tool in every office. Indeed, it is difficult to write anything about the subject without it becoming out-of-date very soon.

In terms of products, the effects are being felt in nearly all sectors of the economy, and not just in the obvious areas of communications and media where new technologies have created entirely new markets such as the mobile phone industry and digital broadcasting. In agriculture, for example, the application of computer power has enabled huge advances in genetics which has produced new strains of disease-resistant plants and created new hybrid specimens, and new fertilisers and insecticides have improved crop yields. In medicine, research is producing new approaches to the treatment of very many diseases and problematic human conditions. In other areas, the microchip has revolutionised the watch industry and the media and leisure industries have witnessed vast changes with the advent of miniaturised music systems, flat screen televisions, High Definition broadcasting and advanced computer games. The rapid development of moulded plastics has allowed electrical and automotive products to be made not only cheaper, but also in more stylish designs.

Changes like these affect a firm's market and each business must adapt to the opportunities or be left behind by more progressive competitors. Advances in science have made some products redundant. For example, in 2011, Sony announced that it was to cease production of the Walkman. What was, just 25 years ago, the cutting edge of technology is now seen to be so out of date that it is no longer financially viable to devote resources to its production.

However, it is perhaps in the areas of production itself and the organisation of work that the greatest impact on business is to be found.

Changed methods of recording, storing and retrieving information, on a scale never previously imagined, have transformed all aspects of business. Computers now play a major role in the design and manufacture of products, particularly through the development of high-speed, fully automated flow production systems – think of the way in which cars are made today as compared with the large numbers of workers employed on assembly lines just forty years ago. The routines of accounting, administration and much of communication are now entirely or partly automated, with consequent savings in cost, largely achieved through shedding staff. For many companies, the emphasis now is on the interpretation and application of this information to gain competitive advantage – for example, through a better understanding of customer needs and wants, developing understanding about their products and increasing their availability through the Internet, and enhancing their brands by creating communities and developing customer involvement through their websites and social media.

The new communications and information technologies have also had a profound effect on employment in general and on the way in which firms are managed:

- Technology has substantially increased manufacturing productivity, so that more people will be involved in service jobs.

- Very few people can expect to remain in the same job, or even the same industry, for all their working lives. Most people will have to change jobs or change the way they do their jobs several times during a normal working life. Whilst the work itself is likely to be more challenging and interesting, at least for most people, employment will be less secure. This has many important social implications.

- Certain sorts of skill, related to the interpretation and manipulation of data and the management of information processes, have become more valued than manual or physical skills. In the UK, this has led to increasingly tight labour markets and competition between employers to attract and retain the technologically competent staff they need (Torrington et al, 2009).

- With the constant change in technology, people must be prepared to retrain and acquire new skills at any time during their working lives. They are likely to find this easier if they have a relatively high level of basic education, particularly in the skills of numeracy and communication. If they do not achieve this before commencing work they may need to do so during their working lives. This has important implications for the education services, which are likely to be asked to provide more and more courses that can be combined with work – courses likely to be making more use of modern information technology.

- An increasing amount of work is now performed individually or by people working in small teams, with workers not necessarily all in the same location. Home working, at least on a part-time basis, is becoming more normal.

- Older forms of management and supervision will give way to self-management and co-ordination in many cases. We have already seen the move towards the 'delayering' of organisational hierarchies (in other words, the reduction of management layers between the senior managers and the workforce). The application of technology provides for workers to take more control over their own work responsibilities.

2.5 The legal environment

Businesses operate within the confines of the rules set out by the governments of the countries within which they operate. This legislation can, on occasions, have a profound effect on how the business functions. Indeed, failure to work within the law can affect a firm's reputation and incur financial penalties. In the UK businesses are subject to legislation from the UK government and from Europe.

By and large, the legislation affecting business has been passed to regulate the way in which organisations carry out their operations with the aim of protecting consumers, employees and other stakeholders from exploitation and harm. Thus, various Acts of Parliament regulate the way in which businesses are set up and run, and their obligations with regard to financial matters, particularly those that are accorded the status of 'companies'. Other Acts regulate the types of goods and services that can be sold, and the way in which they are sold. Here, we can note two other types of legislation which impact on working practices and the management of people in the workplace.

Employment legislation

Businesses must ensure that they work within rules concerning the employment of labour. Legislation first began to be passed in the 19th century to limit the exploitation of the workforce – for example, in respect of the employment of children. There is now a mass of such legislation covering virtually all aspects of the employment relationship, including the following areas:

- Contract of employment – all employees must have a written contract which specifies the conditions under which they are employed, including such issues as hours worked and pay.

- Minimum wage – a feature in many countries and introduced in the UK in 1998.

- Anti-discrimination or equality – to ensure the fair and equal treatment of all employees and prevent discrimination against workers on the basis of, among other things, their sex, ethnic origin or any disability.

- Unfair dismissal – to protect workers against losing their job without good reason.

- Trade unions – giving workers the right to join (and not to join) a trade union and the right of unions to be recognised as representatives of a workforce (although not necessarily for employers to negotiate with them) and to take industrial action, including strikes, in certain circumstances and after certain steps have been complied with.

Health and safety legislation

In simple terms, health and safety legislation is the regulation of the day to day working practices of businesses to prevent dangerous practices from taking place. It does not necessarily aim to promote good health as such, but instead to deter firms from employing dangerous practices.

In the UK, the most important piece of legislation is the Health and Safety at Work Act 1974 (updated in 1996). This created minimum acceptable standards for businesses in their 'duty of care' towards their employees and their handling of certain types of materials. Among the legal responsibilities of employers are the following:

- To provide a safe working environment.

- To provide, at zero cost to employees, appropriate health and safety equipment for all employees who need it.

- If there are more than five workers, to have a written safety policy and for that policy to be put on display.

- To appoint safety representatives (nominated by trade unions if there are any) who are entitled to inspect the workplace to ensure that it constitutes a safe working environment.

Additional legislation is imposed upon UK businesses from being part of the European Union – for example, the Working Time Directive of 2003 gave workers the right to work no more than 48 hours per week, as well as ensuring a minimum number of days holiday each year, paid breaks, and rest of at least 11 hours in any 24 hours' work.

Not surprisingly, the main way in which businesses are affected by this type of legislation is that it imposes additional costs upon them. By exercising their duty of care towards employees, firms must spend additional money which can affect its profitability. On the other hand, it can be used by a firm as a positive and provide a demonstration of its commitment to its employees. This in turn can lead to a more motivated and productive workforce. There is the possibility that if the increased productivity is greater than the increase in production costs then the firm will actually become more profitable.

2.6 The ethical and ecological environment

The 'E' of PESTLE can be taken to stand for either, or both, the ethical standards and concern for the ecological environment demanded by society of the way in which businesses conduct their operations.

Business ethics

Ethics are moral guidelines which govern good behaviour. What constitutes such moral guidelines and good behaviour in business is open to debate, but in western democratic societies it may be taken as relating to the values we noted earlier in respect of cultural values and assuming responsibility for fairness and equality in the treatment of individuals (both those directly in contact with the organisation itself and those affected by its operations) and for the well-being and development of the communities of which the organisation is a part. Note, though, that such values are culturally defined, which means that they may differ between different societies.

Within this definition, then, behaving ethically is doing what is morally right and having high standards of business behaviour based on ethical values. Businesses face ethical issues and decisions almost every day, and in some industries the issues are very significant. These cover a wide area of operations, including the following.

- Production practices – where, for example, attempts to increase profitability by cutting costs may lead to dangerous working conditions, inadequate safety standards in products or exploitative practices (such as employing child labour). This is a particular problem for firms which outsource production to low-cost factories overseas.

- Competitive practices – where, for example, attempts to gain an advantage over competing firms may lead to the payment of bribes, the fixing of markets or lying about facts within advertisements. The controversy over phone hacking by newspapers in the UK in order to get 'better' stories than the competitors can be seen as an example of this, where public outrage about the practice, particularly when it was shown to include violating the privacy of victims of crime, was so strong that one newspaper was effectively forced to close.

- Remuneration strategies – where the payment of high salaries to senior executives is determined by those executives themselves or the payment of bonuses is made irrespective of the performance of the company (as has been the case with many financial institutions).

An important distinction to remember is that behaving ethically is not quite the same thing as behaving lawfully:

- Ethics are about what is right and what is wrong.

- Law is about what is lawful and what is unlawful.

In most of the above examples, there are laws to prevent such practices, but companies have often been found to have had scant regard for them in the pursuit of their own interests.

Ethics is relevant to people management in two major ways. First, there is a need to ensure that employees are treated ethically, in accordance with the obligations imposed by all relevant employment laws, and also in accordance with the broad principles of 'natural justice'. Second, organisations may have to ensure that they conduct themselves ethically so far as their general operations are concerned. This latter issue has become particularly important in recent years, as customers in some countries have articulated their anxieties over such matters as the employment of child labour and the working conditions under which factory operatives have been forced to function in certain countries and locations. The rise of ethical consumerism means that there is a business case for ethical action on the part of employers, and indeed some have responded by introducing schemes to monitor and evaluate their overseas suppliers.

Writing specifically about discrimination in organisations, Stephen Taylor (CIPD, 2010) argues that

> 'Unfair discrimination is just plain wrong. It is socially unjust that some groups should succeed more than others for no good reason. The reluctance of organisations and their managers to take this on board is why there needs to be so much regulation in this area, but there is plenty of evidence to demonstrate that a purely ethical case can sometimes impress even the most hard-nosed and commercially-oriented managers.'

Whilst that may be so, there is also evidence that the ethical values prevailing in some parts of the world can differ, and the practices of people management may have to allow for these differences. For example, the conventional methods of performance appraisal used in Western countries presuppose a more or less equal amount of participation in the process by the subordinate, but this would hardly be practicable in societies which continue to practise very hierarchical and deferential control systems.

ACTIVITY 2   15 mins

In the context of business ethics, consider your response to the following questions.

(a)   Should businesses seek to make profits from problem gambling?

(b)   Should supermarkets sell cider cheaper than bottled water?

(c)   Should businesses make payments to individuals in other companies in order to secure orders, given that there is intense competition between businesses for such orders?

Ecology

We noted above that public concern about the environment is a major feature of the social attitudes that business needs to take account of. Concerns about global warming, the potential exhaustion of natural resources and threats to the diversity of life – plants and animals – are all real and business has a key role in assuring the future of the planet. Concerns are also felt at more local levels, for example in respect of dealing with waste and used products.

Organisations are now much more conscious of the impact that their operations may have for the environment and a whole new concept has arisen – corporate social responsibility (CSR) – to embody their response. This takes the form of companies taking specific actions to ensure that their effect on the planet is as benign as possible. The concept has had some significant effects, not least through the requirement to report actions taken to implement CSR and thus be accountable to a wide variety of stakeholders with interest in these matters. Increasingly, firms are recognising that failure to consider the ecological effects of their activities can lead to consumer boycotts, and that an ethical approach to the environment can be good for business.

THE ROLE OF CSR

A number of companies have made very public declarations of their 'green credentials', reasoning that as well as being genuinely beneficial for the environment, they can gain customer support for their efforts. For example:

(a) IKEA works towards sustainability goals by: providing tips and ideas for a sustainable home life on its website; aiming for zero landfill waste from its packaging, and reduced wastewater treatment and less water use within its production operations; cutting its carbon footprint through less transport and packaging; and showing social responsibility through, for example, its works to support charities.

(b) Marks and Spencer are aiming to cut their carbon footprint to zero by 2012, make all their packaging recyclable and only to use sustainable natural resources in their products.

Not addressing these issues has caused some companies considerable problems. For example, McDonald's has been severely criticised on a number of fronts – for the destruction of rain forests to turn into land for raising cattle (a claim it has consistently denied), and for the use of polystyrene packaging (with a life of a thousand years) for its fast food. In response, the company joined with an environmental pressure group to find ways of reducing the ecological impact of its business. As well as trying systems to recycle used polystyrene, which is possible, the company used a different packaging material which could not be recycled, but which took up much less space in dumps. It has gone on to examine all aspects of its operation to reduce the effects on the environment, a move which has both resulted in cost reductions and pleased its customers.

3 The impact of PESTLE factors on people management

In this section we shall consider some of the ways in which the influences in the general external environment impact on the way in which organisations deal with their employees. We shall then go on to examine in detail one element of this – the psychological contract formed between the employing organisation and those it employs.

3.1 The labour market

The labour market is the sphere in which labour is 'bought' and 'sold', and in which market concepts such as supply, demand and price operate with regard to human resources

The labour market has changed dramatically in the last few decades. Previously, writers suggested that there was 'seller's market' – as technology increased the skills and therefore scarcity value of employees in certain jobs, and as the scale of state benefits blunted the fear of unemployment, the initiative seemed to be with the employee, or with organised groups of employees.

The decline of manufacturing, the increase of women in employment, the globalisation of business (allowing offshoring of production and service provision to low-cost labour countries) and the more general application of technology, among other factors, have changed that situation. A 'buyer's market' for labour now gives employers considerable power, with a large pool of available labour created by unemployment and non-career (temporary, freelance) labour.

On the other hand, even in conditions of high overall employment, particular skill shortages still exist and may indeed be more acute because of economic pressures on education and training. The term 'war for talent' was coined to describe this phenomena, and while the recent economic downturn has seen the phrase used less vigorously, many employees still compete for people. Engineers and software designers, among other specialist and highly trained groups, are the target of fierce competition, forcing a re-evaluation of recruitment and retention policies amongst employers.

Employers may compete for labour and skills in a number of different markets: local, national and international.

- Particular factors in the local labour market (people living in the 'travel to work area' or within reasonable commuting distance) may create pressure for flexibility. For example: geographical dispersion or lack of public transportation may require flexible starting hours, or work-from-home options.

- National/regional skill shortages and wage costs may encourage the outsourcing or 'offshoring' of operations to low-cost labour countries, or the co-opting of overseas team members through 'virtual' collaboration using ICT links.

- Different occupational structures and orientations (at local and national level) may also require different approaches to the employment relationship, career management and so on. Professionally and technically qualified staff, for example, may be treated differently (as 'core' employees) from lower-skilled and high mobility workers (who may be more flexibly contracted).

3.2   The changing workforce

The need for flexibility

A number of factors have come together to create an imperative for working practices to change in order to meet the requirements of business survival in the 21st century.

- Increased global competition has placed an increased emphasis on quality, innovation and reducing the unit costs of production. Job design and the organisation of work must both mobilise employees' energies for quality/innovation and reliable productivity.

- Increased market uncertainty means that organisations need to be more adaptable to changes in demand. This requires them to be able to vary the size and deployment of their workforces to meet demand as effectively and efficiently as possible.

- Technological change, particularly in the computerisation of work processes and information flows, has eroded traditional demarcation boundaries between jobs. Job design and the organisation of work must fit the new technology in order to secure its benefits for efficiency.

In addition, demographic and cultural changes have highlighted the need for flexible job and career designs, in order to meet the needs of dual-income families, women and older workers for 'work life balance' (see below).

These factors all emphasise the need for flexibility to underpinned working practices:

- Increasing managerial ability to adapt the size and deployment of the workforce in line with changing demand and supply.

- Increasing scope for flexible working for individual employees.

- Raising the quality and/or quantity of workforce output.

Diversity in the workforce

At the same time, the increasing diversity of the working population has major implications for working practices, including for example:

- The need to take account of anti-discrimination legislation and best practice in recruitment. As well as legal protection for groups which have traditionally been under-represented in the workplace, heightened sensitivity to such matters means that positive equal opportunity and diversity policies play an important part in building an employer brand which will enable organisations to attract quality labour.

- The need to take account of the needs of increasingly diverse family shapes and circumstances, in order to attract and retain people. Legislation has begun to address the needs of dual income families (for example through parental leave and time off for emergencies) but proactive HR initiatives – such as career breaks and childcare support – contribute importantly to a 'family-friendly' employer brand.

Work-life balance

Work-life balance is a concept which recognises the need for employers to support workers in achieving a balance between the demands of either their work and the demands of home and family or work and their aspirations outside the working environment.

Research for British Telecom Business conducted in 2006 indicated that more than a third of British workers (37 per cent of men and 34 per cent of women) would be prepared to forgo a pay increase for more flexible working options. The survey also found that 43 per cent of 18 to 29-year-olds are interested, compared to 31 per cent of the over-50s.

This research indicated that flexible working policies are valued across the age range, but with an above-average response from young people, more than three-quarters of whom agreed that it is an important benefit. Almost two-thirds of those aged 18 to 29 identified a better work-life balance as the main advantage, followed by less stress and fewer travel problems.

The opinions expressed in 2006 may have changed given the shortages of jobs for young people, however a fundamental change in attitude is evident. There is other evidence to support that graduates select employers on the basis of their attitude towards work-life balance. Work-life balance strategies are often associated with the implementation of flexible working policies.

Flexible working policies, designed to give employees options in regard to their hours and/or locations of work, have been supported in recent years by the range of equal opportunity and family-friendly rights law which we noted above. These have provided a package of entitlements including annual leave, maximum working hours, parental leave and time off for dependent care, maternity/paternity leave and adoption leave; equal rights for part-time workers and so on.

> 'For years, best-practice organisations have taken an informal approach to fielding flexible working requests, with local line managers making decisions that best fit an individual or department, by involving other team members in the matter. In many cases, this method will continue to be the most effective in driving a flexible work culture while avoiding red tape' (Cartwright, 2003).

3.3 The use of non-standard contracts

The Workplace Employment Relations Survey 2004 data shows that the use of non-standard forms of employment has now become 'commonplace' in UK workplaces. 83% of workplaces employed part-time employees (less than 30 hours per week), up from 79% in 1998. Almost one third of workplaces had employees on temporary contracts. It is worth noting that those working on part time contracts is now 5% higher than before the economic downturn. Whilst this may be less attributable to a general change in working styles and more to do with the needs to control employment costs, it has meant that many people have remained in employment and continued to develop their skills.

The increase in the service sector has seen an increase in non-traditional full-time jobs. Compared to traditional manufacturing type employment there is not the requirement for the workforce to be in one place at one time. Service sector jobs often require a longer working day that cannot be undertaken by someone in a single shift – for example, in retail outlets and call centres. Also by splitting such jobs the employer is able to make themselves available to a wider market of those seeking non-full-time hours.

There has also been an increase in temporary contracts. Research by Ford and Slater (2006) discovered that the use of temporary workers was less of a strategic people planning decision by employers but more driven by meeting short-term needs and managing costs. They also concluded that these type of contracts were mostly focused on low-paying entry level clerical and operative type work.

Another developing practice is the increase in the contracting out or outsourcing of services such as cleaning, transport, security – and, indeed, HR and training.

4 The psychological contract

Many of the environmental changes and influences we have discussed above have impinged on the working environment. In particular, the attitudes and expectations of both employers and their employees have changed, though not universally and not in a homogeneous fashion.

4.1 The theory of the psychological contract

The idea of the psychological contract is an important area of theory and research in HRM, helping to explain and predict some aspects of behaviour in the employment relationship. Torrington et al (2009) offer a working definition, describing the psychological contract as: '. . . a set of expectations or obligations between employer and employee, which serve to govern the employment relationship.' (p15)

(a) The psychological contract differs from the legal contract of employment. The contract of employment is binding in law and is normally in written form. The psychological contract exists only in the minds of the employer and the employee.

(b) The psychological contract works at an individual not at a collective level, which is to say it is not established by trade union activity such collective bargaining.

In their discussion, Torrington et al (2009) also remark that HR practices such as recruitment, training and reward are expected to be influential in creating a psychological contract where trust is high and fairness prevails and which leads to positive outcomes such as employee commitment, motivation and performance. However, it is equally the case that if an employer is perceived as being in breach of the contract, negative outcomes such as poor motivation and performance will result.

Rayner and Adam-Smith (2009) provide further useful background.

(a) The psychological contract is influenced by both organisational policy and procedures and by the attitudes and behaviour of individual managers and employees.

(b) The contract is based on 'perceptions of mutual obligations' (p94). That is to say, the details of the contract are not recorded anywhere; they exist only in the consciousness of the people concerned. This means that it is very likely that different people will have different perceptions of the obligations involved.

4.2 Types of psychological contract

It is possible to discern at least two main kinds of psychological contract: the difference depends on how the employment relationship is perceived. As with many aspects of human behaviour, these are not really strict categories: many contracts will have characteristics that fall somewhere between these two types or fall outside the range altogether.

(a) The transactional contract. The transactional contract is largely concerned with more or less tangible aspects of the employment relationship. Typically, in this kind of contract, the employer provides a job involving well-defined work, which carries with it the reward of pay, which may be related to performance. The employee expects to work for the hours and in the way required by the employer. Neither party expects a high degree of commitment and the duration of the contract may be perceived to be of fairly short duration.

(b) The relational contract. While the relational contract will include expectations about basic and tangible matters such as pay and work requirements, it will focus on expectations relating to less tangible aspects of the relationship. Employers will provide job security, good career prospects and opportunities for personal training and development, while employees will be loyal, committed to the organisation and motivated to perform to high standards. Both parties will perceive the relationship as stable and long-term.

Case study research from 1990 onwards suggested that the environmental pressures already discussed, particularly globalisation, have led to a change in the general nature of the psychological contract, making it possible to identify 'old' and 'new' versions. The essence of this change appeared to be a shift away from the relational type of contract and towards a more transactional type focussed on pay and replacing employee loyalty and conformance with long hours and high performance.

However, research based on surveys during the same period contradicted this impression.

4.3 The psychological contract and flexible working

Three important pressures lead employers to expect greater work flexibility.

(a) One of the effects of globalisation has been an increase in environmental uncertainty. Existing markets shrink and new ones develop; technical innovation brings new products that disrupt markets and new methods that reduce costs. Such rapid change requires prompt action and this often must take the form of adjustments to work roles and methods, working hours and job numbers.

(b) At the same time, the costs of installing and using technologically advanced plant and machinery make it important to run such equipment continually, or with no more than short breaks for maintenance.

(c) A requirement for flexible working tends to be inherent in many service industry jobs, particularly those involving knowledge work. Services cannot be kept in stock, for example, and provision must match patterns of varying demand.

Employers dealing with such problems now expect appropriate flexibility from staff and see acceptance of the need for such adjustments as part of the psychological contract.

Torrington et al (2009) describe three aspects of the required labour flexibility.

(a) Numerical flexibility allows rapid adjustment to the size of the workforce and is achieved by confining traditional permanent, full-time contracts to a core of staff and supplementing them with short-term contracts, rolling contracts and outworkers. The core employees are concentrated in crucial roles, are well-regarded by the employer, well-paid and have improved career prospects. In return they provide the other two forms of flexibility discussed below. Various groups of peripheral workers must look to the external labour market for continuing employment; turnover among these groups is probably fairly high, which enhances numerical flexibility.

(b)   Temporal flexibility responds to varying business requirements by varying the number of hours worked and the times at which they are worked. This can be achieved by the use of part-time workers, by flexibility in the number of hours worked by full-time workers and by the use of annual hours contracts. Annual hours contracts recognise the seasonal nature of much commercial activity and allow for increases and decreases in the length of the working day and week, usually without the payment of an overtime premium.

(c)   Functional flexibility is achieved when employees are able to undertake more than one type of work. This type of flexibility will normally be provided by the core workers described above.

One important aspect of the development of labour flexibility has been the demise of the 'job for life'. In many organisations, employees had a reasonable expectation of a high degree of job security. This is now far less common, which is clearly to the detriment of the employees concerned. Employers have responded to concern about this disadvantage by undertaking action to enhance the employability of their work people. In short-term emergencies, such as periods of major down-sizing and redundancy, this has taken the form of counselling and coaching in job search and interview skills, often provided by external 'outplacement' consultants. For the longer term, there has been increased attention to providing training and experience that will enhance employability in more general terms.

Chapter Roundup

↳ The business environment comprises everything outside an organisation's boundaries, and organisations are subject to various influences from that environment which affect all aspects of its operations, including those associated with people management.

↳ PESTLE is a useful mnemonic to identify these various influencing factors – political, economic, social (and cultural), technological, legal and ethical/ecological.

↳ Political factors are significant in that the government sets the overall tone for society and is ultimately responsible for shaping the economic and legal environments. Organisations make representations to government in the hope of influencing policy and decisions in their favour.

↳ Economic factors include both the overall state of the economy at any particular time and the extent of competition, particularly in international trade. The major influences on the state of the economy, as they affect business operations, are the level of inflation, the availability of credit and the level of interest rates, and the overall level of unemployment. Globalisation, fuelled by the relaxation of trade barriers and the use of advanced communication and information technologies, has led to significantly increased levels of competition across the world. This has driven down costs in nearly all sectors of the economy, although competition is also intense in product attributes other than price. This has had a major impact on the workplace as organisations seek to reduce labour costs and apply skilled labour more efficiently through new, more flexible working practices.

↳ The social environment is characterised by the demographic makeup of particular societies and the influence of culture (and subcultures) within them. Western developed societies are notable for their aging populations and their increasingly diverse ethnic and cultural composition. There has been a major change in the role of women in society and in work. Social attitudes have also been changing in recent years and there is an increased emphasis on individualisation and personal fulfilment which has affected working practices.

↳ The technological environment is characterised by constant change as advances are made in the application of communication and information technologies to all aspects of society, including the workplace. This has had a significant impact on both the products businesses produce and the processes and working practices used in their production.

↳ The legal environment regulates the activities of business organisations, primarily to protect employees and customers from exploitation. In terms of people management, employment and health and safety legislation is designed to ensure fair and equitable treatment of all employees and the provision of a safe working environment.

↳ Organisations must be aware of cultural change and adjust their methods and strategies to take it into account. One further factor which has emerged from this general area in recent years is the pressure on business to maintain standards of 'good' behaviour in the way in which they operate. This includes the application of ethical standards in business decision making as well as a concern for the environment in its broadest sense.

↳ The psychological contract takes the form of a set of unspoken perceptions and assumptions about the relationship between employer and employee, in terms of expectations and obligations. It differs from the contract of employment, which is specific, legally binding and usually in writing. Psychological contracts may be divided into two types: relational (stable in the long-term and providing co-operation and security) and transactional (probably assumed to be impermanent and relating to immediate duties and rewards).

↳ Environmental pressures, such as globalisation, the cost of advanced technology and the move to service industries have led to changes in many psychological contracts, largely to provide for flexibility in employment. Numerical flexibility is achieved by establishing a core of permanent employees, supplemented as required by short-term and part time workers; temporal flexibility requires permanent staff to accept variation in their hours of work and is enhanced by part-time staff and annual hours contracts; Functional flexibility is achieved when employees are able to undertake more than one kind of work.

↳ Flexibility has led to the demise of the 'job for life' and, as a result, increasing concern about employability.

Quick Quiz

1   What do the letters PESTLE stand for?

2   How can organisations influence government?

3   Why is the availability of credit so important to business?

4   A country experiences a surge in birth rate. What might it expect to experience in about 25 years' time?

5   Which region has the highest rates of women's participation in the economy?

6   What is the purpose of anti-discrimination and equality legislation?

7   What is the psychological contract?

8   How does the psychological contract differ from the contract of employment?

9   If you identified a transactional type of psychological contract, what time scale would you expect the parties to have in mind?

10   What is temporal flexibility?

Answers to Quick Quiz

1 Political, economic, social, technological, legal and natural environmental factors of the general business environment.

2 They can employ lobbyists and public relations specialists to influence decision makers and public opinion.

3 It provides the means for organisations to fund investment through the taking on of debts.

4 Increased demand for housing and, possibly, inflation as a consequence

5 Scandinavia

6 To ensure the fair and equal treatment of all employees and prevent discrimination against workers on the basis of, among other things, their sex, ethnic origin or any disability.

7 A set of expectations or obligations between employer and employee, which serve to govern the employment relationship

8 The contract of employment is binding in law and is normally in written form. The psychological contract exists only in the minds of the employer and the employee.

9 Probably a fairly short one

10 Temporal flexibility responds to varying business requirements by varying the number of hours worked and the times at which they are worked.

Answers to Activities

Activity 1

The firm's market is shrinking. There is an absolute fall in the number of school leavers. Moreover, it is possible that the increasing proportion of school leavers going to higher education will mean there will be fewer who can afford Club Fun's packages. That said, a higher disposable income in the population at large might compensate for this trend. People might be encouraged to try destinations other than Club Fun's traditional resorts if these other destinations are publicised on television. Growing access to the Internet makes it easier for other suppliers to compete.

Activity 2

The answers to these ethical questions will depend very much on your personal views. However, they all raise issues of weighing up actions which are in the interests of the company itself and the pursuit of its profit objective, against moral standpoints as to what may be considered right and wrong in other circumstances. There are also legal issues involved.

Chapter 4

The motivation to work

In this chapter we begin our examination of why people work. This is a complex topic and the subject of a range of ideas and theories. We start by considering the nature of the work ethic and then proceed to a description of some of the theories that attempt to explain motivation. In the next chapter we will round off our discussion by examining the relationship between financial reward and motivation.

1 The nature of the work ethic

Your Chief Examiner has provided a brief definition of the **work ethic:** 'the belief that individuals have a moral responsibility to seek, gain and keep employment'.

and has pointed out the religious origins of the concept. The Concise Oxford Dictionary underlines these origins, describing the phrase as 'another term for "protestant ethic"', which it defines as 'the view that a person's duty and responsibility is to achieve success through hard work and thrift'. The term appears in the title of Max Weber's important early sociological text *The Protestant Ethic and the Spirit of Capitalism*, originally published in 1905. In this book, Weber suggested that the growth of capitalism as a widely successful economic system could be traced to the influence of Protestantism on attitudes to work. An important implication of the work ethic is that people should work even it is not strictly necessary for economic survival or even for prosperity, because it is the right thing to do.

ACTIVITY 1   15 mins

(a)   Contrast this view with the 'instrumental' attitude to work described by Goldthorpe *et al* and discussed in Chapter 1 of this book.

(b)   Consider your own attitude to work of all kinds; include academic work, paid work and the effort you expend on recreations and hobbies. Ask yourself how well the work ethic fits with your own attitudes.

2 The relevance of the work ethic

An important point of view about the work ethic is that it influences not just the way people view work, but also, by extension, the way that managers deal with the people who work for them. The implication is that, if the work ethic applies, the **role of management** in motivating people to work is diminished, since they will supply their own motivation.

The problem with this view is exposed if we take it to an extreme: if the work ethic applies, do employers need to pay their employees to work? Certainly, many people will work voluntarily for a cause they believe in, and some people are sufficiently wealthy not to have to work to secure a living. However, most people do have to work to **secure an income**, so for them the motivation to work is at least partly economic. They will therefore have an interest in the nature and extent of the economic rewards of work. Having established that the work ethic does not provide a full explanation of why people work, it is reasonable to ask if there might be other factors involved as well, such as the motivation provided by management.

This would be a commonsense view of a complex topic: people's motivation to work is probably influenced by several factors, including economic reward, management policy and job satisfaction.

Nevertheless, many people's attitudes to their work situations are likely to be coloured to a greater or lesser extent by moral considerations, whether explicit or present in a vaguer form.

(a)   A person may subscribe to the work ethic.

(b)   The psychological contract may be satisfactory to the employee, leading to an obligation to work as directed and to a proper standard.

(c)   Even if the psychological contract is unsatisfactory overall, individuals may be motivated by feelings of personal loyalty to colleagues or to individual managers.

3 Motivation

3.1 What is motivation?

Motivation is 'the cognitive decision-making process through which goal-directed behaviour is initiated, energised, directed and maintained.' (Huczynski and Buchanan, 2007, p242).

Like many definitions of complex things, this definition is itself rather complex, but you should note that it mentions both **goals** and **decisions**. This reflects the view that both **innate drives** and **cognitive processes** can influence motivation.

In practice, the words **motives** and **motivation** are commonly used in different contexts to mean the following.

(a) **Goals or outcomes** that have become desirable for a particular individual. We say that money, power or friendship are motives for doing something. **Content theories** of motivation are based on this idea.

(b) The **mental process of choosing desired outcomes**, deciding how to go about them (and whether the likelihood of success warrants the amount of effort that will be necessary) and setting in motion the required behaviours. **Process theories** of motivation address this process of **decision-making**.

(c) The **social process** by which other people motivate us to behave in the ways they wish. Motivation in this sense usually applies to the attempts of organisations to get workers to work in a satisfactory way. From a manager's point of view, motivation is the controlling of the work environment, rewards and sanctions in such a way as to encourage desired behaviours and performance from employees.

3.2 What does motivation achieve?

The argument is that if individuals can be motivated, they will perform better and more willingly – **above mere compliance** with rules and procedures. If their personal needs and goals are integrated with those of the team and organisation, individuals will work more efficiently (so that productivity will rise) or produce a better quality of work, or might contribute more of their creativity and initiative to the job.

There is continuing debate about exactly what motivation strategies can aim to achieve in the way of productivity, quality and other business benefits, but it has become widely accepted that **committed** employees add value to the organisation. This is particularly true in environments where initiative and flexibility are required of employees in order to satisfy customer demands and keep pace with environmental changes.

> **MOTIVATION IN ACTION: THE JOHN LEWIS PARTNERSHIP, SINGAPORE AIRLINES AND THE RITZ-CARLTON HOTEL GROUP**
>
> Here are a few examples of organisations which have proved extraordinarily successful in attracting and keeping their staff, and equally successful in attracting and keeping their customers. In truth, there is a logical connection between keeping staff and keeping customers, because long-standing staff become more experienced and can develop strong personal links with important customers.
>
> The **John Lewis Partnership** is an unusual collection of around 25 department stores in the UK – unusual in the sense that all its employees are 'partners' in the business. That is to say, they actually own the business themselves, so of course they have a personal stake in the success of the company. Each year part of the profits is returned to the employees as a dividend, and almost every year there is a huge cheer from the staff if the profit-share amount exceeds the figure from the previous year. Obviously that doesn't happen every year, but nothing seems to dent the loyalty of the John Lewis workforce.

One of the key elements in the John Lewis philosophy is the expectation that people in the organisation will look for and perform 'random acts of kindness' for each other and also for customers – in an effort to encourage corporate team-working and unselfish collaboration internally, and memorable service for customers externally.

In one John Lewis store recently, for instance, an assistant in the ladies shoe department was asked to find a pair of elegant shoes to harmonise with a suit which the customer had just purchased in Ladies Fashions.

'Is this a special occasion, madam?', enquired the assistant.

'Yes it is,' replied the customer. 'It's my 50th birthday today, my husband has organised a special dinner for me this evening, and I need to look my best.'

Whereupon the assistant stood on a chair and sang 'Happy Birthday To You' to the customer!

Now clearly we can't know how you might have reacted had this happened to you, but the fact is that the customer was so impressed that she subsequently wrote to the Chairman of the John Lewis company in praise of the treatment she received that morning in the shop's shoe department. And of course the whole incident could have gone horribly wrong – but the point is that the staff of John Lewis are strongly encouraged to use their initiative – and that means they must sometimes take risks (the only way to ensure that people don't take risks is to prevent them from taking any decisions at all, but that simply turns them into robots – and probably makes them alienated). Risk-taking is, well, risky; when it works it's brilliant, as in the example above; when it fails you must simply learn from the experience and move on. It would be disastrous to conclude, however, that the best thing to do is not to take risks any more.

Staff are certainly encouraged to take risks when they work for the **Ritz-Carlton Hotel** group, where the care and comfort of hotel guests is everyone's top priority. If a guest has a problem or a special need, employees break away from their regular duties to resolve the issue. Indeed, the employee who first hears the complaint becomes responsible for resolving it to the guest's satisfaction – and in this company staff are required to respond with a 'Yes' to all customer requests: they must seek managerial permission before they can answer 'No'. That's diametrically the opposite of what happens in many other companies, whether hotel firms or not, where the standard response to a customer complaint is to ask the customer to complete a complaints form. This then means that the complaint can be passed onwards and upwards, perhaps to the company's Head Office, until it reaches someone who is judged to have the appropriate authority to enable the complaint to be resolved. But that's not the style in the Ritz-Carlton group.

Every day, employees of every department in every Ritz-Carlton hotel gather for a 15-minute staff meeting where they share 'Wow stories'. These are true stories of employee heroics that go above and beyond conventional customer service expectations. For example, a hotel chef in Bali found special eggs and milk in a small grocery store in another country and had them flown to the hotel for a guest with food allergies.

Singapore Airlines is another company with an exceptional reputation for service excellence, and yet to fly with SIA (Singapore International Airlines) costs no more than flying with any other airline - disproving those who try to argue that world-class customer service costs more. In fact, like total quality, world-class customer service costs *less* than 'ordinary' customer service because the airline spends much less on dealing with customer complaints and with the need for service recovery.

The only problem experienced by SIA is that its customers have such high expectations. That being so, even excellent service is taken for granted and the company has to work very hard to find new ways to create 'wow' experiences for its customers.

3.3   Theories of motivation

Many theories try to explain motivation and why and how people can be motivated. We will divide them into **content** and **process** theories.

(a)   **Content theories** assume that we all have a set of **needs** that we wish to satisfy or **goals** and desired outcomes that we wish to achieve.

(b)   **Process theories** explore the **process** through which outcomes become desirable. This approach assumes that people are able to select their goals and choose the paths towards them, by a conscious or unconscious process of calculation.

4   Content theories of motivation

4.1   Maslow's hierarchy of needs

Abraham Maslow described **five innate human needs** or motives (Maslow, 1943) which he suggested were related to one another by their place in a hierarchy of 'relative pre-potency'. This has two implications.

(a)   Starting at the bottom of the pyramid, each level of need is **dominant until satisfied**; only then does the next level of need become a motivating factor.

(b)   A need that has been satisfied no longer motivates an individual's behaviour.

The diagram below illustrates this pyramid.

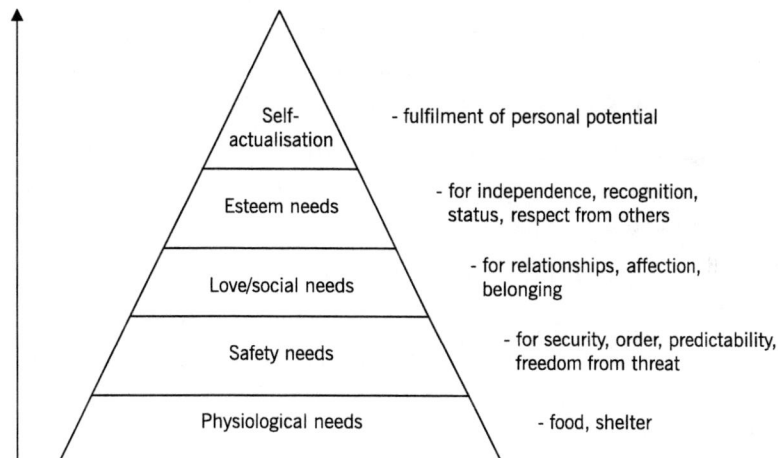

Figure 4.1: Maslow's hierarchy of needs

Maslow did not present his ideas as a set of rules or as scientific fact but as a speculative model in which personalities could be discussed. For example, he made it clear that the various levels of the need hierarchy overlap to some extent, and for some people the needs may apply in a different order.

(a)   The most common apparent difference is that some people seem to need self-esteem before love, though aggressive, confident behaviour may disguise a need for love.

(b)   Very creative people may be driven by the need for self-actualisation even when lower needs are unsatisfied.

(c)   Some people do not seem to be affected by higher needs and may continue to seek satisfaction of lower needs.

(d)   Conversely, a lower need that has always been satisfied may be regarded as unimportant and the satisfaction taken for granted.

Maslow also pointed out that the satisfaction of a need may be only partial; this means that higher needs may emerge gradually as the ones below them approach satisfaction.

ACTIVITY 2

Decide which of Maslow's motivating need categories the following fit into.

(a)   Receiving praise from your manager
(b)   A family party
(c)   An artist forgetting to eat
(d)   A man washed up on a desert island
(e)   A pay increase
(f)   Joining a local drama group
(g)   Being awarded a national honour

The **implication for management** of this theory is that a satisfied need is unlikely to motivate and once this state has been achieved, motivational effort should be directed to the satisfaction of higher needs. There is a certain intuitive appeal to this. After all, you are unlikely to be concerned with status or recognition while you are hungry or thirsty - primary survival needs will take precedence. Likewise, once a person has achieved a reasonable standard of living, we might expect love and esteem needs to predominate.

However, there are various problems associated with using Maslow's theory.

(a)   People seek satisfaction in other places than work and the same need may cause different behaviour in different individuals. One person might seek to satisfy his need for esteem by winning promotion, while another might place more value on respect within a religious context. Yet another might prefer leading a challenge against authority.

(b)   The hierarchy ignores the concept of **deferred gratification** by which people are prepared to forgo the immediate satisfaction of needs in order to fulfil a long-term goal; a good example is the long studentship of the medical profession.

(c)   Different people have different views of the importance of individual needs.

(d)   Research does not bear out the proposition that needs become less powerful as they are satisfied, except at the very primitive level of 'primary' needs like, hunger and thirst.

(e)   It is difficult to predict behaviour using the hierarchy: the theory is too vague.

(f)   Research has revealed that the hierarchy tends to reflect UK and US cultural values, which may not transfer to other contexts.

Despite these problems, Maslow's theory remains popular and has stimulated awareness of the range of motivations that people may have. We see the influence of the theory in many aspects of the work situation.

Need	Example of satisfaction at work
Physiological	Pleasant working conditions
Safety	Job security
Social	Friendly work group
Esteem	Job status
Self-actualisation	Task achievement

4.2 Alderfer's ERG theory

Alderfer presents a simpler analysis of needs into three areas or groups.

(a) **Existence needs** relate to survival and combine physiological and safety needs of a material kind.

(b) **Relatedness needs** concern social relationships and include needs for love, esteem, a sense of belonging and a sense of being safe.

(c) **Growth needs** focus on achieving individual potential and include the needs for self-esteem and self-actualisation.

Research indicates that if the lower-level needs are unsatisfied they will increase in force, but, conversely, if they approach satisfaction they will tend to diminish in force.

While accepting the basic idea that individuals try to satisfy their needs in the order existence – relatedness – growth, Alderfer suggested that they should be seen as a continuous spectrum rather than a hierarchy, in that more than one set of needs may be active at the same time. Also, frustration of one group of needs may lead to extra emphasis on the other groups. This idea can be used by managers in work situations where one of the groups of needs is frustrated; typically, if a job frustrates the need for personal development, this can to some extent be overcome by providing opportunities for the satisfaction of needs in the existence and relatedness groups.

4.3 McClelland's need theory

David McClelland identified three types of motivating need.

(a) **The need for power** (nPow) corresponds, roughly, to the status and recognition elements of Maslow's esteem need. People with a high nPow usually seek positions in which they can influence and control others, but they may lack the flexibility and people skills needed by managers.

(b) **The need for affiliation** (nAff) corresponds, roughly to Maslow's love/social need. People with a high nAff value a sense of belonging and tend to be concerned with maintaining good personal relationships. This may affect their ability to make difficult management decisions concerning people.

(c) **The need for achievement** (nAch). People who need to achieve have a strong desire for success and a strong fear of failure.

Much of McClelland's work was concerned with the need for achievement, since he considered that people with high nAch scores made the best managers. He found that such people set realistic goals and found achievement to be more motivating than material reward. Their weakness as managers was a tendency to concentrate on results to the detriment of the interests and needs of their subordinates.

McClelland developed both tests to detect nAch and programmes of training to develop it.

4.4 Herzberg's two-factor theory

In the 1950s, Frederick **Herzberg** interviewed engineers and accountants in Pittsburgh to find out what had given them positive or negative feelings about their work. Analysis revealed two distinct sets of factors: those that **created dissatisfaction**, which Herzberg called **hygiene** or **maintenance** factors, and those that **created satisfaction**, which Herzberg called **motivator** factors. Hygiene factors are, generally, aspects of the **work environment**, whereas motivator factors are aspects of the **work itself**. Hygiene and motivator factors correspond very roughly to the lower and upper parts of Maslow's hierarchy.

Hygiene factors	Motivator factors
Company policy and administration	Recognition
Salary	Responsibility
Supervision	Challenging work
Interpersonal relations within the team	Achievement
Working conditions	Growth and development in the job
Job security	

Herzberg related these groups of factors to two basic needs of individuals.

(a)   The need to **avoid unpleasantness**. Hygiene factors satisfy this need, temporarily – in the same way that hygiene or sanitation minimises threats to health. Hygiene factors can be manipulated to prevent dissatisfaction in the short term, but cannot offer lasting satisfaction or motivation.

(b)   The need for **personal growth and fulfilment**. Motivator factors satisfy this need, and actively create job satisfaction, motivating the individual to superior performance and effort.

The implication of this analysis is that satisfaction and dissatisfaction at work are **not simple opposites**: the opposite of satisfaction is lack of satisfaction, while the opposite of dissatisfaction is lack of dissatisfaction. This means that it is not possible to move seamlessly from dissatisfaction to satisfaction by the application of a single stimulus or group of stimuli. Two different need systems are involved and each must be considered separately.

It would be possible to experience **apparently contradictory states** such as simultaneous (if unspoken) satisfaction with hygiene factors and dissatisfaction with motivator factors. This would probably be the case with well-paid workers engaged in dull, repetitive, unchallenging work in ideal working conditions. The typical reaction to this situation would be a lack of motivation and a tendency to demand even better pay and conditions. However, even if granted, these improvements would not achieve anything in relation to the feelings of dissatisfaction.

It is possible to link Herzberg's model to **McClelland's** theory in that people with high nAch are particularly responsive to motivator factors – which, of course, include achievement among their number.

Herzberg suggested that 'when people are dissatisfied with their work it is usually because of discontent with environmental factors... Satisfaction can only arise from the job.' He recommended various approaches to **job design** that would build motivation potential into the work.

Like Maslow's hierarchy, Herzberg's model is simple and accessible, and embraces a wide range of possible rewards and working conditions, but it has been criticised on a number of grounds.

(a)   **Empirical verification** of the claim that motivator factors increase productivity has been hard to find.

(b)   The research findings are **context-specific**: they describe specific groups of workers in a single cultural context, whose values cannot necessarily be generalised to other contexts.

(c)   The original study was based on an inadequately **small sample size** to draw conclusions.

The model's main contribution is highlighting the potential **intrinsic rewards** of work, contributing to job design and the 'quality of working life' movement.

ACTIVITY 3   2 mins

Herzberg's **hygiene** factors and **motivator** factors is a well-known model of motivation. Which of the following is likely to be a **motivator** factor?

A   Salary

B   Job security

C   Achievement

D   Team relationships

4.5   Theory X and Theory Y

We introduced McGregor's Theory X and Theory Y in Chapter 1. We said that McGregor suggested that managers in the USA tended to behave as though they subscribed to one of **two sets of assumptions about people** at work: Theory X and Theory Y. (McGregor, 1960)

(a)   **Theory X** suggests that most people dislike work and responsibility and will avoid both if possible. Because of this, most people must be coerced, controlled, directed and threatened with punishment to get them to make an adequate effort. Managers who operate according to these assumptions will tend to supervise closely, apply detailed rules and controls, and use 'carrot and stick' motivators.

(b)   **Theory Y** suggests that physical and mental effort in work is as natural as play or rest. The ordinary person does not inherently dislike work: according to the conditions it may be a source of satisfaction or dissatisfaction. The potentialities of the average person are rarely fully used at work. People can be motivated to seek challenge and responsibility in the job, if their goals can be integrated with those of the organisation. A manager with this sort of attitude to his staff is likely to be a consultative, facilitating leader, using positive feedback, challenge and responsibility as motivators.

Each theory is intended to illustrate an extreme case rather than describing actual groups of managers.

Theory X and Theory Y do not really form a theory of motivation but rather a description of management attitudes to **control** (Schein, 2006). Theory X managers do not trust their subordinates and control them closely; Theory Y managers expect their subordinates to work properly and provide honest feedback when things go wrong. This promotes 'responsible, open, team-oriented behaviour' (Schein, 2006, p xiv).

McGregor's Theory Y can be seen as leading to modern management practices such as empowerment, team working, self-management and the manager as coach. However, it is not ubiquitous. Many successful companies habitually use identifiably Theory X practices, including Samsung, General Electric and Wal-Mart (Cutcher-Gershenfield, 2006).

McClelland's approach can also be linked to Theories X and Y. Their high degree of concentration on achieving the task in hand makes many high nAch people tend to adopt Theory X, though not all, and even those who do can be trained to appreciate the value of the Theory Y approach. High nPow managers are very likely to adopt Theory X, while high nAff managers typically adopt Theory Y.

5   Process theories of motivation

Content theories in their most basic forms tend to explain motivation in terms that seem to apply to everyone, with individual differences explained as special cases. Process theories acknowledge individual differences by taking into account both personal choice and social influence in the processes that determine individuals' goals. They are inevitably more complex than content theories for this reason.

Your syllabus does not call for detailed coverage of process theories, so we will restrict our coverage to brief summaries of three main approaches.

- **Expectancy theory**
- **Equity theory**
- **Goal theory**

5.1   Expectancy theory

The basis of expectancy theory is that our motivation to act depends on the results we expect to our acts to achieve in relation to our personal needs or goals.

Victor Vroom stated a formula by which human motivation could be assessed and measured. He suggested that the strength of motivation is the product of two factors.

(a)   **The strength of preference for a certain outcome**. Vroom called this **valence**: it can be represented as a positive or negative number, or zero – since outcomes may be desired, avoided or regarded with indifference.

(b)   **The expectation that the outcome will in fact result** from a particular behaviour. Vroom called this **expectancy**. As a probability, it may be represented by any number between 0 (no chance) and 1 (certainty).

In its simplest form, the expectancy equation may be stated as:

$$F = V \times E$$

Where

$F =$ the force or strength of the individual's motivation to behave in a particular way,

$V =$ valence: the strength of the individual preference for a given outcome or reward, and

$E =$ expectancy: the individual's perception that the behaviour will result in the outcome/ reward.

In this equation, the lower the values of either valence or expectancy, the less the motivation. An employee may have a high expectation that increased productivity will result in promotion (because of managerial promises, say), but if he is indifferent or negative towards the idea of promotion (because he dislikes responsibility), he will not be motivated to increase his productivity. Likewise, if promotion was very important to him – but he did not believe higher productivity would get him promoted (because he has been passed over before, perhaps), his motivation would also be low.

5.2   Equity theory

Equity theory focuses on people's sense of whether they have been fairly treated in comparison with the way others have been treated.

It is based on exchange theory, which suggests that people expect certain **outcomes** or rewards in exchange for their **inputs** or contributions. If they perceive that the ratio of their outcomes to inputs is unfair in comparison with those of other people, they experience a sense of **inequity**. This may be positive, if they feel they have not earned favourable treatment they have received, or negative, if they feel they have not received the favourable treatment they deserve. For example, people who feel that they are not paid enough for their work, compared with others, will have a sense of negative inequity.

A sense of inequity causes unpleasant tension, or dissonance, which motivates people to attempt to remove or reduce the perceived inequity by any of six types of behaviour.

(a)   Changing their inputs (eg reducing their hours or quality of work)
(b)   Changing the outcomes (eg demanding better pay)
(c)   Cognitive distortion (eg believing they aren't really working as hard as they are)
(d)   Withdrawal (eg absenteeism or resignation)
(e)   Influencing others to do any of the above (eg getting co-workers to put in extra hours)
(f)   Changing the comparison (eg comparing themselves with a different set of people)

5.3   Goal theory

Goal theory is based on the idea that people's behaviour is influenced by their goals or intentions. This may sound like content theory, but the application of goal theory has much more in common with process theory in that it is chiefly concerned with goals and motivation in a specifically work environment; the goals concerned are not the wider goals or needs of the individuals concerned but the achievement targets that are set for them at work.

Research supports four propositions about individual goals and work achievement in situations where clear and quantifiable short-term goals can be set.

(a)   Challenging goals lead to higher performance than easy goals, though the proper degree of challenge can be tricky to set.

(b)   Specific goals lead to higher performance than vague goals.

(c)   Participation in setting goals may lead to increased commitment and thus to higher performance. However, adequate explanation and justification of management-set goals can also lead to high performance.

(d)   Feedback on performance is necessary for high achievement.

It is less clear that these techniques are valid for team working, for longer-term goals or for work that is difficult to quantify, such as managerial work.

Chapter Roundup

- ↳ The **work ethic** is the belief that work of any kind is virtuous and idleness is morally undesirable. Individuals therefore have a moral responsibility to seek, gain and keep employment.

- ↳ However, people's attitudes to their work are also likely to be influenced by other factors, including loyalty, economic reward, management policy and job satisfaction.

- ↳ **Motivation** is the cognitive decision-making process through which goal-directed behaviour is initiated, energised, directed and maintained. Motivation is important to managers because motivated individuals perform better than those who merely comply with rules and procedures.

- ↳ **Content theories** of motivation assume that we all have a set of needs that we wish to satisfy or goals and desired outcomes that we wish to achieve.

- ↳ **Process theories** explore the process through which outcomes become desirable. This approach assumes that people are able to select their goals and choose the paths towards them, by a conscious or unconscious process of calculation.

- ↳ **Maslow** identified a hierarchy of needs which an individual will be motivated to satisfy, progressing from physiological needs through safety, social and esteem needs to self-actualisation.

- ↳ **Alderfer's** analysis was simpler, including existence, relatedness and growth groups of needs and suggesting that more than one set of needs may be active at the same time.

- ↳ **McClelland** identified three types of motivating need: the **need for power**, the **need for affiliation** and the **need for achievement**. People who need to achieve have a strong desire for success and a strong fear of failure. McClelland considered that such people made the best managers.

- ↳ **Herzberg** identified two basic need systems: the need to avoid unpleasantness and the need for personal growth. He suggested factors which could be offered by organisations to satisfy both types of need: these are hygiene and motivator factors respectively.

- ↳ **Theory X** and **Theory Y** do not really form a theory of motivation but rather a description of management attitudes to **control**. Theory X managers do not trust their subordinates and control them closely; Theory Y managers expect their subordinates to work properly and provide honest feedback when things go wrong.

- ↳ **Process theories** of motivation go beyond analysis of needs to consider in addition both personal choice and social influence in the processes that determine individuals' goals. There are three main process theories:

  - **Expectancy theory**
  - **Equity theory**
  - **Goal theory**

Quick Quiz

1   What is the work ethic?

2   What are the three main ways in which the word motivation is used?

3   What are the two main groups of motivation theories?

4   What are the five main groups of needs described by Maslow?

5   What are the three groups of needs described by Alderfer?

6   What arc the three main needs described by McClelland?

7   Herzberg described groups of factors affecting feelings about the work situation. What are they? Give two examples of each group.

8   What are the main process theories of motivation?

Answers to Quick Quiz

1 A belief that work of any kind is virtuous and idleness is morally undesirable and that individuals therefore have a moral responsibility to seek, gain and keep employment.

2 (a) A goal or desired outcome

   (b) The mental process of selecting a goal

   (c) The social process of influencing others' behaviour toward our own aims

3 Content theories and process theories

4 Physiological, safety, love/social, esteem and self-actualisation

5 Existence, relatedness and growth

6 Need for power, need for affiliation and need for achievement

7

Hygiene factors	Motivator factors
Company policy and administration	Recognition
Salary	Responsibility
Supervision	Challenging work
Interpersonal relations within the team	Achievement
Working conditions	Growth and development in the job
Job security	

8 Expectancy theory, equity theory and goal theory

Answers to Activities

Activity 1

(a) The essence of the instrumental attitude to work was that it provided no satisfactions in itself; it was undertaken simply as a method of obtaining the money which could be used to obtain satisfactions elsewhere, such as in family life. The protestant work ethic view is, essentially, the opposite of this: while work is an economic activity, it is also good in itself.

(b) Obviously, only you can provide this analysis. It is not unusual for people to have very mixed feelings about the various forms of work they undertake and even for their feelings to vary from time to time. Generally speaking, most people will find that they enjoy some forms of work and dislike others. The reasons for both liking and disliking are complex. An understanding of your own feelings will help you to understand some of the concepts and theories dealt with later in this book.

Activity 2

Maslow's categories for the listed circumstances are as follows.

(a)   Esteem needs

(b)   Social needs

(c)   Self-actualisation needs

(d)   He will have physiological needs

(e)   Safety needs initially; esteem needs above in a certain income level

(f)   Social needs or self-actualisation needs

(g)   Esteem needs

Activity 3

The correct answer is C, achievement. Motivators satisfy the need for personal growth and fulfilment and actively motivate the individual to superior performance. The other choices are hygiene factors which satisfy the need to avoid unpleasantness. However they do not offer lasting motivation.

Activity 2

Chapter 5

Money and motivation

In the previous chapter we examined some theoretical ideas about motivation in general. In this chapter we will look more closely at some more specific ideas about motivation in the context of work. These ideas revolve around the notion of rewards, but this is only a different way of talking about the satisfaction of needs and you should keep the theories we have already discussed in the forefront of your mind while you are thinking about this new material.

1   The nature of rewards

Rewards offered to the individual at work may be of two basic types.

(a)   **Extrinsic rewards** are separate from (or external to) the job itself, and dependent on the decisions of others (that is, also external to the control of the workers themselves). Pay, benefits, cash and non-cash incentives and working conditions are examples of extrinsic rewards.

(b)   **Intrinsic rewards** are those which arise from the performance of the work itself. They are therefore emotional rather than material and relate to the concept of job satisfaction. Intrinsic rewards include the satisfaction that comes from completing a piece of work, the status that certain jobs convey, and the feeling of achievement that comes from doing a difficult job well.

We discuss these two types of reward in more detail below.

2   Pay as a motivator

Historically, monetary reward has a central, but somewhat ambiguous, role in management ideas about motivation.

2.1   Scientific management and instrumentality

It is almost intuitive to suppose that people enter into employment with the specific aim of securing an income. Simple economic theory is based on the concept of utility, which may be understood in terms of maximum economic reward for minimum economic outlay. This simple approach is one of the bases upon which FW Taylor and his contemporaries developed the approach known as **scientific management**. One of Taylor's fundamental assumptions was that the improved efficiency of his methods would increase the cash returns to both worker and employer and would therefore be eagerly taken up by both. He said, 'What the workmen want from their employers beyond anything else is high wages, and what employers want from their workmen most of all is a low labor cost of manufacture.' (Taylor, 1911)

When thinking about Taylor's work and assumptions it is important to remember when he was working. His first managerial responsibility was in the late 1870s, that is, over 130 years ago. At that time, there was no doubt that a lack of income meant destitution: **pay** was the means to satisfy the basic need for **survival**. Since that time, in the developed world, greater prosperity and schemes of social welfare have largely abolished the immediacy of the need for pay simply to survive. Nevertheless, the principle remains.

We mentioned the idea of an **instrumental** approach to work in Chapter 1. Instrumentality is the attitude adopted by people when they do one thing in order to achieve or bring about another. An instrumental orientation to work sees it purely as a means to an end, a source of income that may then be expended in obtaining the things that the worker really wants. Goldthorpe *et al* found that highly-paid Luton car assembly workers accepted that their work was tedious and unfulfilling, but had made a rational decision to enter employment offering high monetary reward rather than intrinsic interest.

The intuitive approach that people work in order to receive pay is thus supported by the research of Goldthorpe *et al*. There are many organisations that work on this basis and use reward systems based exclusively on pay, or very nearly so. The natural outcome is that these organisations attract people who take instrumentality to a very high level and are thus difficult to motivate in any other way.

Nevertheless, the picture is complex and there is not a simple linear relationship between pay received and effort expended. For instance, Goldthorpe *et al's* work also suggested that people will seek a suitable balance of two things.

(a)   The rewards that are important to them
(b)   The deprivations they feel able to put up with in order to earn them

Even those with an instrumental orientation to work have **limits to their purely financial aspirations**, and will cease to be motivated by money if the disadvantages of their employment – in terms of long working hours, poor conditions and so on – become too great.

ACTIVITY 1 20 mins

Think about your own attitudes to work and reward. In particular, think about working conditions such as noise, smell, confined spaces, dirt, onerous protective clothing, working hours, isolation and so on. Can you think of a job that does not attract you but which you would do if the pay was adequate? What would you refuse to do even if offered a great deal of money? If you have an opportunity, discuss this with friends, colleagues and fellow students.

2.2 Pay and group processes

We also find that, since very little work is entirely solitary, the interaction of people in **groups** also influences behaviour with regard to pay.

Taylor's approach to management was in part based on his early experience of workers' practice of restricting output. He called this 'soldiering' because of its resemblance to marking time as opposed to making progress. Soldiering took advantage of management's incomplete knowledge of how long a given piece of work should, in fact, take. Workers soldiered, Taylor felt, partly from a natural human tendency to avoid exertion, but more importantly, to **defend their income**, since they were generally paid at piecework rates and faster work would inevitably lead to **rate cuts**. There was great solidarity among the workforce in this respect and, when he first became a supervisor at Midvale Steel, Taylor struggled to increase output.

The importance of group pressures was further demonstrated by the long series of experiments at the Western Electric Company's works at Hawthorne in Chicago, carried out under the general supervision of Elton Mayo. Among other findings, these experiments clearly demonstrated that output was determined by a range of factors other than pay. These factors included, as assumed by Taylor, shared anxiety about piecework rates and the prospects of layoff or dismissal in the then prevailing poor economic conditions. **Social pressure** was exerted to discourage high levels of output in individual workers. (Roethlisberger and Dickson, 1939)

2.3 Assessing the importance of pay

Pay is not mentioned explicitly in any need list, but clearly it can allow or support the satisfaction of various needs. According to Herzberg, it is the most important of the hygiene factors: valuable not only in its power to be converted into a wide range of other satisfactions, but also as a **consistent measure** of worth or value, allowing employees to compare themselves with other individuals or occupational groups. This can be very important in terms of the **need for esteem**, in that high pay is a measure of achievement.

High pay can also be particularly important to people at specific stages of their careers, typically when setting up house and starting a family.

Nevertheless, pay is still generally seen as a hygiene factor: it gets taken for granted, and becomes a source of dissatisfaction (particularly by comparison with others) rather than satisfaction.

Individuals may have needs unrelated to money, with which the pay system of the organisation may conflict or be irrelevant; an example would be a reward package based on regular overtime to the detriment of work-life balance. Although the size of their income will affect their standard of living, most people tend not to be concerned to *maximise* their earnings. They may like to earn more but are probably more concerned with other aspects of their rewards.

(a) Earning **enough** to meet their needs and aspirations

(b) Knowing that their pay is **fair** in comparison with the pay of others in comparable groups both inside and outside the organisation. This aspect has been highlighted in recent decades by legal requirements for equal pay for men and women.

We will return to the topic of pay and discuss it further, later in this Study Manual.

THE DANGERS OF CREATING INCENTIVES THAT PULL IN TWO DIRECTIONS AT ONCE

One of the major problems of relying on financial incentives and targets as mechanisms to improve performance is that **people do what is rewarded**. That may sound fine, but it also means that **people don't do what isn't rewarded** – so important parts of the job and important priorities for the organisation may be ignored or neglected.

A good example concerns the UK electrical retailer Currys, which until recently rewarded its salespeople with commission payments based on their sales volumes (e.g. a bonus for each refrigerator or electric kettle sold). As a result, customer service was neglected, and indeed customers were ignored if it appeared likely that they only wanted to purchase a very low-cost item such as a pack of batteries. The quality of customer service wasn't an issue if the good purchased actually worked once they were taken out of their boxes, but if they didn't then it was often very difficult to secure proper post-sales support.

Currys have now changed their incentive system and service performance (based on feedback from customers) is now a key element in the reward package for their sales-people.

---

3 Intrinsic rewards

3.1 Herzberg's approach

In Chapter 4 we discussed Herzberg's very important findings about the nature of satisfaction and dissatisfaction at work. You will recall the elements that he found led to a sense of satisfaction.

- Recognition
- Responsibility
- Challenging work
- Achievement
- Growth and development in the job

Herzberg suggested that motivation to perform well would be enhanced if jobs were adjusted to introduce or enhance the presence of these elements. He proposed **vertical loading** as a way of doing this. Vertical loading is conceptually similar to **empowerment** and has several elements that work together. Some formal controls would be removed and replaced by increased individual accountability; this would require enhanced feedback on performance. Other aspects of vertical loading are the allocation of new tasks and special assignments; and the allocation of work in natural units rather than breaking it down into smaller, incomplete, repetitive tasks that remove any possibility of satisfaction at the completion of a piece of work. These considerations led Herzberg to suggest three techniques that might be used to design more satisfying work.

- **Job enrichment**
- **Job enlargement**
- **Job rotation**

Job enrichment

Job enrichment is planned, deliberate action to build greater responsibility, breadth and challenge of work into a job. Job enrichment represents a **vertical extension** of the job into greater levels of responsibility, challenge and autonomy. A job may be enriched by:

(a) Giving the job-holder **decision-making tasks** of a higher order
(b) Giving the employee greater **freedom** to decide how the job should be done
(c) Encouraging employees **to participate** in the planning decisions of their superiors
(d) Giving the employee regular **feedback**

Job enlargement

Job enlargement is the attempt to widen jobs by increasing the number of operations in which a jobholder is involved. It is a **horizontal extension** of the job into increased task variety and reduced task repetition.

(a)   Tasks that span a larger part of the total production work should reduce boredom and add to task meaning, significance and variety.

(b)   Enlarged jobs might be regarded as having higher status within the department, perhaps as stepping-stones towards promotion.

Job enlargement is, however, potentially limited in its intrinsic rewards; for example, asking workers to complete three separate tedious, unchallenging tasks is unlikely to be more motivating than asking them to perform just one tedious, unchallenging task.

Job rotation

Job rotation is the planned transfer of staff from one job to another to increase task variety. It is a **sequential extension** of the job. It is also sometimes seen as a form of training, where individuals gain wider experience by rotating as trainees in different positions.

Job rotation can reduce the monotony of repetitive work, but the enhancement of motivation may be at the expense of reduced productivity while new techniques are learned.

> **JOB ROTATION**
>
> Tollit & Harvey, a manufacturer of stationery and office supplies, investigated its rates of absence and sickness and, alongside other measures, it started a project to multi-skill the workforce.
>
> 'Workers were previously trained on only one type of machine, but they now have the opportunity to train on two, three, four or more machines. As a result, deliveries are no longer held up as they were in the past when the one person who could operate a particular machine was off sick or on holiday.
>
> Workers are less likely to develop the upper limb disorders associated with repetitive assembly-line work if they do a number of different jobs. Job rotation also helps to relieve the tedium of this type of work, and may also have helped to reduce absence levels.'
>
> *People Management*, 18 April 2001

3.2   Job design

Herzberg was carrying out his research and making his recommendations in the 1950s and 1960s. A great deal of work has been done on work motivation and job design since then. Essentially, **job design** is the incorporation of the tasks the organisation needs to be done into a job for one person, but the potential of job design to enhance or diminish personal motivation must be carefully considered. The term **job enrichment** is now generally used to signify those aspects of job design that tend to enhance motivation. Job enlargement and rotation still have their place, but the concept of job enrichment overall now incorporates new thinking.

Hackman and Oldham (1980) suggest that high motivation, performance and satisfaction occur when workers experience three **critical psychological states**.

(a)   **Experienced meaningfulness** depends on the extent to which the work is regarded as inherently valuable and worthwhile.

(b)   **Experienced responsibility** depends on the extent to which workers feel accountable for their work performance.

(c)   **Knowledge of results** exists when workers understand how well they are performing.

These critical psychological states are stimulated and enhanced by improvements along five core **job dimensions**.

(a)   **Skill variety** exists when a job involves the use of several different skills and talents.

(b)   **Task identity** exists when a job involves completing an entire, meaningful piece of work from beginning to end.

(c)   **Task significance** exists when the job is believed to have an impact on other people, whether inside or outside of the organisation.

(d)   **Autonomy** exists when the worker feels freedom and discretion in areas such as job planning, target setting and work methods.

(e)   **Feedback** exists when workers are provided with information on the effectiveness of their performance and the results of their work.

The extent to which enhancements to the five core job dimensions stimulate the critical psychological states and thus promote the desirable outcomes of high motivation, performance and satisfaction depends on three further **moderating factors**.

(a)   **Context satisfaction** is, essentially, the same thing as Herzberg's concept of hygiene factors.

(b)   Workers must perceive that their **knowledge and skill** are adequate to enable them to perform satisfactorily.

(c)   Workers may place a low value on personal growth and development in the job and take an instrumental approach to work. A person in whom the strength of the need for growth is low is said to exhibit low **growth-need strength**. Such people are unlikely to respond well to job enrichment: they may become anxious about expanded responsibility or even demand increased pay to compensate for it.

ABILITY, MOTIVATION, OPPORTUNITY

Professor John Purcell's celebrated research into the 'black box' connecting HR practices with organisational outcomes, published in 2003, also re-emphasised the notion that employee performance equals Ability + Motivation + Opportunity. As an equation, this translates into: EP = A + M + O. Each element is explained as follows:

ABILITY

Employees have the skills, experience and knowledge to perform effectively and efficiently

MOTIVATION

The organisation has provided an infrastructure comprising financial, social and psychological rewards and recognition for progress, success and achievement

OPPORTUNITY

How the job is done (on-line participation) and

How the employee operates as a team member and 'citizen' (off-line participation)

ACTIVITY 2   10 mins

Think about your own need for personal growth and development. Try to analyse your own motives in pursuing this course of study, for example.

4 Emergent needs

A number of factors have brought new emphasis to various higher-order needs that would generally be considered to be linked to the intrinsic nature of work. Your syllabus mentions five such needs.

(a) **Self-actualisation**, or the fulfilment of personal potential in all respects is the highest need presented in Maslow's hierarchy. As well as the achievement of personal goals, there is also an element of contentment inherent in the state of self-actualisation, since it can only be attained when personal ambitions are thoroughly understood.

(b) **Self-development** is an aspect of education or training: individuals take action to equip themselves with the skills and knowledge they require for their work, to further their careers and for wider purposes of self-fulfilment.

(c) **Self-determination** is defined by Field et al (1998) as a combination of skills, knowledge, and beliefs that enable a person to engage in goal-directed, self-regulated, autonomous behaviour. An understanding of one's strengths and limitations, together with a belief of oneself as capable and effective are essential to self-determination. When acting on the basis of these skills and attitudes, individuals have greater ability to take control of their lives and assume the role of successful adults in our society. (p 2)

(d) **Involvement** and **participation** are features of the modern, non-autocratic management style typified by practices such as empowerment and consultation. This style accepts that individuals at all levels have creative and innovative potential and is expressed by such practices as involvement of subordinates in decision-making and their participation in planning and the setting of budgets.

The emergence of these individual needs and their consequent recognition may be traced to a range of developments in the work environment and in wider society.

(a) We discussed the pressures of **globalisation** in Chapter 1 and the response of organisations in the form of empowerment, flexible working and the utilisation of new technology in Chapter 2. These policies have directly encouraged the development of self-determination, involvement and participation among the workforce. In particular, participation is widely believed to enhance commitment and thus lead to higher performance.

(b) At the same time there have been extensive changes in organisations of all kinds including, in particular, major programmes of redundancy; as noted earlier, there is now little expectation of a 'job for life'. People have responded to this new reality by seeking qualifications and career experience that will enhance their **employability**. Responsible employers have supported such ambitions. Tymon & Mackay (2010) say that:

> 'The self-managed career emphasises the individual as master of his or her own destiny rather than the organisation . . . As the business environment evolves and requirements change, individuals . . . must similarly adapt by renewing their skills and updating their knowledge.' (p206)

(c) There is now a widespread assumption of entitlement to personal development and fulfilling experience at work and in life generally. This has emerged as a consequence of the adoption of 'child-centred' policies in education and increased government spending on and promotion of training; and further and higher education. Participation in higher education by 17 to 30 year olds has increased from 5% in 1960 to 35% in 2001 (Chowdry et al, 2010). Speaking of participative management, Huczynski and Buchanan (2007) say it is:

> '. . . part of a wider social and political trend which has raised expectations concerning personal freedom and the quality of working life. These social and political values encourage resistance to manipulation by impersonal bureaucracies, and challenge the legitimacy of management decisions.'

IT'S NOT ALL ABOUT MONEY

A new book [*A Guide to Non-Cash Reward* by Michael Rose, Kogan Page, 2011] supports two simple ideas:

(1)   Organisations should recognise the great things that people do; and

(2)   Organisations should use more non-cash rewards to help recognise and incentivise their people.

Non-cash rewards can be far more effective than cash. Non-cash rewards can have memory value, so their impact last longer than the cash reward (especially bearing in mind that cash on its own only motivates for about three weeks). The perceived value of a non-cash reward can also be much higher than its actual cost to the organisation or a cash equivalent, particularly if the firm can buy the rewards at special rates or can use their own products and services as part of the reward.

However, there are six ingredients for the successful management of a non-cash reward system:

- Be genuine – if you don't mean it, then don't say it;

- Be timely – make the reward as close to the event as you can;

- Be personal – use the recipient's name;

- Make it specific – refer exactly to what the individual did;

- Be clear – explain why it is appreciated; and

- Make it public – find a way to let others know about it.

Rose also makes the important point that any reward or recognition scheme must ultimately be judged by the degree to which it stimulates extra levels of productivity and/or quality without incurring excessive costs that outweigh any benefits received.

Chapter Roundup

↳ Rewards from work may be **extrinsic** or **intrinsic**. Extrinsic rewards are separate from the job itself and include pay and benefits. Intrinsic rewards arise from the performance of the job itself and are emotional rather than material.

↳ Scientific management assumed that pay was the only motivator; the affluent worker study confirmed that for some people at least this is effectively true. However, early experience demonstrated that **group processes** would influence the ability of pay to motivate.

↳ Pay can support the achievement of a range of emotional needs, which is the basis of the **instrumental** approach to work. It is also a consistent measure of worth and can satisfy the need for esteem. Rather than maximising their income, people may be concerned that they have **enough pay** for their needs and that their **pay is fair**.

↳ Satisfying work provides intrinsic rewards such as Herzberg's motivating factors. Herzberg suggested **job enrichment**, **job enlargement** and **job rotation** as ways of making work more satisfying.

↳ The term **job enrichment** is now used to mean those aspects of design that that tend to enhance motivation. Hackman and Oldham suggest that high motivation, performance and satisfaction occur when workers experience three critical psychological states. These are

- **experienced meaningfulness**
- **experienced responsibility**
- **knowledge of results**.

↳ These are stimulated and enhanced by improvements along five core **job dimensions**.

- **skill variety**
- **task identity**
- **task significance**
- **autonomy**
- **feedback**

↳ Three factors moderate the effect of enhancements

- **context satisfaction**
- **knowledge and skill**
- **growth-need strength**

↳ Certain higher order needs have emerged as a result of modern pressures. Among these are

- **self-actualisation**
- **self-development**
- **self-determination**
- **involvement**
- **participation**

↳ The pressures leading to this development include

- organisations' response to **globalisation**
- the need for improved **employability**
- social and political emphasis on personal development and fulfilment

Quick Quiz

1   What are the two classes of reward that may be available to individuals at work?

2   What did FW Taylor believe his methods would achieve for wages and costs?

3   What is an instrumental approach to work?

4   How can pay satisfy the need for esteem?

5   What is job enlargement?

6   What are the three critical psychological states described by Hackman and Oldham?

7   What is self-actualisation?

Answers to Quick Quiz

1   Intrinsic and extrinsic

2   Wages would rise and costs would fall.

3   Acceptance of unfulfilling work because it provides high levels of material reward

4   High pay is an acknowledgement of individual worth or value.

5   A horizontal extension of the job to provide increased task variety

6   Experienced meaningfulness, experienced responsibility and knowledge of results

7   The fulfilment of personal potential in all respects

Answers to Activities

Activity 1

Clearly, this is a question that you can only answer for yourself. Make sure that your answer takes into account all the circumstances that might apply. For example, if you dislike the thought of boring and repetitive work, even for high pay, ask yourself if you would do it if you really needed the money, for important family reasons and there was nothing else available?

Activity 2

This is a very difficult and rather large task, since responding to it properly involves thinking hard about your own personality. If you think you have a clear view of your own motivation and ambitions, go a little further and ask yourself if you can identify the forces that created them. Some may well come from within yourself, but you may find that some are external, such as other people's expectations.

Chapter 6

Employer expectations

In this chapter we review the development of employer attitudes to their employees and their work. It would be an oversimplification to say that there has been a general movement away from regarding workers as extensions of machinery and towards understanding their motivations and attitudes. There are still organisations that take the former view and there have always been employers who understood human nature and managed in a way that drew the best out of people.

Nevertheless, the general trend of theory expressed by managers and academics has been to move from an early engineering approach to a much greater understanding of human factors in work.

TOPIC LIST	LEARNING OUTCOMES
1 Scientific management	4.1, 4.2, 4.3
2 Human relations	4.1, 4.2, 4.3
3 Modern thinking	4.1, 4.2, 4.3

1 Scientific management

We have already mentioned Frederick W Taylor and discussed some of his work. He is remembered as a pioneer of what he called **scientific management**. Taylor's approach to management was in part based on his early experience. He was of middle-class New England stock and originally destined to study law at Harvard. However, his vision was impaired and his doctor advised that he should avoid close study. Instead, in 1874, he was apprenticed as a pattern-maker and machinist and in 1878 started work at the Midvale Steel Company. Within eight years he was Chief Engineer.

Taylor is generally remembered for his contribution to the practice of management. However, he was also an innovator in the technology of engineering, developing improved belt drives for machinery and playing a prominent role in the invention of high speed steel cutting tools, which vastly improved the performance of machine tools.

His experience of manufacturing convinced him that the industrial managers of the time had no idea of the production potential of the machinery they installed, nor any means of establishing it. He spent much of his professional life developing ways of solving this problem.

He was among the first to argue that management should be based on 'well recognised, clearly defined and fixed principles, instead of depending on more or less hazy ideas.' He subsequently laid down four principles of scientific management.

(a) The development of a true **science of work**. 'All knowledge which had hitherto been kept in the heads of workmen should be gathered and recorded by management. Every single subject, large and small, becomes the question for scientific investigation, for reduction to law.' The assumption behind this was that there was 'one best way' to deal with any problem of production and that it was management's job to establish what it was and then make sure that it was used.

(b) The **scientific selection** and **progressive development** of workers: workers should be carefully trained and given jobs to which they are best suited. 'The new way is to teach and help your men as you would a brother; to try to teach him the best way and to show him the easiest way to do his work. This is the new mental attitude of the management towards the men....'

(c) The application of techniques to **plan**, **measure and control work** for maximum productivity.

(d) Constant and intimate **co operation between management and workers**: 'the relations between employers and men form without question the most important part of this art.'

In practice, scientific management techniques included the following key elements.

(a) **Work study techniques** were used to analyse tasks and establish the most efficient methods to use. No variation in method was permitted in the way work was done, since the aim was to use the 'one best way'.

WORK STUDY

It is useful to consider an application of Taylor's principles. In testimony to the House of Representatives Committee in 1912, Taylor used as an example the application of scientific management methods to shovelling work at the Bethlehem Steel Works.

Facts were first gathered by management as to the number of shovel loads handled by each man each day, with particular attention paid to the relationship between weight of the average shovel load and the total load shifted per day. From these facts, management was able to decide on the ideal shovel size for each type of material handled in order to optimise the speed of shovelling work done. Thus, scientific technique was applied to deciding how work should be organised.

By organising work a day in advance, it was possible to minimise the idle time and the moving of men from one place in the shovelling yard to another. Once again, scientific method replaces 'seat of the pants' decisions by supervisors.

Workers were paid for accepting the new methods and performance standards and received 60% higher wages than those given to similar workers in other companies in the area.

Workers were carefully selected and trained in the technique of shovelling properly; anyone consistently falling below the required output standards was given special teaching to improve his performance.

At the Bethlehem Steel Works the costs of implementing this method were more than repaid by the benefits. The labour force required fell from 500 men to 140 men for the same work.

(b)   **Planning and doing were separated**. It was assumed that the persons who were intellectually equipped to do a particular type of work were probably unlikely to be able to plan it to the best advantage: this was the manager's job.

(c)   Workers were **paid incentives** on the basis of acceptance of the new methods and output norms; the new methods greatly increased productivity and profits. Pay was assumed to be the only important motivating force. Remember the quotation from Taylor in Chapter 5 - 'What the workmen want from their employers beyond anything else is high wages, and what employers want from their workmen most of all is a low labor cost of manufacture.' (Taylor, 1911)

Taylor was a very skilled engineer and he took an engineering efficiency approach to management. The essence of his approach was that scientific investigation would allow managers to state exactly how work should be done, how long each element of a job should take and, almost as an afterthought, what the pay rate should be for each job.

Inevitably, this approach met a lot of opposition from organised labour, since it allowed no role whatever for collective bargaining. Nevertheless, the ideas of Taylor and other leaders of scientific management such as Gilbreth and Gantt spread rapidly and widely: perhaps the most significant application of the general approach was by Henry Ford in his development of assembly line techniques between 1908 and 1915.

Scientific management as practised by Taylor and his contemporaries was very much about the efficiency of **manual work**. However, the general ideas were subsequently applied to many other kinds of work, including office and administrative tasks. The principles and techniques continue in use today under such names as industrial engineering, work study and organisation and methods. They may also be discerned in recent widely adopted efficiency programmes such as total quality management, business process re-engineering and Six Sigma.

📎 **EXAMPLES OF SCIENTIFIC MANAGEMENT**

Elements of scientific management such as close attention to standards, micro-design of jobs, strict control of working time and close supervision can be seen in the management of junior staff in businesses such as:

(a) Large fast-food franchises

(b) Call-centres, where calls are scripted, timed and monitored

---

Scientific management and Theory X

We introduced you to Douglas McGregor's Theory X and Theory Y in Chapter 1. It is possible to discern some aspects of the scientific management approach in Theory X.

Let us look more closely at what McGregor said constituted Theory X. There were **three main propositions** (McGregor, 1957).

1 Management is responsible for organising productive resources.
2 This includes directing, controlling and modifying the behaviour of people.
3 If management did not do this, people would be passive or resistant.

Behind these propositions were a set of beliefs about people.

4 The average person lacks ambition, dislikes responsibility, is indolent, resistant to change, gullible and indifferent to organisational needs.

We can see that the assumptions of scientific management fit quite well into this mould. Proposition 1 is an unspoken but essential condition. Proposition 2 lies behind all of the work of Taylor and his peers in the fields of time study, motion study and methods design. Proposition 3 is fundamental to Taylor's views on 'soldiering'.

However, proposition 4 may be a step too far. We have quoted Taylor's remark about workers' attitude to pay already. Let us look at what else he said in that context. Here is a longer quotation.

> 'It is safe to say that no system or scheme of management should be considered which does not in the long run give satisfaction to both employer and employee, which does not make it apparent that their best interests are mutual, and which does not bring about such thorough and hearty cooperation that they can pull together instead of apart. It cannot be said that this condition has as yet been at all generally recognized as the necessary foundation for good management. On the contrary, it is still quite generally regarded as a fact by both sides that in many of the most vital matters the best interests of employers are necessarily opposed to those of the men. In fact, the two elements which we will all agree are most wanted on the one hand by the men and on the other hand by the employers are generally looked upon as antagonistic.
>
> What the workmen want from their employers beyond anything else is high wages, and what employers want from their workmen most of all is a low labor cost of manufacture.
>
> These two conditions are not diametrically opposed to one another as would appear at first glance. On the contrary, they can be made to go together in all classes of work, without exception, and in the writer's judgment the existence or absence of these two elements forms the best index to either good or bad management.'

(Taylor, 1911)

This makes it clear that Taylor did not overtly subscribe to proposition 4, though his enemies would have had no doubt at all that he did.

2 Human relations

In the 1920s, research began to show that managers needed to consider the complexity of **human behaviour**. It was recognised that an exclusive focus on technical competence (under scientific management) had resulted in social incompetence: managers were not taught how to manage people. At the same time, it emerged that current management approaches were experienced as alienating and demoralising by workers, whatever the financial incentives offered. A more complex picture of human motivation began to emerge.

2.1 The Hawthorne experiments

This was demonstrated by the long series of experiments at the Western Electric Company's works at Hawthorne in Chicago between 1924 and 1932, carried out by Roethlisberger and Dickson under the general supervision of Elton Mayo, professor of Industrial Research at the Harvard Business School. These studies were originally firmly set in the context of scientific management in that they began with an experiment into the **effect of lighting on work output**.

This experiment involved the creation of an experimental work group, for whom lighting was varied and a control group, for whom lighting was held at a constant level. The researchers were intrigued to find that productivity in the experimental group tended to increase, whatever they did with the lighting, and what is more, it also increased in the control group. This led to further research.

The **relay assembly test room** experiment involved six female workers segregated into a separate room. The general working conditions were the same as in the main assembly shop, but the test room workers were subjected to a variety of changes in their hours of work and rest periods; in some experimental periods, refreshments were provided. The experiments were supervised by an observer who behaved in a pleasant and friendly manner to the workers, consulting them about the experiments and keeping them informed. Generally, output increased steadily and it was concluded that the observer's interaction was seen as a change in supervisory technique, reflecting an increase in management attention and interest; as a result, the group's attitude to work became more positive and this accounted for the increased output.

A programme of **confidential interviews** was subsequently set up to investigate workers' views about management and working conditions. This programme was intended to provide information about potential improvements in what we would now call management style, though it also had a positive effect on morale simply by allowing workers to express their feelings and opinions. However, the severe fall in business that occurred as the economy moved into recession in 1931 led to the termination of this programme.

The **bank wiring observation room** experiment was designed to investigate the social behaviour of employees in a work group. It involved observation of 14 men involved in wiring equipment for telephone exchanges. Among other things, this experiment documented the **informal organisation** of the work groups in the observation room: the patterns of relationships, behavioural norms and informal influence that exist separately from the organisation's official authority and communication structures. The workers involved in the experiment were anxious about piecework rates and the prospects of layoff or dismissal in the then prevailing poor economic conditions. The experiment was noteworthy for its demonstration of the power of group pressure to overcome financial incentives and cause individuals to restrict output.

With the benefit of hindsight, the methodology, assumptions and conclusions of the Hawthorne studies are now widely regarded as flawed. However, they did bring the significance of human relationships and emotional response into the foreground of thinking about work and management and formed the basis of what is now called the **human relations** school of management studies. In particular, they demonstrated both the importance of informal work relationships and the inadequacy of the belief that people work exclusively for money.

2.2 Neo-human relations

Subsequent inquiry into the topics brought forward by the Hawthorne experiments included extensive research into motivation, some of which we have already discussed in detail. This work and its investigations into informal organisation are referred to as the **neo-human relations** school.

3 Modern thinking

Scientific management saw people as engineering assets to be utilised in the most efficient manner by proper planning and control. Money reward was assumed to be the main factor in motivation, though coercion was also available. As we have seen from the early Hawthorne experiment on light levels, this approach came to consider working conditions as important, though at first the object was to achieve an optimum – another version of the 'one best way'.

Human relations acknowledged the complexity of human responses to work and, particularly, their expression in group processes. This approach has emphasised the need for management to understand and provide some satisfaction for the human needs to their work force.

Neo-human relations suggested that management should go further than this and take steps to ensure that work should be a mutually beneficial activity that people would undertake as part of their personal scheme of fulfilment. This would lead to the kind of enhanced commitment that employers desire.

Modern organisations have sought improved methods of management in order to deal with problems arising from global-scale economic, technological and social change. Your Chief Examiner has mentioned the following specific pressures.

(a) **Global competition**. There are two important aspects of global competition that relate to production costs.

  (i) **Labour cost competition** from developing countries where labour costs are typically much lower than in developed countries. This has been particularly apparent in the textiles and clothing industries. The UK cotton industry has disappeared and, with the end of the protection given by the international Multi-fibre Arrangement, similar industries in other EU countries such as Greece and Portugal are in decline. Developed countries can, in some industries, exploit superior technology and innovation as a counter to low labour cost, but this is no longer a default position as developing countries catch up.

  (ii) **Manufacturing efficiency competition**. The source of competition here has been Japan, though similar technology has spread to other countries such as Taiwan and China. The classic example is the **Toyota manufacturing system** which has enhanced quality and driven down costs to such an extent that Toyota rose from a very minor place to being the most successful car manufacturer in the world.

(b) **Shortages of skilled labour**. Technological change and labour cost competition have made established skills obsolete and required the deployment of new ones. Providing labour with the right mix of skills, including flexibility to cope with rapid change has been made more difficult in the UK by the failure of the education system to ensure wide achievement of basic numeracy and literacy. Employers have been forced to increase investment in training in order to overcome skill shortages of all kinds (Paton, 2008).

(c) **Rising customer aspirations**. Consumers have come to expect gradually increasing standards of living, because that is what they have experienced for 60 years. Continuing growth is caused by market competition, which drives increases in quality standards while bringing down prices. The effect on employers is a need for constant innovation, efficiency improvements and cost control. Staff naturally play their part in these developments, but they have to be managed properly.

(d)   **Global management examples**. There is a widespread tendency among strategic managers to emulate the methods of the most successful companies. This emulation often takes the form of adopting the schemes and methods recommended by consultants, such as 'excellence' and the various quality management schemes, some of which are discussed below.

Responding to these pressures, employers want systems that will release the creativity, commitment and skill of their people since this will be mutually beneficial. The operations of the organisation will be transformed by improved and innovative working practices, while the lives of the staff will be enhanced by the satisfactions they gain from their work. Reduced staff turnover, absence and sickness; improved training outcomes and enhanced workplace flexibility will be valuable side-effects.

A wide variety of ideas and approaches have addressed this conundrum.

CORE BEHAVIOURS AT DIRECT LINE INSURANCE

Direct Line Insurance is a UK-based provider of insurance services and it is totally dedicated to an 'added value' culture for all employees. One of its 'Core Competencies' that is applicable to every member of the workforce is '**Continuous Improvement**', which translates into the following behaviours – which, again, are expected for everyone in the business, no matter how mundane their jobs:

- *Seeks ways to improve activities and processes*

- *'Gets it right first time, every time'*

- *Willing to try new things and adapt own behaviour (to new situations)*

- *Understands the need for change*

- *Reacts positively to requests for change*

- *Proposes ways to comply with requests for change or improvement*

3.1   Employee involvement

Employee involvement concentrates mainly on individual employees and the degree to which they can be encouraged to identify with the goals of the organisation. It can be distinguished from employee participation, which concerns the extent to which employees are involved in management decision-making.

The aims of involvement may be:

(a)   To generate commitment to the organisation

(b)   To help the organisation improve performance, especially in the face of change

(c)   To enable the organisation to better meet changing customer requirements

(d)   To improve the challenge and satisfaction of the work experience

(e)   To aid the organisation in attracting and retaining skilled labour

(f)   To develop the business awareness of labour at all levels

(g)   To increase employee incentives and accountabilities through tying reward to company performance and profitability, and/or

(h)   To marginalise trade unions.

3.2 Upward communication

Upward communication is rarer than downward – but vital to many modern organisations in:

(a) Providing feedback on progress and performance, so that plans can be adjusted where necessary

(b) Harnessing the experience and know-how of employees for innovation, problem-solving and decision-making

(c) Giving management insight into employees' needs, interests and problems, to help them manage better

(d) Demonstrating the value management places on employees, establishing the mutual trust and commitment that underpins constructive employee relations.

Mechanisms for upward communication include attitude surveys, questionnaires, interviews and focus groups.

Attitude surveys

Surveys of employee opinions are a useful source of feedback (especially if there are no other direct avenues for employees to express their satisfactions and dissatisfactions). Attitude surveys may be carried out via:

(a) **Questionnaires**, whether standardised or tailored to the particular organisation or issue concerned. These may be paper-based or (increasingly) posted online on a company intranet. Questionnaires have the advantage of being quick and relatively cost-effective to administer, although they must be carefully designed if they are to elicit honest, meaningful and comparable responses.

(b) **Interviews**, either completely free-flowing or structured to a specific agenda of issues. Interviews are time-consuming and costly, but may also be more revealing, allowing a skilled interviewer to probe.

(c) **Focus groups**, allowing a structured response to interview questions by a representative sample of employees on specific issues

ACTIVITY 1   15 mins

How would you respond to the following objections from a management traditionalist to employee surveys?

(a) Good managers already know their staff's opinions.
(b) Surveys are superficial, impersonal and bureaucratic.
(c) Surveys open cans of worms and raise false hopes.
(d) Surveys contain built in bias because of the unknown opinions of the many who do not respond.

> **VODAFONE**
>
> 'What's the big idea, Vodafone?
>
> Vodafone is running a campaign to promote innovation: in the workforce. "My big idea" has already generated 500 ideas from employees aimed at improving customer experience, products and services.
>
> The ideas amassed so far will be whittled down to five with the finalists presenting their suggestions to the board later this month. The winning idea will be assessed for feasibility and rolled out next year.
>
> Dawn McIntyre, an HR business partner at Vodafone, told PM: 'It's important to encourage staff to come up with ideas, and firms that don't do that are missing out as it's key to employee satisfaction.'
>
> (*People Management*, 9 November 2006)

3.3 Modern thinking in action at Toyota

It is well known that the assembly-line system of production originated with Henry Ford, but it is an approach that is now largely discredited, at least in its basic form which followed the principles of work organisation first outlined by Frederick Winslow Taylor, the so-called 'father' of Scientific Management. Taylor argued that the task (say, the construction of a motor car) should be broken down into as many jobs as possible so that the skill required to perform each is minimal. This then means that human beings need very little training before they become competent, and also that they are easily interchangeable between jobs.

Scientific Management along these lines may have been appropriate at a time when workers were poorly educated and had very low expectations about work. Whether we like it or not, that isn't the situation today, and Toyota has been one of the pioneers in creating an entirely different approach to the business of making motor cars. Toyota operates in accordance with the principles of 'The Toyota Way', which are: Challenge, Kaizen (improvement), Genchi Genbutsu (go and see), Respect, and Teamwork.

In turn these five principles are translated into 14 operational practices. Listed here are the ten practices that are specifically relevant to the management and development of people.

(1)   Base your management decisions on a long-term philosophy, even at the expense of short-term goals.

(2)   Build a culture of stopping to fix problems, to get the quality right all the time.

(3)   Standardised tasks are the foundation for continuous improvement and employee empowerment.

(4)   Use only reliable, thoroughly tested technology that serves your people and your processes.

(5)   Grow leaders who thoroughly understand the work, live the philosophy, and teach it to others.

(6)   Develop exceptional people and teams who follow your company's philosophy.

(7)   Respect your extended network of partners and suppliers by challenging them and helping them to improve.

(8)   Go and see for yourself to thoroughly understand the situation (genchi genbutsu).

(9)   Make decisions slowly by consensus, thoroughly considering all options, but implement decisions rapidly.

(10) Become a learning organisation through relentless reflection and continuous improvement.

3.4   Empowerment

Empowerment has two key aspects. It involves giving workers discretion to make decisions about how to organise work in order to achieve task goals *and* making workers responsible for achieving production and quality targets.

The purpose of empowerment is:

(a)   To free employees from rigorous control by instructions and orders, which contributes to job satisfaction *and* learning and flexibility

(b)   To give employees opportunities for growth and job satisfaction through taking responsibility for their ideas and actions

(c)   To release and develop resources in the workforce that would otherwise remain inaccessible, including creativity and initiative

(d)   To harness employee commitment by allowing them to share in the process of target-setting and work organisation

(e)   To decentralise decision-making and problem-solving initiative to 'front line' customer-facing roles, to enhance the flexibility and responsiveness of customer service.

Empowerment goes hand in hand with:

(a)   **Delayering**, or a cut in the number of levels in the organisation hierarchy: This is facilitated by modern ICT systems, which reduce the need for managers to filter information and compile reports. Some responsibility previously held by managers is devolved down the organisational chain

(b)   **Flexibility**, since giving responsibility to the people closest to the product or customer encourages responsiveness

(c)   **New technology**, since skilled knowledge workers need less supervision, being better equipped to identify and control the means to clearly understood ends

(d)   **Employee development**, since the personal and interpersonal skills needed to meet the challenges of responsibility and participation in decision-making need to be developed

(e)   **Unitarist employee relations**, since empowerment rests on the belief that employees will recognise and commit themselves to the business goals of their unit and organisation.

Empowerment implies a shift in the role of both **line managers** (who effectively become coaches and facilitators in team decision-making processes, setting parameters and providing information and guidance where required) and **HR practitioners** (who increasingly share responsibility for delivering HR policy outcomes not only with line managers but with employees themselves).

3.5   Self-managed teams

Self-managed teams are the most highly-developed form of team working. They are permanent structures in which team members collaboratively decide all the major issues affecting their work: work processes and schedules, task allocation, the selection and development of team members, the distribution of rewards and the management of group processes (problem-solving, conflict management, internal discipline and so on). The team leader is a member of the team, acting in the role of coach and facilitator: leadership roles may be shared or rotated as appropriate.

Self managed teams generally have the following features.

(a) They contract with management to assume various degrees of **managerial responsibility** for planning, organising, directing and monitoring (which may increase as the team develops). Team members learn and share the jobs usually performed by a manager. They often report to 'absentee' managers with broad responsibilities for several functions, whose role is to act as integrators and facilitators.

(b) They perform **day-to-day planning and control functions**: scheduling and co-ordinating the daily and occasional tasks of the team and individuals; setting performance goals and standards; formulating and adopting budgets; collecting performance data and reviewing results.

(c) They perform **internal people management functions**: screening and interviewing candidates to join the team, and contributing to selection/hiring decisions; providing orientation for new members; coaching and providing feedback on member performance; designing and conducting cross-training on all tasks.

(d) Team members **cross-train** in all the tasks necessary for a particular process, and members rotate flexibly from job to job.

(e) **Weekly team meetings** are used to identify, analyse and solve task and relationship problems within the team: reviewing team working and progress; getting team members to research and present team issues and so on.

ACTIVITY 2 · 10 mins

What do you think are likely to be the advantages of self-managed team working for the organisation?

3.6 Quality management

The drive for improved quality has been a major influence on the development of modern management practice. This is because the various schemes adopted have generally done away with separate inspection of output and recommended that individuals take responsibility for the quality of their work. This has enhanced work along all five Hackman and Oldham's core dimensions, which we discussed in Chapter 5.

(a) **Skill variety** is enhanced because workers must be able to assess output as well as produce it.

(b) **Task identity** is enhanced since inspection is no longer carried out elsewhere.

(c) **Task significance** is enhanced because someone further along the value chain will depend on the output.

(d) **Autonomy** is enhanced since workers are no longer being checked up on.

(e) **Feedback** is enhanced since workers will themselves assess the effectiveness of their performance and the results of their work.

Much of modern quality management methods may be traced back to the work of W Edwards Deming. Deming's first job in this field was to use **statistical process control** to raise productivity in US factories during World War II. His ideas were widely adopted in Japan, once he was able to convince Japanese business leaders of their merits. Deming's book *Out of the Crisis* listed fourteen points for managers to adopt to improve quality and competitiveness. Several of these are directly relevant to our theme of modern management

(a) Train people so they are better at working, and understand how to optimise production.
(b) Lead people.
(c) 'Drive out fear.'
(d) Break down barriers between staff areas.
(e) Get rid of slogans, exhortations, targets. These can be alienating.

(f) Get rid of numerical quotas. These encourage the wrong attitude to production.

(g) Enable people to take pride in work.

(h) Encourage 'education and self improvement for everyone'.

Quality management schemes have introduced a range of techniques and procedures.

Quality circles

The quality philosophy has been implemented most famously in Japan.

Kaoru Ishikawa is noted for proposing **quality circles**, which are groups of six to ten employees from different levels and disciplines within an organisation. They meet regularly to discuss problems of quality, customer care and related issues in their area of work. Success requires a commitment from the circle's membership, and a management willingness to take a back seat.

The circle is facilitated by a leader who directs the discussion and helps to orient and develop members in quality control and problem-solving techniques. It is important that the group is made up of volunteers, in order to harness genuine commitment and enthusiasm.

Quality circles do not generally have responsibility for making, implementing or following up recommendations. Even as discussion groups, however, they may have significant benefits, as members return to their departments as ambassadors for quality, customer care and employee involvement.

Total quality management (TQM)

TQM is a Japanese-inspired orientation to quality in which quality values and aspirations are applied to the management of *all* resources and relationships in order to seek continuous improvement and excellence in all aspects of performance.

Mullins (2007) defines TQM as expressing: 'a way of life for an organisation as a whole, committed to total customer satisfaction through a continuous process of improvement, and the contribution and involvement of people' (p761).

An important aspect of TQM is **total involvement**. Quality requires the commitment of all staff, and needs to be modelled from the top by senior management. It needs to be supported and reinforced by HRM policies for recruitment, training, appraisal, reward and development. It also emphasises the importance of people: communication, awareness and problem-solving are more important than mere systems.

Chapter Roundup

- **Taylor** was an engineer and sought the most efficient methods of work organisation and control, forming the basis of what became known as the scientific management school.

- **Mayo** and his colleagues investigated individual and group behaviour at work, as a factor in productivity. This became the focus of the human relationship school of management.

- Employee involvement is the process of informing and consulting employees about, or associating them with, one or more aspects of running an organisation. It may be accomplished by two-way communication, financial participation, representative participation, empowerment and inclusion in cultural programmes such as quality management and organisational learning.

Quick Quiz

1   What did Taylor say were the four principles of Scientific Management?

2   What, in one word, is the general nature of Scientific Management?

3   In the Hawthorne experiments, what happened to output in the lighting experiment work group when light levels were reduced?

4   What social mechanism observed in the bank wiring observation room was able to restrict output?

5   What are the two main aspects of empowerment?

6   What is delayering?

7   Who first proposed quality circles?

8   What is TQM?

9   What are the purposes of empowerment?

Answers to Quick Quiz

1 The development of a true science of work; the scientific selection and progressive development of workers; the application of techniques to plan, measure and control work for maximum productivity; and constant and intimate co operation between management and workers.

2 Engineering

3 It increased.

4 The informal organisation of the workers

5 Giving workers discretion to make decisions about how to organise work in order to achieve task goals and making them responsible for achieving production and quality targets

6 Cutting the number of levels in the organisation hierarchy

7 Kaoru Ishikawa

8 Total Quality Management: a whole-organisation approach to managing quality through the application of quality values, continuous improvement and total involvement.

9 See paragraph 3.3 for a full answer.

Answers to Activities

Activity 1

(a) How do managers know if their reading of opinions is correct?

(b) Yes, they are no substitute for good personal communications, but 'Thanks for asking us' is a common response.

(c) Cans of worms probably should be opened. If problems cannot be resolved because of cost, for example, management should explain why.

(d) Bias is modest when return rates of over 50% are achieved, and a well-designed and carefully introduced survey can expect returns of 65% or more.

Activity 2

(a) Savings in managerial costs

(b) Gains in quality and productivity, by harnessing the commitment of those who perform work

(c) Encouraging individual initiative and responsibility, enhancing organisational responsiveness (particularly in front-line customer service units)

(d) Gains in efficiency, through multi-skilling, the involvement of fewer functions in decision-making and co-ordinating work, and (often) the streamlining of working methods by groups

However, self-managed teams are a comparatively recent (and rare) phenomenon, and require skilled leadership and culture change (particularly in former 'command and control' organisations) in order to be effective.

Chapter 7

The basic framework factors

In this chapter we introduce the concept of basic framework and differentiator factors. This provides a slightly different approach to Herzberg's theory of hygiene and motivator factors. It also provides a background for our later discussion of leadership, engagement and high performance working.

1 Factors affecting performance

In Chapter 4 we discussed the motivational theory developed by **Frederick Herzberg**. Herzberg's research was designed to ascertain the nature of the factors that lead to positive or negative feelings about work. Analysis revealed two distinct sets of factors: those that created dissatisfaction when they were inadequate and those that created satisfaction when they were present. Herzberg called the first group **hygiene** or **maintenance** factors and the second group **motivator** factors. Hygiene factors are, generally, aspects of the **work environment**, whereas motivator factors are aspects of the **work itself**.

Hygiene factors	Motivator factors
Company policy and administration	Recognition
Salary	Responsibility
Supervision	Challenging work
Interpersonal relations within the team	Achievement
Working conditions	Growth and development in the job
Job security	

Herzberg suggested that 'when people are dissatisfied with their work it is usually because of discontent with environmental factors... Satisfaction can only arise from the job.'

The lecture guide for your course calls for you to be familiar with what it calls the 'basic framework' and 'differentiator' factors. Basic framework factors are sometimes referred to as **infrastructure** factors since they relate to the organisation's routine systems and practices. Differentiator factors are so-called because they enable an organisation to differentiate itself from others in the eyes of serving and potential employees. These two sets of factors **correspond exactly** with Herzberg's hygiene and motivator factors respectively.

This is a very important analysis since both categories of these factors influence people's attitudes and behaviour at work. High levels of organisational performance depend on their proper management. Unfortunately, this is not always a simple matter, as is illustrated by modern trends in **employee remuneration**. We have already looked at the rather difficult topic of reward and motivation; now we must return to it and develop our ideas a little further.

2 Pay and other rewards

Herzberg identified pay as a hygiene factor, with limited capacity to provide positive motivation. This view is easy to apply to simple pay systems under which a flat rate is paid and even to more complex systems that include premiums for shift work, enhanced rates for overtime and gratuitous payments such as bonuses. For most of us, whatever our income, there is a need to budget and make choices about how we will use our limited resources. Inevitably, we think about what we might do if we had more disposable income and so the natural human tendency is always to **want more pay**, whatever its current level. Few of us are ever completely **satisfied** with our pay and thus the relevance of Herzberg's analysis is clear.

However, Herzberg also identified **recognition** as a potential motivator. For many people and on many occasions, a simple verbal or written statement of thanks for a job well-done will constitute recognition. However, something more tangible is often **more appreciated** and therefore **more effective**. One of the most obvious and valued ways for an employer to recognise good performance is through monetary reward. A very common example is sales commission. Equally common are various kinds of output-related payments: these may recognise individual performance or the performance of a group. **Incentive payments** such as these can form a major element of remuneration schemes.

A rather different kind of monetary reward is provided by schemes of **profit-sharing**. Profit-sharing schemes are generally intended to encourage employees to identify with the interests of the organisation but they may also be seen as recognising valuable employee input.

ACTIVITY 1   15 mins

Consider your own experience of being recognised as having done a good job. What form did the recognition take? Were you pleased? Did you think the extent and nature of the recognition were appropriate to your achievement? If you had been in your manager's shoes, what would you have done?

Benefits provide valuable but non-monetary rewards. There is a wide variety of such rewards. Commonly encountered benefits are cars, healthcare, pensions, subsidised meals, recreational facilities and various kinds of entertainment, such as office parties. Benefits are often used as forms of recognition, with some, less expensive ones, such as recreational facilities being provided to all staff, but more expensive ones such as cars, healthcare and pensions being restricted by staff seniority in terms of length of service or position in the hierarchy.

The rather complex nature of valuable reward means that its motivational potential is not completely clear. Torrington *et al* (2009) identify opposing views on the usefulness of **incentive payments** in particular.

(a)   In addition to Herzberg's analysis, there is the possibility that such payments will be perceived by employees as manipulative and tending to reduce their personal autonomy. There is also a practical objection, in that incentive schemes are typically costly and complex to set up and operate.

(b)   The expectancy theory of motivation, which we discussed briefly in Chapter 4, suggests that employees will respond positively to a reasonable probability that more or better work will lead to larger rewards. This supports the view that incentives are both fair and effective in encouraging the behaviour that employers desire.

Total reward

A further complexity appears in the concept of **total reward**. Torrington *et al* (2009), discussing earlier work by Armstrong and Brown (2006) and the Towers Perrin consultancy model of reward, suggest that employees **value the intangible rewards** of work and that employers should take this into account. An organisation' competing for high quality staff but also seeking to contain employment costs may design a total reward package that recognises the importance of such intangibles. This concept is illustrated using the ever-popular two axis matrix. The axes of differentiation here are transactional-relational (or tangible-intangible) and individual-communal.

Transactional rewards are so-called because they are the result of an **economic transaction** between the employee and the organisation: the employee undertakes work and, in exchange, the organisation provides tangible rewards. **Relational** rewards are so-called because they arise from the nature of the intangible relationship between the employer and the organisation.

Four kinds of reward may be considered: pay; benefits; learning and development; and the work environment.

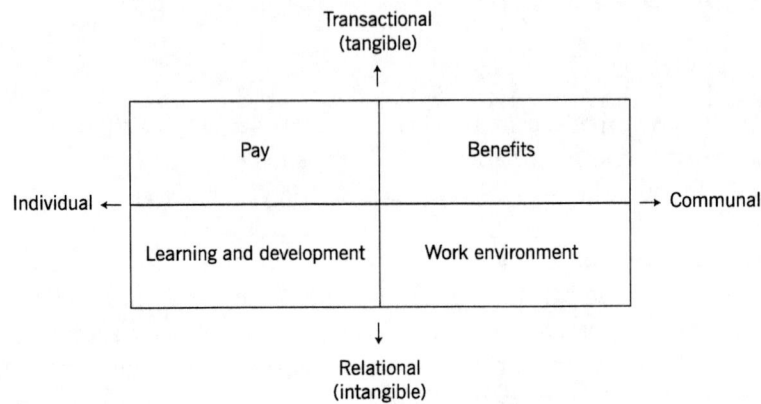

```
                        Transactional
                          (tangible)

                              ↑

              ┌──────────────────┬──────────────────┐
              │                  │                  │
              │       Pay        │     Benefits     │
              │                  │                  │
Individual ←  ├──────────────────┼──────────────────┤  → Communal
              │                  │                  │
              │    Learning and  │  Work environment│
              │    development   │                  │
              └──────────────────┴──────────────────┘

                              ↓

                         Relational
                         (intangible)
```

Figure 7.1: Total reward model

Pay and benefits might be called **extrinsic rewards** since they mostly fall into Herzberg's hygiene category, though, bearing in mind our discussion of recognition and achievement above, perhaps not entirely.

(a)   **Pay** includes all forms of pay, incentives, bonuses and profit sharing.

(b)   **Benefits** includes pensions, holidays, health care and flexible working hour schemes.

(c)   **Learning and development** includes workplace training, performance management, career development opportunities and support for gaining qualifications. These might be called **intrinsic rewards** since they appear to fall into Herzberg's motivator category.

(d)   **Work environment rewards** is a very wide group, including recognition, achievement, work-life balance, job design (responsibility, autonomy and so on), leadership and organisational values. This is a particularly interesting category, since it includes elements from **both sides of Herzberg's analysis**.

     (i)   Achievement and recognition are motivating factors and job design was, of course, recommended by Herzberg as a means of increasing job satisfaction. These would therefore qualify as **intrinsic rewards**.

     (ii)   However, leadership, organisational values and work-life balance would appear to be closely related to company policy and administration, working conditions and supervision, which are specified by Herzberg as hygiene factors. They do not, therefore, count as **intrinsic rewards**.

A slightly different analysis of work environment rewards is provided in Higgs (2006). This paper refers to this group of factors as 'climate' and describes it as the experienced reality of working in the organisation (p8). It classifies the group quite firmly as containing **intrinsic rewards** only and thus identifies a rather different set of factors. These include clear vision and purpose, manager concern for well-being, challenging work and resources, open management style, involvement, empowerment, strong communities and flexibility.

Implications

We can see from the discussion above that the concept of valuable reward is rather complex.

(a) Herzberg identifies pay as a **hygiene** factor; in the classification we are using, it is part of the **basic framework**.

(b) However, various forms of pay can be used to provide recognition, which is a **motivation** factor in Herzberg's analysis and a **differentiator** in our terms.

(c) Furthermore, some aspects of the work situation, while clearly **motivator** (or **differentiator**) factors, are regarded in modern writing as aspects of **total reward and may be viewed as such by employees**. Such factors include career development opportunities, recognition, achievement and aspects of job design.

What are we to make of this complexity? The first point to make is that it is important to approach any given employment situation with an open mind, since circumstances are likely to alter cases. Secondly, while it is important to know and understand the theory, it is the attitude of the employees in question that is most important in deciding which category a given factor falls into.

> **TOTAL REWARD AT ARUP**
>
> Rees & French (2010) illustrate total reward with a discussion of how it is implemented at Arup, a global design and engineering consultancy. Arup is employee-owned and the organisation wanted employees to understand in detail the make-up and value of their reward package. An important feature of the approach is the total reward statement prepared for each employee which shows the monetary value of a range of employee entitlements. Other items, such as holidays are mentioned on the statement but not given a monetary value. A further feature is that training and development opportunities, while viewed as important parts of the employment package, do not appear on the statement at all.
>
> Arup clearly appreciates the concept of total reward, but does not emphasise communal or relational rewards.

3 The performance infrastructure

The performance infrastructure, or basic framework, consists of factors that must be present if dissatisfaction is to be avoided. In themselves, they are **not sufficient** for motivation to be achieved, but their presence is **necessary** for that purpose. High levels of productivity and satisfaction are unlikely if these factors are not present to an at least acceptable degree.

The list of hygiene factors given above is no more than a summary and it is necessary to explore the **performance infrastructure** in more detail. In general terms, this infrastructure might be seen as the more formal systems, processes and procedures that impinge on employees individually and collectively as part of their relationship with the organisations. In organisations that have well-developed HRM functions, these matters will probably be seen as aspects of routine people management and staff administration, though responsibility for some of them will, in some organisations, reside with operations managers.

3.1 HRM compliance

The employment relationship is subject to a high degree of external control, partly because of the potential for abusive exploitation by the parties involved. While abuse by the employee is not uncommon, we are not concerned with that topic here, but with the converse: the organisation's duties to the employee.

There is a wide range of rules of various kinds that employers must comply with.

(a) **Employment law** in most countries is both voluminous and complex. Typically it will govern many aspects of the employment relationship, including such matters as recruitment, holiday entitlement, pay, redundancy and dismissal. The long-term trend in the UK has been to constrain the employer's freedom of action. Non-compliance with law is a dangerous course for any organisation to take.

(b) **Corporate social responsibility, ethics and professional standards** will also affect an organisation's behaviour. Unlike law, the standards expected under these headings are not clearly enforceable against the organisation, but moral pressure will cause most organisations to comply with them most of the time. It is on the occasions that these standards are eroded that the danger of employee dissatisfaction arises.

ASPECTS OF SOCIAL RESPONSIBILITY

Danish clothing and workwear company **Mascot** has shown its formal commitment to being a socially responsible employer at its Vietnamese subsidiary by gaining the international certification SA8000. It is one of the few Danish companies to gain this recognition.

To achieve this certificate, companies must provide documentary proof that they do not use child or forced labour, that they have a good working environment adapted to local conditions and that employment policies allow freedom of association, do not discriminate and ensure that working hours and wages are fair. They must also have an efficient management system that ensures that sub-contractors also comply.

Mascot moved production to Vietnam in 2008 and the factory now has over 1,000 employees, mostly seamstresses.

Michael Grosbøl, Mascot's managing director said that a company's ability to prove corporate social responsibility is becoming increasingly important for customers. 'Having our own factory with European management helped achieve an increase in efficiency and product quality. We also ensure that our products are manufactured under good and safe working conditions, which is crucial for us'.

Laundry and Cleaning News, 5 May 2011
http://www.laundryandcleaningnews.com/story.asp?sectioncode=138&storyCode=2059550
accessed 15 May 2011

3.2 Working conditions

Working conditions are governed by law in many countries, but sometimes only to a minimum standard. Employees are likely to have reasonably firm expectations of what working conditions should be like, even if they are 'adapted to local conditions', as in the example given above. The requirement for satisfactory working conditions extends beyond the basic working environment: an important aspect is the health and safety of employees. Many aspects of this topic are regulated by law, but, especially in the matter of safe working practices, it is necessary for employers to be active in monitoring developments that may lead to accident and injury.

ACTIVITY 2   10 mins

Think about your own working conditions and those you may have seen in any other organisation. Can you identify good aspects and bad? Are there any physical hindrances to good work performance? How about factors that might affect motivation?

3.3 Job security

Job security is a major concern for employees and this is reflected in the widespread adoption of employment protection legislation. The impact of job loss depends on several factors, including the general state of the economy and the employability of the person concerned, both of which will have a major influence on the ease with which alternative employment can be found. The classification of job security as a hygiene or infrastructure factor goes back Herzberg's work. However, there is little doubt that when economic conditions are poor, the need to retain employment can be a powerful **motivator** to good performance.

3.4 Quality of management and leadership

Herzberg identified supervision as a hygiene factor, though not a particularly powerful one (Herzberg, 1968). We will discuss management and leadership in detail later in this Study Manual. Here it will be enough to remark that leadership of sufficiently high quality to **inspire high performance** may occasionally be encountered, but this is unlikely to be a common occurrence.

> **PERSONAL LEADERSHIP**
>
> Stella David, Chief Executive of Bacardi-Martini was described as 'inspiring' by employees in The Sunday Times' 2004 list of the best 100 companies to work for. She eats in the staff canteen, is on first name terms with staff at all levels, and sends each one a birthday card and a gift each year.

Sound, competent managerial leadership is probably the best that most of us will ever encounter; leadership of such a workmanlike standard may well come to be taken more or less for granted. Problems will arise when leadership is inadequate and, to an even greater extent, when it is actually bad. Practices such as harassing, insulting and bullying employees are not unknown and will lead rapidly to withdrawal of trust and co-operation and eventually to active obstruction.

Leadership is therefore, properly classified as a hygiene factor, with the provisio that it may, on some occasions, be capable of providing motivation.

3.5 Culture

We mentioned culture briefly in Chapter 3. There, we were concerned with the culture of the wider society surrounding the organisation. Here we are concerned with the special culture that exists within organisations. The two are linked, of course, but different organisations are likely to have different cultures because of the different influences operating within them. **Organisational culture** in this sense consists of the beliefs, attitudes, practices and customs to which people are exposed during their interaction with the organisation. All managers will be more or less aware of the influence of culture, but those responsible for people management should understand its nature; how it arises and is continued; and what its influence is likely to be upon specific problems.

Culture can be very important for motivation and its influence can be positive or negative. Informal interactions in the workplace will rapidly spread impressions and attitudes about new developments and managerial actions. Work groups may develop their own standards of acceptable and unacceptable behaviour and, in particular, levels of output. We saw a classic example of this in Chapter 6 when we examined the bank wiring room part of the Hawthorne experiments.

3.6 Pay

We have already discussed the limitations of pay as a motivator in some detail, both earlier in this chapter and in Chapter 5. It will therefore be sufficient here to remind you that the ability of pay to motivate is subject to considerable debate. Organisations that set out to create commitment and high performance will probably pay at least reasonably well but they will not rely on pay as their main means of motivation.

4   The dysfunctional side-effects of money as the sole motivator

It is naïve to imagine that workers are motivated by money and nothing else, or that organisations can function successfully by manipulating financial incentives without offering anything else. Let's look at both of these dangerous and misleading beliefs.

4.1   'People are motivated by money and nothing else'

Of course, there will always be individuals who will respond to financial incentives and will either ignore or deliberately neglect the other aspects of their employment, like the nature of the job itself, the job security and the working conditions. These individuals fall into one or more of the following categories:

- They live in subsistence or near-subsistence societies without any 'cushion' from social services like unemployment benefit or disability allowances, so they have to work in order to earn money for survival. No wonder they are motivated by money in these circumstances: all of us would be.

- They are at a particular period in their lives when the need for money takes precedence over all else, perhaps because they have just entered into a long-term relationship with someone else and/or have children in their care and/or have begun a monetary commitment for house purchase. For a while, then, these individuals will seek highly-paid employment and will be willing to sacrifice other 'benefits', like working hours, location and a stimulating, satisfying job. They will accept shift work (which normally pays a premium) and take jobs in uncomfortable surroundings (e.g., down a mine), or work very long, unsociable hours.

- They belong to a special group of people who are instrumentally motivated all their lives, so they will always seek opportunities to maximise their earnings and will regularly move from one employer to another in search of higher wages or bonus payments. In most societies this group of the instrumentally motivated is a small minority, because most people will ultimately want more than money alone. As an extreme example we could cite people who are employed smuggling drugs across international borders: these may be drug users themselves, of course, but many do it simply for the money, and the money is meant to be quite attractive, certainly sufficient to compensate them for the risks they run. Such people don't smuggle drugs for the whole of their lives, however.

All the major motivation theories recognise the importance of money (it's especially important when you don't have enough, or don't have any), but they all acknowledge that there's more to life – for most people. There comes a time when we're prepared to give up monetary gain because we also want, say, a job which is stimulating and even enjoyable, working conditions that are tolerably pleasant, some job security which goes beyond the end of the week, and workmates or colleagues whom we can look forward to meeting each day.

4.2 'Organisations can motivate people solely by offering money – and nothing else'

In reality it is very rare to find organisations that do try to motivate people solely through pay, bonuses and other incentives, though there are some that come close. The problems with such a strategy are massive, however.

- As Herzberg points out, a pay rise may be sufficient to cause the recipients to be 'satisfied', though much depends here on the expectations of the recipients prior to the pay award. If their expectations were high, then the pay rise may leave them more dissatisfied than before – so nothing has been achieved except a raised level of worker disillusionment.

- Research has shown that if there is a period of genuine, conscious 'satisfaction', **it lasts for no longer than an average of three weeks**. This means that for three weeks the employer may experience an increase in productivity, commitment and overall performance – but then the employees' actions typically recede, 'normality' returns until an appetite for the next pay rise begins to emerge. This will be noticeable after about six months.

- So here's the most damaging news of all: the next pay rise has to exceed the one given earlier if it is to generate anything like its predecessor's surge of 'satisfaction'. This is because exactly the same event, repeated, seldom achieves the pleasure of the initial experience.

- Ultimately, therefore, motivating people exclusively through pay increases becomes unaffordable. No organisation can keep on handing out ever larger pay increases. [And even the organisation which can print its own money will fail because each issue of money will be devalued.]

A major study into the efficacy of pay as a motivator [*Rewarding Customer Service: Using Reward and Recognition to Deliver your Customer Service Strategy*, by Professor Michael West et al, CIPD, 2005] shows convincingly that pay is hardly ever a sufficient motivator on its own. This is for two reasons. First, it is not the physical quantity of the pay which matters, but rather the employee's perception about that pay level: some may regard any given level of earnings as adequate whilst others believe it to be an insult and still others are delighted.

Second, the research found that employees' feelings about their pay were closely linked to their perceptions about other dimensions of the working environment. Thus people were more likely to be satisfied with their earnings if they also believed that the organisation did these things as well:

- Looked after its workforce and treated its members fairly;
- Encouraged employees to be involved in decision-making; and
- Promoted discussions about ways of working and how to improve.

Chapter Roundup

↳ Herzberg identified two sets of factors affecting satisfaction and dissatisfaction at work, which he called **motivator** and **hygiene** factors respectively. Hygiene factors must be acceptable if dissatisfaction is to be avoided but only motivator factors can provide satisfaction at work. The hygiene factors are related to an organisation's **infrastructure** of routine systems and practices, while motivator factors enable an organisation to **differentiate** itself from others in the eyes of serving and potential employees.

↳ **Pay** in its simplest aspect is regarded as a hygiene factor but it is actually a complex matter. Expectancy theory suggests that valuable reward can help to produce desired employee behaviour and that incentive payment schemes, bonuses and benefits can provide recognition and a sense of achievement. However, such payments and schemes may be seen as manipulative and administering them can be costly and complex.

↳ The concept of **total reward** regards both monetary and intangible rewards as equally important. Four groups of reward may be considered.

- **Pay** including all forms of pay, incentives, bonuses and profit sharing.

- **Benefits** such as pensions, holidays, health care and flexible working hour schemes.

- **Learning and development** includes the full range of training and development opportunities, including career and professional development opportunities.

- **Work environment rewards** include recognition, achievement, work-life balance, job design, leadership and organisational values.

↳ The **performance infrastructure** consists of the more formal systems, processes and procedures that impinge on employees individually and collectively as part of their relationship with the organisation.

↳ **HRM compliance** is important to the employment relationship; legal provisions must be respected, but considerable influence is also exerted by social responsibility aspirations, business ethics and professional standards.

↳ **Working conditions** include the basic nature of the working environment as well as the health and safety of employees.

↳ **Job security** was seen by Herzberg as a hygiene factor but it can be a major concern for employees, especially when the economy is sluggish or in recession, and the need to retain employment can be a powerful motivator to good performance.

↳ **Supervision** was also identified as a hygiene factor and poor leadership by managers can rapidly destroy any potential for high performance. On the other hand, good leadership may inspire, though it is rarely encountered. Sound, competent management will probably be taken for granted.

↳ **Culture** can have a positive or a negative effect on motivation.

Quick Quiz

1   Who identified hygiene and motivator factors?

2   What is the name given to payments designed to motivate by recognising high levels of performance?

3   Apart from the theoretical status of pay as a hygiene factor, what are the objections to schemes of incentive payments?

4   What are relational and communal rewards?

5   Organisations must obey the law. What other kinds of external pressure influence their behaviour, in terms of right and wrong?

6   Is supervision a hygiene factor?

Answers to Quick Quiz

1   Frederick Herzberg

2   Incentives

3   The can be seen by employees as manipulative and they can be costly and complex to set up and operate.

4   In Armstrong & Brown's scheme of total reward, relational rewards consist of various aspects of training and development, while communal rewards include recognition, achievement, work-life balance, job design, leadership and organisational values.

5   Corporate social responsibility, business ethics and professional standards

6   Almost always, though there will be a few occasions when it provides motivation.

Answers to Activities

Activity 1

Clearly this activity will depend on your own experience. However, you should try to be aware that different people respond in different ways both to being recognised and to the need to show recognition. You should also think about organisational policy and the extent to which it affected you.

Activity 2

Many physical factors can have a direct effect on work performance, as was identified and studied over a century ago in the era of Scientific Management. These include light quality and level; sound and temperature levels; the space available for work; the positioning of equipment and tools; and the effectiveness of communication systems. The effect of working conditions on motivation would be expected to follow the theory for hygiene factors, of course, which is to say that while poor conditions may demotivate, the best conditions can never really lead to satisfaction. However, this is a complex subject and good working conditions may, to some extent, be an indication of organisational commitment to the individual and thus have some indirect motivating effect.

Chapter 8

The differentiator elements

In this chapter we continue our examination of the factors making up the employee's workplace experience. This time we concentrate on the differentiator factors. A very important theme running through this chapter is the contribution people management can make to the success of the organisation. Keep in mind the basic nature of the organisation as explained in Chapter 1 and remember that organisations employ people for a purpose: to achieve the organisation's aims. People management is about organisational success.

We commence with a discussion of the nature of differentiation as a concept borrowed from the world of business strategy. This leads us into a consideration of both critical success factors and competences, both of which are of great importance in practical people management terms.

After a discussion of the differentiator factors themselves, we conclude the chapter with a brief discussion of employer branding, which exploits the advantages to the organisation of differentiators.

1   Differentiation

Differentiation means the process of making something we are interested in noticeably different from other similar things. We have to create some kind of effect that will distinguish our 'something' from everyone else's. Differentiation in this sense is an important concept in the world of business strategy, where it is a well-established route to take in seeking sustainable competitive advantage. The essence of the concept is that the organisation makes its market offering so **distinctive and desirable** in the eyes of potential customers that it is able to charge premium prices. The classic means of doing this with consumer goods is to build a brand that both promises and delivers something of value to the customer. The value may be largely or entirely intangible, as in the case of fashion goods, or it may be tangible, or have tangible effects, as in the case of brands that deliver value for money or consistently high quality. For example, there are many different car manufacturers, but BMW's products are distinguished from their competitors' by their quality and performance.

What has this to do with people management? We will address this question in detail later in this chapter, but first we must look in more detail at the wider concept of differentiation in a business setting.

This concept is illustrated in detail by Johnston and Clark (2008) in their discussion of factors that affect the **delivery of services**. They do not speak in terms of differentiation, but that is, effectively the subject of their analysis.

They say that the factors affecting the **service delivery** may be divided into four groups, depending on their impact on the quality of the service delivered. These four groups are, inevitably, analysed using the kind of two-axis matrix we encountered in Chapter 7. Here the axes are **potential to dissatisfy** the customer and **potential to delight** the customer (p120).

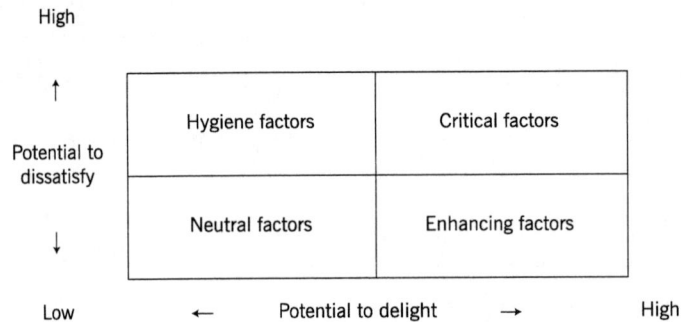

High

	Hygiene factors	Critical factors
Potential to dissatisfy	Neutral factors	Enhancing factors

Low   ←   Potential to delight   →   High

Figure 8.1: Factors affecting service delivery

(a)   **Hygiene factors**. The terminology here is clearly derived from Herzberg's work. In Johnston and Clark (2008)'s analysis, hygiene factors have **high potential to dissatisfy** but are unlikely to delight the customer even when over-provided.

(b)   **Critical factors** will dissatisfy if they are of low standard but have the **potential to delight** if they are of high quality.

(c)   **Neutral factors** have little effect on either satisfaction or delight.

(d)   **Enhancing factors** have the **potential to delight** the customer, but their absence is unlikely to dissatisfy.

> **SERVICE DELIVERY FACTORS IN ACTION**
>
> We can illustrate these categories by reference to a public transport system such as a **local bus network**.
>
> An example of **hygiene factor** would be the reliability of the service. If the buses rarely arrive on time, there will be widespread dissatisfaction. However, even a very high rate of on-time departures are likely to be taken for granted rather than provide delight – or even very much satisfaction.
>
> An example of an **enhancing factor** would be friendliness on the part of bus drivers. If the drivers were widely acknowledged to be friendly and helpful, there would be great potential for delighting travellers. However, the simple absence of friendliness would be unlikely to dissatisfy and even consistent grumpiness might simply be accepted as a characteristic of the service.
>
> Elegant design of buses would be an example of a **neutral factor**. Customers are unlikely to be either pleased or dissatisfied by the visual aspect of the buses.
>
> Speed of travel might be an example of a **critical factor** for a bus service. If travel is universally slow, especially when compared to alternatives, such as rail, customers are likely to be dissatisfied. However, noticeably fast journey times may well have the capacity to delight.

The point of this kind of analysis is its implication for the management of the organisation, especially if it is concerned with a **strategy of differentiation** – in the sense of achieving a market advantage by making the product stand out from its competitors. Each of the factor groups requires a different management approach.

(a)   **Hygiene factors** must be managed so that they do not create dissatisfaction. They must be provided in sufficient quantity and quality to achieve this end, but there is no point in going beyond this requirement, since these factors cannot delight customers or differentiate the product.

(b)   **Critical factors** must receive great attention since they have the potential both to delight and to dissatisfy. They must be managed so as to achieve the former and preclude the latter. This is one possible basis for achieving differentiation in the marketplace.

(c)   **Neutral factors** need not be a great concern to management.

(d)   Wise managers will consider **enhancing factors** carefully. If the organisation is doing well and this is expected to continue, or if resources are particularly scarce, these factors may merely be monitored to see if their status is likely to change or if competitors seem likely to exploit them. However, they offer an opportunity to enhance the service offered, and thus the degree of differentiation achieved, which might be useful if competition is severe or if the cost/benefit ratio is sufficiently advantageous.

2   Critical success factors and competences

2.1   Critical success factors

We will stay with the field of market success or failure a little longer: the relevance of this will become apparent later on in this chapter. In the meantime, remember that while this discussion deals specifically with commercial, profit-making organisations, the ideas are equally relevant to not-for-profit and public sector organisations, since they too have customers to satisfy and, if possible, impress.

Johnson *et al* (2008) provide a more traditional account of the factors affecting customer perceptions of organisations and their outputs. They remark that there is likely to be a wide range of opinion among customers as to the features of the organisation's market offerings that provide them with the greatest satisfaction, but, equally, it is also likely that some features will be widely regarded as **particularly important**. These features, the satisfactions they provide and the demands they make on the organisation's way of doing business constitute **critical success factors**: the organisation must get these things right if it is to be successful in what it does.

They go on to define critical success factors as 'those product features that are particularly valued by a group of customers and, therefore, where the organisation must excel to outperform competitors' (p597). This definition is particularly useful since it contains both of the elements discussed above: the **potential to delight the customer** and the **need for careful management** to ensure that this happens.

2.2   Competences

This approach to critical success factors puts them squarely in the perception of the customer, which inevitably provokes this question: how does the organisation ensure that its products continue to possess these features? The answer is that it is necessary to deploy appropriate **competences**. Johnson *et al* (2008) say that strategic capability consists of resources, such as machinery and technical information, and competences. In the field of people management we are primarily concerned with the strategic capability that flows from **competences**.

Johnson *et al* (2008) define competences as 'the skills and abilities by which resources are deployed effectively through an organisation's activities and processes' (p596). **Threshold competences** are 'needed to meet customers' minimum requirements and therefore for the organisation to continue to exist' (p96), while **core competences** 'underpin competitive advantage and are difficult for competitors to imitate or obtain' (p96).

KISTLER'S CORE COMPETENCE

Established in Winterthur (Switzerland) in 1957, the Kistler Group now has a worldwide presence with 23 group companies and 30 distributors ensuring prompt, local application support and short delivery times. With a staff of more than 1,000, the Kistler Group is one of the world's leading providers of dynamic measuring instrumentation.

Kistler's core competence is the development, production and use of sensors for measuring pressure, force and acceleration. Kistler's know-how and electronic systems can be used to prepare measuring signals for use in analyzing physical processes, controlling and optimizing industrial processes, improving product quality in manufacturing and improving performance in sports and rehabilitation.

---

http://www.manufacturingtalk.com/news/kst/kst000.html

accessed 17 May 2011

ACTIVITY   10 mins

Think about any organisation you are familiar with. What do you consider to be its threshold and core competences? To what extent does it achieve them?

Using these definitions, we can discern a direct link between the definitions of hygiene factors and critical factors given by Johnston and Clark (2008) on the one hand and threshold and core competences on the other. Hygiene factors, you will remember, have high potential to dissatisfy. To avoid disappointing the customer in the matter of hygiene factors, **threshold competences** must be in place. However, the proper management of critical factors (or critical success factors) ideally demands the possession and proper deployment of **core competences**.

2.3   People management

We may now take a further logical step and link these ideas to the conceptual basis of people management that we introduced in Chapter 7: the basic framework or performance infrastructure factors and the motivating or differentiating factors.

We said that the performance infrastructure (or Herzberg hygiene) factors must be adequate if worker dissatisfaction is to be avoided. This means that this group of factors **supports both threshold and core competences**; they are **not sufficient** for motivation to be achieved, but their presence is **necessary** for that purpose. This is an important point and you should make sure you understand it: the adequacy of these factors does not guarantee organisational success, but inadequacy is likely to lead to organisational failure.

The status of the motivating or differentiating factors is rather more complex. It is tempting to see them as specifically linked to core competences, since such competences 'underpin competitive advantage and are difficult for competitors to imitate or obtain'. However, you should not make this mistake; these factors support high levels of performance *of any kind* and it may be that the particular circumstances of a given organisation require particularly high levels of performance to achieve even threshold competence.

For example, a very high level of service will be **taken for granted** by the guests of any luxury hotel: personal service in such a place will be a hygiene factor, in the terms of Johnston and Clark (2008). A high level of service will be no more than a threshold competence but staff will require a high level of motivation to achieve it. In such a setting, critical success factors and the core competences that support them will relate to something else, such as the particular recreational activities provided by the hotel. A high level of motivation will be needed here, as well. Thus, the motivating factors **support both threshold and core competences**.

(You will have noted that this example illustrates one very important trap that you must not fall into if you are thinking about the analysis in Johnston and Clark (2008). In their model, hygiene factors are aspects of the service provided to customers, whereas in the people management concept we are concerned with here, hygiene factors are aspects of the worker's experience of work. Keep this distinction in mind.)

2.4 In summary

In the first two sections of this chapter we have attempted to set the idea of the basic framework and differentiator factors in the context of the work of the organisation. We have discussed some fairly complex ideas, such as competences and critical success factors, and tried to point out the ways in which confusion can arise from the **careless use of the terminology** concerned. Here is a summary of that rather complex terminology.

In people management, Herzberg's **motivator** factors = syllabus **differentiator** factors, while Herzberg's **hygiene** factors = syllabus **basic framework** factors = syllabus **infrastructure** factors.

In Johnston and Clark (2008), service delivery **hygiene factors** have high potential to dissatisfy but are unlikely to delight the customer, even when over-provided.

In Johnston and Clark (2008), service delivery **critical factors** will dissatisfy if they are of low standard, but have the potential to delight if they are of high quality.

In Johnson *et al* (2008), **critical success factors** in any organisation 'are particularly valued by a group of customers and, therefore, where the organisation must excel'.

In organisational activity, both basic framework and differentiator factors support both threshold and core competences, which in turn both support critical success factors.

3 Differentiators in people management

We have now looked at the basic concept of differentiation with respect to the market offering and shown how achieving it depends on the existence of both basic framework, and differentiator or motivator factors in the workplace. In Chapter 7 we examined the basic framework factors, so we must now look in more detail at the differentiator factors.

3.1   Why differentiate in people management?

Product (or service) differentiation is widely seen as a route to successful engagement with existing and potential customers, as we have already explained. The importance of the concept in people management is that it is seen as a means to achieve successful engagement with people within the organisation. Engaged employees are loyal and productive. They undertake in what is known as **discretionary behaviour**, that is, behaviour that goes beyond normally accepted minimum standards of performance. They put in extra effort, co-operate well and help others and they take the initiative in providing customer satisfaction, in solving problems and in developing systems of work. This kind of behaviour constitutes '**organisational citizenship**'.

In order to build an engaged workforce, we think in terms of employees (and potential employees) as customers and the work experience as a kind of product. We want people to 'buy' this 'product' by working enthusiastically and well. We want to recruit and retain the ablest, most highly-qualified and most energetic people in the job market and we are in competition with other employers to do so. To succeed in this quest for employee engagement, we **differentiate** the workplace experience. When we differentiate a product, we incorporate desirable marketing features into it, such as style, speed, colour and value for money. When we differentiate our workplace we do just the same thing: we incorporate the various people management differentiator features into the workplace experience.

3.2   Features of differentiation

You are already familiar with Herzberg's summary list of motivating factors.

- Recognition
- Responsibility
- Challenging work
- Achievement
- Growth and development in the job

This is useful as far as it goes, but we need to look in more detail at the policies and practices that are necessary to achieve people management differentiation in the modern workplace. The fundamental point is that **a high value is placed on people** and this leads to policies and practices that promote differentiation and engagement.

(a)   **Recruitment and selection**. Recruitment is focussed on finding people who will support the organisation's style and benefit from it. Such people welcome change and continuing improvement and they willingly undertake programmes of learning and development. They are loyal to the organisation and feel a sense of responsibility both in terms of their own input and the behaviour of the teams and departments of which they are members. This sense of responsibility extends beyond the workplace into ethical conduct generally.

(b)   **Management and leadership**. High standards of management and leadership are expected by the organisation and managers at all levels are expected to focus on high performance from their staff. Job descriptions based on lists of tasks are not used; instead accountability profiles that identify outputs and key result areas are used.

(c)   **Communication**. Great care is taken over the way the organisation communicates with its members. In addition, the importance of employee voice and involvement are recognised and techniques such as briefings, discussion, suggestion schemes and surveys are used.

(d)   **Opportunity**. The organisation actively promotes learning and development, both in the work situation and externally. Career development is important as task-related learning. Also, there are opportunities for advancement, possibly based on a policy of promotion from within. Promotion brings enhanced responsibilities; purely notional 'promotion' that merely enhances status is avoided.

(e) **Employee commitment and engagement**. We will look more closely at the concepts of commitment and engagement later in this Study Guide; here it will suffice to say that there will be clear mechanisms in place to encourage and recognise employee effort, but only when it leads to increased organisational success and value added. These may include incentive payments, praise, employee of the month schemes and so on.

(f) **Job design**. The basic ideas of Herzberg and the principles established in Hackman and Oldham (1980) were explained in Chapters 4 and 5 respectively; these ideas are utilised to create, as far as is practicable, work that is satisfying.

(g) **Self-actualisation**. Self-actualisation, or growth to fulfil personal potential, is widely seen as an innate human need with significant potential to motivate people to action in its pursuit. Not all people will see the workplace as the sphere in which they might achieve self-actualisation, but for those who do perceive some element of this possibility it will be important. Enlightened employers will bear this in mind and, as a minimum, do what they can to remove obstacles to self-actualisation. Also, the various measures discussed above may provide opportunities for some degree of self-actualisation.

4 Building an employer brand

Let us restate the basic principle of people management differentiation. Just as organisations sell their products and services in the marketplace, so too they participate in the employment marketplace. In the product marketplace, they seek revenue by attempting to convince potential customers to accept their wares and pay for them with money. In the employment marketplace they do something very similar: they seek high quality work by attempting to convince potential employees to accept employment and contribute their talents, skills and experience. The two cases are exactly parallel and that is why the concept of **employer branding** has arisen.

As we have remarked, building a brand is an accepted way of differentiating a product or service in order to attract a premium price and keep customers coming back for more. Why not use this idea to attract and retain premium employees? Even when the economy is sluggish it will not be easy to find and keep the best people and employer branding is an extra stimulus to encourage their initial attention and their eventual loyalty.

The differentiating factors we have discussed above will form the foundation of a successful employer brand. The Chartered Institute of Personnel and Development has published a guide that goes into more detail.

MCDONALDS, MCJOBS AND NEW CUSTOMER ASPIRATIONS

McDonald's restaurants are found in 119 countries and territories around the world and serve 58 million customers each day. There are over 31,000 McDonald's restaurants worldwide, employing more than 1.5 million people.

A new (2009) edition of the Oxford English Dictionary contains, for the first time, the word 'McJob', which is defined as 'an unstimulating, low-paid job with few prospects, especially one created by the expansion of the service sector'. The term 'McJob', however, was coined by a sociologist, Amitai Etzioni, in 1986, and was later popularised by Douglas Coupland's 1991 novel, *Generation X: Tales for an Accelerated Culture*, in which a 'McJob' was described as a 'low-pay, low-prestige, low-dignity, low-benefit, no-future job in the service sector.'

The appearance of the word 'McJob' in a reputable dictionary excited the hostility of David Fairhurst, a Senior Vice-President for McDonalds, who wrote: 'It's time the dictionary definition of "McJob" was changed to reflect a job that is stimulating, rewarding and offers opportunities for career progression and skills that last a lifetime'. In 2006 McDonald's undertook an advertising campaign in the UK, based on some research by Professor Adrian Furnham, in an attempt to show the benefits of working for the company.

What we have here is an example of the tensions caused by a massive change in expectations about work and employment. At one time, 'Taylorism' (named after Frederick Winslow Taylor, the 'father' of Scientific Management) meant that tasks were broken down into their smallest possible component jobs so that they could be performed by people with virtually no training at all and by people who could be replaced at a moment's notice. This was the thinking behind Henry Ford's assembly line. However, it is an approach which has its drawbacks, not least that it produces a workforce which is alienated and disillusioned – scarcely appropriate for a world which is fast-moving, dynamic, demanding and interactive. Today customers expect personalised service, they want customer-facing employees to be empowered, they want fast responses and they seek a one-stop shop culture for handling all customer-related issues like complaints and queries.

4.1 The History of Employer branding

The phrase 'employer branding' was invented in the early 1990s, and was recently defined by Walker as 'a set of attributes and qualities – often intangible – that makes an organisation distinctive, promises a particular kind of employment experience, and appeals to those people who will thrive and perform to their best in its culture'. Undoubtedly there are some organisations which could legitimately claim to be 'employer brands' (or 'employers of choice', which is the other phrase sometimes used), because they attract vast numbers of speculative job applications, because they experience very low levels of voluntary labour turnover, and because, as a result, they can be very selective when choosing which candidates will actually be offered jobs. In the UK, these 'employer brands' include such companies as Procter & Gamble, PriceWaterhouseCoopers, and Tesco; internationally they embrace Singapore Airlines, Standard Chartered Bank and British American Tobacco.

There are many benefits in becoming an 'employer brand', but first of all we need to understand that an organisation does not become an 'employer brand' by simply claiming that it is. As with the marketing of any brand, the value of the brand is dependent on the value given to it by its customers, so in that sense the customers 'own' the brand: thus the brand value for Tesco is the value given to the Tesco brand .by its customers: it is they who decide whether it has a value or not. It's the same with an 'employer brand': the 'brand value' is the value of the brand *as perceived by its employees, its suppliers and its job applicants*. An organisation may claim that it is an 'employer brand', but if that isn't how it is viewed by outsiders, then it isn't a true 'brand'.

4.2 The benefits of becoming an 'Employer Brand'

(a) Quality of Recruitment. The organisation is more attractive to potential recruits and becomes an 'employer of choice' in the labour market.

(b) Reduced Recruitment Costs. It follows that if the organisation receives a large number of unsolicited yet quality applications, it doesn't have to spend so much on recruitment advertising or recruitment literature, and doesn't have to pay recruitment agencies any fees.

(c) Increased Retention. Given that the organisation's employees feel good about their employer and are proud to work there, they are more likely to stay. With Tesco, 87% of its workforce say they would happily recommend others (including friends and relatives) not just to apply for jobs with the company but also to shop there as customers.

(d) Better Performance. Typically, an employer brand will experience lower levels of employee absence, lower levels of unexplained sickness, and improved productivity figures including enhanced customer feedback because they now transact business with more dedicated and enthusiastic employees.

(e) Reputational Advantages. Achieving the status of an employer brand can bring benefits with customers, too, because the public believes that the organisation is a 'good' employer and therefore is likely to sell 'good' products and services.

4.3 Purposes of employer branding

A successful **employer brand** brings three main benefits.

(a) It achieves **differentiation**. Potential employees have a better idea of what working for the organisation will be like if there is a well-established employer brand.

(b) It inspires **loyalty**. If the right work has been done, the reality of the new employee's situation will reflect the brand. A sense of affinity and bonding will lead to a loyal relationship.

(c) Just as in the market for goods and services, an employer brand supports **premium pricing**. In the employment marketplace, the organisation with the strong brand is not forced to compete on exclusively monetary terms to attract and keep the recruits it wants. Its reputation makes people want to work for it.

4.4 Keeping the brand promise

Of course, it is vital that the **brand promise** is kept. The actual experience of working for the organisation must confirm the story the employer brand tells. If it does not, the extent of dissatisfaction, disillusion and alienation that will result will exceed anything that might have occurred if not promises had been made.

4.5 Managing the brand

In effect, all organisations except, perhaps, the tiniest, have employer brands whether they realise it or not, in the sense that each already has a **reputation in the labour market**. It may be vague and of little importance, but it exists. The aim of managing the brand is to ensure that its effects are positive and significant.

PERCEIVED REPUTATION

The **London Fire Brigade** found that its recruits almost all came from white working class families that had a tradition of fire brigade work. Clearly this compromised its duty in respect of diversity and it had to overcome the perception this created among potential recruits.

A basic aspect of employer brand management must therefore be to establish just what the current brand situation is by means of **market research techniques** such as surveys and focus groups.

A project to establish an employer brand must identify and define the distinctive features that will identify it to existing and potential employees. These attributes must be carefully considered: they must be attractive, but they must also be feasible.

(a) They must be supported by managers at all levels, especially at the very top.

(b) Establishing them will require money to be spent, so there must be an adequate budget

(c) They must fit reasonably well with the way the organisation does things: the greater the change to culture and practice, the less likely that the branding project will succeed.

4.6 Measuring brand power

Creating an employer brand requires effort and expense; it is therefore necessary that its effectiveness should be subjected to proper assessment and review. This will involve measuring the extent to which it achieves its purposes; in the simplest terms, that means measuring its effect on recruitment and retention of high quality staff. Simple measurement of application numbers and staff turnover will be supplemented by exit interviews and employee surveys.

Chapter Roundup

⤷ The concept of differentiation in HRM is borrowed from business strategy, where differentiation of products is a means to achieving competitive advantage. Such differentiation may be analysed in terms of four groups of product characteristics.

- **Hygiene factors** have high potential to dissatisfy but are unlikely to delight the customer even when over-provided.
- **Critical factors** will dissatisfy if they are of low standard but have the potential to delight if they are of high quality.
- **Neutral factors** have little effect on either satisfaction or delight.
- **Enhancing factors** have the potential to delight the customer but their absence is unlikely to dissatisfy.

⤷ **Critical success factor**s are product features that are particularly valued by a group of customers and, therefore, where the organisation must excel to outperform competitors.

⤷ **Threshold competences** are needed to meet customers' minimum requirements and therefore for the organisation to continue to exist.

⤷ **Core competences** underpin competitive advantage and are difficult for competitors to imitate or obtain.

⤷ In HRM terms, **infrastructure factors** and **differentiator factors** are both required to support threshold competences and core competences.

⤷ Differentiator factors promote employee engagement, motivation, loyalty, discretionary behaviour and organisational citizenship.

⤷ Herzberg's motivator factors are important for HRM differentiation, but more extensive analysis is necessary.

⤷ Important differentiator factors relate to specific approaches to a range of organisational functions.

- **Recruitment and selection** focuses on finding people who welcome change, willingly undertake programmes of learning and development and are both loyal and responsible.
- **Management and leadership** must be of a high standard and focus on high performance.
- **Communication** is thorough and effective, both up and down the organisation.
- **Opportunity** is extensive; learning and development are promoted and there are opportunities for advancement.
- **Employee commitment and engagement** are encouraged by mechanisms that encourage and recognise employee effort leading to increased organisational success and value added.
- **Job design** is utilised to create, as far as is practicable, work that is satisfying.
- **Self-actualisation** is nurtured.

⤷ A positive, powerful **employer brand** helps to achieve differentiation, inspires loyalty and overcomes the default position of competing exclusively with monetary rewards to attract and keep high quality recruits.

⤷ The brand promise must be kept.

⤷ All organisations have employer brands but many do not know what they are; this is established by market research techniques.

⤷ An employer branding project must be supported by top management and properly financed. The new brand should not require too great a change to existing culture and practice if it is to succeed.

⤷ The success of an employer brand can be measured by its effect on recruitment and staff turnover.

Quick Quiz

1 Why do companies seek to differentiate their products and services in the marketplace?

2 What categories do Johnston & Clark use to analyse the factors that affect the quality of service delivery?

3 What are critical success factors?

4 What are core competences?

5 Why should organisations feature differentiation factors in people management?

6 Which writers established widely applied principles of job design to achieve motivation?

7 What are the purposes of employer branding?

8 How is the success of employer branding measured?

Answers to Quick Quiz

1 To make them offering sufficiently distinctive and desirable in the eyes of potential customers to be able to charge premium prices.

2 Hygiene factors, enhancing factors, neutral factors and critical factors

3 Those product features that are particularly valued by a group of customers and, therefore, where the organisation must excel to outperform competitors

4 Competences that underpin competitive advantage and are difficult for competitors to imitate or obtain

5 To encourage engagement, loyalty, motivation and discretionary behaviour among employees

6 Herzberg originally and Hackman & Oldham

7 Differentiation, loyalty and premium pricing

8 By its effect on the recruitment and retention of high quality staff

Answer to Activity

Activity

Clearly, it is not possible to give a full debrief to this activity, but you should note that many organisations have definite weaknesses in both core and threshold competences, as their reputations and ability to add value show.

Chapter 9

Management and leadership

We have already made frequent reference to managers and management, but we have treated them as basic ideas that everyone understands. Now it is time to look more closely at the nature of management as a function within the organisation and what it is that managers do. This leads us on to a consideration of the authority of managers and their role as leaders within the organisation.

1   The role of the manager

In Chapter 1 we said that organisations are, in essence, groups of people working together for a common purpose. They exist in order to achieve results that individuals cannot achieve by themselves. They enable people to be more **productive**. However, organisations do not succeed simply by goodwill and co-operation: it is fundamental that a number of **managerial functions** are discharged.

(a)   **Objectives** have to be set for the organisation.

(b)   Somebody has to **monitor progress and results** to ensure that objectives are met.

(c)   Somebody has to communicate and sustain **corporate values**, **ethics** and **operating principles**.

(d)   Somebody has to look after the interests of the **organisation's owners** and other **stakeholders**.

ACTIVITY 1   10 mins

John, Paul, George and Ringo set up in business together as repairers of musical instruments. Each has contributed £5,000 as capital for the business. They are a bit uncertain as to how they should run the business, and, when they discuss this in the pub, they decide that attention needs to be paid to planning what they do, reviewing what they do and controlling what they do.

Suggest two ways in which John, Paul, George and Ringo can manage the business assuming no other personnel are recruited.

Five functions of management: Henri Fayol

A more detailed picture of what managers must do was presented by Henri Fayol, a prominent nineteenth century manager). Fayol was a French industrialist who put forward and popularised the concept of the '**universality of management principles**': in other words, the idea that all organisations could be structured and managed according to certain rational principles (Fayol, 1961).

Fayol classified five **functions of management** which apply to any organisation.

Function	Comment
Planning	This involves determining **objectives**, and strategies, policies, programmes and procedures for achieving those objectives, for the organisation and its sub-units.
Organising	Establishing a **structure of tasks** which need to be performed to achieve the goals of the organisation; grouping these tasks into jobs for individuals or teams; allocating jobs to sections and departments; **delegating** authority to carry out the jobs; and providing **systems of information** and communication, for the co-ordination of activities.
Commanding	Giving **instructions** to subordinates to carry out tasks, for which the manager has authority (to make decisions) and responsibility (for performance).
Co-ordinating	**Harmonising** the goals and activities of individuals and groups within the organisation. Management must reconcile differences in approach, effort, interest and timing, in favour of overall (or 'super-ordinate') shared goals.
Controlling	**Measuring** and **correcting** the activities of individuals and groups, to ensure that their performance is in accordance with plans. Deviations from plans are identified and corrected.

You may be struck by two key 'omissions' from Fayol's classification, from a more modern viewpoint.

(a)   **Motivating** is not mentioned. It is assumed that subordinates will carry out tasks when 'commanded' or instructed to do so, regardless of whether or how far they may want to do so.

(b)   **Communicating** is not mentioned, although it is implied by the process of commanding (giving instructions), co-ordinating (sharing information) and controlling (giving feedback).

This reflects the **classical view** of the function of management as a matter of controlling resources and processes rather than dealing with people. More recent writers have analysed the role of management in rather different ways and included these elements. Nevertheless, Fayol's list remains useful, especially if we are aware of its omissions. It makes it clear that organisations must have managers and those managers must be able to discharge their functions. This implies the use of some kind of **authority**.

2   Authority relationships

2.1   Power and authority

Power and **authority** as concepts are closely linked. For example, Huczynski & Buchanan (2007) provide these definitions.

Authority: the right to guide or direct the actions of others and extract from them responses that are appropriate to the attainment of an organisation's goals (p831).

Power: the capacity of individuals to overcome resistance on the part of others, to exert their will and to produce results consistent with their interests and objectives (p845).

The main difference between these definitions is that authority is presented as a right established by the need to achieve an **organisation's goals**, whereas power is a **personal capacity** and related to the exerciser's own purposes. Nevertheless, in general use, the words are almost interchangeable, unless great precision is required, as in the case of the analysis below.

French and Raven (1958) classified power into six types.

Type of power	Description
Coercive power	The power based on fear of punishment or other undesirable outcomes such as withdrawal of support or allocation of unpleasant tasks.
Reward (or resource) power	The power based on the subordinates' perception of access to or control over valued resources. For example, managers have access to information, contacts and financial rewards for team members. The amount of resource power a person has depends on the scarcity of the resource, how much the resource is valued by others, and how far the resource is under the manager's control.
Legitimate (or position) power	The subordinate believes that the superior has the right to exercise the power associated with a particular position in the organisation. This is authority as defined above by Huczynski & Buchanan (2007).
Expert power	Power based on subordinates' recognition of experience, qualifications or expertise in an area which they need or value.
Referent (or personal) power	Based on respect, esteem and force of personality, which can attract, influence or inspire other people.
Negative power	The power to disrupt operations, for example, by failure or refusal to communicate or co-operate, or in extreme cases, by industrial action such as strikes or working to rule.

This analysis supports a widely held view that authority is all very well, but power is needed to back it up.

Power and authority are not things a superior has in isolation: they are exercised over other individuals or groups and depend on their *recognising* the superior's power over them.

Managers' authority is generally limited to specific purposes and groups of subordinates. Limits are often functional, in that they relate to specific aspects of work, or financial; financial limits may be specified in the form of a budget.

THE CONCEPT OF 'NEGATIVE POWER'

You may be curious about 'negative power', which is mentioned briefly in the above classification of 'types of power'. The following note should help to explain what 'negative power' means and why it is important in today's organisations.

Already in this book you should have noticed occasional use of the words 'discretionary behaviour' and 'organizational citizenship'. These are meant to refer to the willingness of employees to 'go the extra mile' in support of their organisation, their colleagues, their managers and their customers. Examples include:

- Helping colleagues to cope whenever one of their number is off sick;

- Acting resourcefully when seeking to resolve a serious customer complaint, by agreeing to provide compensation or a replacement product;

- Supporting the organisation when it wishes to introduce new methods of working or new technologies; or

- Co-operating with the manager when special commitments have to be honoured.

The notion of 'discretionary behaviour' arises out of the fact that every job has two elements:

(1)   THE PRESCRIBED – defined by the job description; and

(2)   THE DISCRETIONARY – defined by the way in which the more ambiguous elements of the job description are interpreted, the speed, care and style of job delivery, and the extent to which the job-holder is willing to exercise initiative in the exercise of his/her accountabilities.

In turn, there are two types of 'discretionary behaviour'. The employee can act positively – for the benefit of the organisation – or may function negatively. It is important to acknowledge that **all employees have the power to act negatively**:

- By refusing to remain at work after the end of a shift in order to finish an uncompleted task (such a refusal may be technically legitimate, especially if hours of work are spelt out in the job description, but can often appear hostile).

- By claiming that a customer's complaint is nothing to do with him or her, and should be addressed elsewhere – instead of taking the responsibility for transferring the complaint the right department.

- By wilfully neglecting to pass on important information to the manager or other colleagues.

- By allowing machinery to continue to malfunction beyond the point at which the original defect was first noticed.

The concept of 'negative power' is very important in understanding the realities of people management and people leadership, because arbitrary methods of management and leadership can easily tempt employees into acting negatively. What's more, they can often get away with it because their actions can seldom be traced. Positive leadership and management, on the other hand, more commonly produces positive responses in the form of value-added 'discretionary behaviour' and 'organisational citizenship'.

2.2 Responsibility and accountability

Responsibility is the **obligation** a person has to fulfil an assigned task.

Accountability is a person's **liability** to be called to account for the fulfilment of assigned tasks.

The definitions given above are useful because the term 'responsibility' is used in two ways.

(a) A person is said to be responsible *for* a piece of work when he or she is required to ensure that the work is done.

(b) The same person is said to be responsible *to* a superior when he or she is given work by that superior: in this sense, the term 'accountable' is often used.

One is thus accountable *to* a superior *for* a piece of work for which one is responsible.

LACK OF ACCOUNTABILITY WITHIN THE CIVIL SERVICE

The civil service lacks a culture of accountability, with lines of responsibility all too often unclear, according to a report from an independent think tank.

Staff and ministers are disappointed that incompetence goes unpunished, according to a qualitative survey of 65 civil service personnel by the Institute for Public Policy Research (IPPR). It found that staff were frustrated because improvements within the sector were so slow.

'Lines of accountability in Whitehall are ill-defined and too often responsibility falls between the cracks,' said Nick Pearce, director of IPPR. 'Politicians and civil servants duck and dive behind each other and no one takes clear responsibility for driving improvement. The civil service will never achieve consistently high performance without effective performance management.'

James Brockett, *People Management*, 7 August 2006

Delegation of authority is the process whereby a superior gives to a subordinate part of his or her own authority to make decisions.

The principle of **delegation** is that a manager may make subordinates *responsible for* work, but remains *accountable to* his or her own superior for ensuring that the work is done. Appropriate decision-making authority must be delegated alongside the delegated responsibility.

Responsibility/authority mismatch

In practice, matters are rarely clear-cut, and in many organisations responsibility and authority are ambiguous and shifting because of, for example, departmental 'empire-building' or changes in jobs or structures.

Authority without responsibility is a recipe for arbitrary and irresponsible behaviour: the person has the right to make decisions without being held accountable for them.

Responsibility without authority places subordinates in an impossible and stressful position: they are held accountable for results over which they have no control.

2.3 Power centres

The **degree** of power people exercise, and the **types** of power they are able to exploit, differ depending in part on their position in the organisation hierarchy.

Senior management

Senior managers enjoy high position power: in theory, they take the major decisions and set constraints over the decisions taken by other people. In practice however, this power is never absolute. Senior managers depend on decisions and information supplied by subordinates, and it is quite possible that the information is shaped at a lower level. Quite junior or even informal leaders such as experts may have upward or sideways influence.

Senior managers have high resource powers which they exercise over budget allocations and strategic direction.

Middle managers

Middle managers have limited reward power over their own subordinates; they will often have expert power and perhaps negative power to delay or subvert decisions taken by senior managers. They need legitimate power, hence the need for formal job descriptions, authorisation limits and so on. They may also gain influence from networking, by obtaining useful information or the support of influential people and coalitions.

Interest groups

Formal interest groups represent the interests of their members and may wield greater power than their individual members. Examples include trade unions and professional associations.

3 Management and leadership

The terms 'management' and 'leadership' are often used interchangeably. However, there have been many attempts to distinguish meaningfully between them. We can summarise these ideas in the table below.

	Manager	Leader
Exercises influence over	Subordinates	Followers
Nature of authority	Derived from role and position	Exists in the perception of others
Concerned with	Logic, structure, resources, activities, projects	People, opportunities for change
Activities	Plan, control , decide communicate	Inspire, motivate, excite

Managers as leaders

While it is possible to distinguish management from leadership, it is not a useful distinction to make in practice. Any person occupying an office of authority in an organisation must inevitable combine management with leadership. We generally refer to such people as managers, but they will nearly all have to be leaders as well. It is only a very small number of managers who have no responsibility for subordinates that can afford to ignore the need for leadership.

ACTIVITY 2   5 mins

Can you think of a theoretical example of such a manager and what he or she might do?

In fact, management and leadership are the two sides of a single coin. Managers must be leaders and leaders, if they are to achieve anything at all must pay close attention to basic management functions such as planning and controlling the use of resources. Indeed, managers should display the attributes and perform the activities listed in both columns of the analysis shown above.

Management, leadership and motivation

In Chapter 7 we briefly considered the idea that supervision falls into Herzberg's category of hygiene factors. There is no doubt that quality of management is an important aspect of the basic framework of factors that must be of an acceptable standard if they are not to adversely affect people's attitudes to work. Here and in the next chapter, however, we are concerned with the management attitudes and techniques that can make a positive difference to both performance and satisfaction.

Managers and change

The increasing complexity and rapid change typical of the current business environment mandate a leadership approach to management in order to achieve transformation within the organisation as a response.

(a) Leaders energise and support **change**, which is essential for survival in highly competitive and fast-changing business environments. By setting visionary goals, and encouraging contribution from teams, leaders create environments that:

   (i)   Seek out new information and ideas
   (ii) Allow challenges to existing procedures and ways of thinking
   (iii) Invite innovation and creativity in finding better ways to achieve goals
   (iv) Support and empower people to cope with the turbulence

(b) Leaders secure **commitment** to change, mobilising the ideas, experience and motivation of employees – which contributes to innovation and improved quality and customer service. This is all the more essential in a competitive, customer-focused, knowledge-based business environment.

(c) Leaders set **direction** in implementing change, helping teams and organisations to understand their purpose, goals and value to the organisation. This facilitates team-working and empowerment (allowing discretion and creativity about how to achieve the desired outcomes) without loss of co-ordination or direction.

(d) Leaders support, challenge and develop **people**, maximising their contribution to the processes of change. Leaders use an influence-based, facilitate-empower style rather than a command-control style, and this is better suited to the expectations of empowered teams and the need for information-sharing in modern business environments.

ACTIVITY 3   15 mins

Reflect on your own experience of working under the direction of others. Identify the best leader you have ever followed. Think about how this person behaved and interacted with you and others.

What qualities make you identify this person as a good leader, from your point of view as a follower?

Chapter Roundup

↳ Organisations cannot function without managers. The earliest contributions on the science of management were offered by Fayol. He defined five functions of management: planning, organising, commanding, co-ordinating and controlling.

↳ **Power** is the ability to get things done. There are many types of power in organisations: position or **legitimate power**, expert power, personal power, resource power and negative power are examples.

↳ **Authority** is related to position power. It is the right to take certain decisions within certain boundaries.

↳ **Responsibility** is the obligation a person has to fulfil a task (s)he has been given. Responsibility can be delegated, but the person delegating responsibility still remains **accountable** to his or her boss for completion of the task.

↳ **Authority/responsibility mismatch** or **ambiguity** is stressful for the individual, and may be risky for the organisation's control over decision-making.

↳ There are many different definitions of **leadership**. Key themes (which are also used to distinguish leadership from management) include: interpersonal influence; securing willing commitment to shared goals; creating direction and energy; and an orientation to change.

↳ Leadership offers key **benefits** in implementing the changes demanded by a competitive, turbulent environment: activating commitment, setting direction, developing people and energising and supporting change.

↳ In practical terms, management and leadership are different aspects of the same thing. Managers must be leaders and leaders must be able to manage.

Quick Quiz

1 What did Fayol consider to be the functions of management?

2 What is authority?

3 What is legitimate power?

4 What is responsibility?

5 What is accountability?

6 How does the authority of a manager differ from that of a leader?

Answers to Quick Quiz

1   Planning, organising, commanding, co-ordinating and controlling

2   The right to guide or direct the actions of others and extract from them responses that are appropriate to the attainment of an organisation's goals

3   Much the same thing as authority

4   The obligation a person has to fulfil an assigned task

5   A person's liability to be called to account for the fulfilment of assigned tasks

6   Managerial authority is derived from the position the manager holds in the organisation; the authority of a leader exists in the perception of other people.

Answers to Activities

Activity 1

John, Paul, George and Ringo have a number of choices. Here are some extreme examples.

(a)   They could give all of the management activities to one person.

In this case, Paul, for example, could plan direct and control the work and the other three would do the work.

(b)   They might divide the management tasks between them, so that, for example, repairing drums *and* making plans would be Ringo's job, while controlling progress and stringing guitars might be John's role, and so on.

(c)   They could choose to manage by committee, each of them contributing to planning, reviewing and controlling. In a small business with equal partners this is likely to be the most effective approach.

Activity 2

It is possible that a senior person's direct responsibilities might be confined to material resources, such as buildings, or even immaterial matters such as press relations or risk, and it is likely that such a person would have the title of manager, or even director. However, it is likely that such a person would have at least one assistant, making some requirement for leadership unavoidable, and may on occasion have to provide instruction or guidance for staff who generally report to other managers.

Activity 3

We will not provide a debrief for this exercise here. However, you should make a note of your thoughts and revisit them after studying the next chapter, which looks in detail at what managers do.

Chapter 10

Leadership models

Leadership has been the topic of much research for many years. Academics have been interested in how leaders go about their work and the relative success of the approaches they use. It has also been appreciated within organisations that the quality of their leadership has a profound effect on their functioning and success.

There have been numerous theories put forward. A favourite theme that appears in many studies and programmes of leadership training is the need to balance concern for task achievement with concern for the needs of the people being led. John Adair has extended this dichotomy in his famous and widely adopted scheme by raising the needs of group maintenance to parity with task and individual needs.

Some theories have explicitly recognised the importance of situational factors in leadership, which has led to a realisation that a single style will not be effective at all times and that an important leadership skill is judging which style is appropriate to given circumstances.

The most recent thinking has been concerned with rather different aspects of leadership, perhaps because of the extreme demands that have been made on organisations subject to intense global competition and rapid change. The role of inspiring, visionary, charismatic leadership has been explored, though this work is still at an early stage.

1   Theories of leadership

In this section we will introduce six basic approaches to the nature of leadership.

School	Comment
Trait theories	Based on analysing the personality characteristics or preferences of successful leaders.
Leadership functions	Based on the activities leaders must undertake if they are to be successful.
Leadership behaviour	Based on the behaviour of leaders with respect to their subordinates and the task they have been set.
Style theories	Based on the view that leadership is an interpersonal process whereby different leader behaviours influence people in different ways. More or less effective patterns of behaviour (or 'styles') can therefore be adopted.
Contingency theories	Based on the belief that effective leaders adapt their behaviour to the specific and changing variables in the leadership context: the nature of the task, the personalities of team members, the organisation culture and so on.
Recent thinking	Based on vision, charisma and the inspiration of commitment.

We will look at each of these in turn.

2   Leadership traits

Early study of leadership concentrated on examining what was known about acknowledged leaders of the past and trying to establish the personal qualities they had in common. Various studies have attempted to determine exactly *which* traits are essential in a leader.

The idea of leadership traits continues to be very popular.

LEADERSHIP TRAITS

Being an effective leader requires having a set of beliefs, knowing your own strengths, having a support team and being genuinely concerned about your fellow man.

These were some of the leadership traits former New York City Mayor Rudy Giuliani offered during his keynote presentation at the National Automatic Merchandising Association (NAMA) One Show at Chicago's McCormick Place North.

---

http://www.vendingmarketwatch.com/online/article.jsp?siteSection=1&id=29751&pageNum=1
accessed 17 May 2011

Nevertheless, this has proved to be an unsatisfactory approach, partly because it has never been substantiated that any of the qualities considered is essential for effective leadership. Also, it has not been possible to produce a single acknowledged list of desirable qualities; this problem is compounded if sex and culture are considered. Studies of successful female leaders identify traits that differ than those identified for men, while national and regional cultures differ in the qualities they find appropriate. A further problem is that this approach ignores the fact that different situations appear to affect the nature of leadership that is required. A more practical approach is required.

3 Leadership functions

John Adair's model (variously called 'action-centred', 'situational' or 'functional')is based on an analysis of what effective leaders do rather than what they are. This approach has the great advantage of providing a solid basis for training people to lead and has been adopted by the UK armed services as the basis of their initial officer training programmes.

Functional leadership is based on satisfying needs in three interrelated areas. The analysis is that leaders must do practical things in three areas. The **task** they have to achieve is what drives the whole thing and brings its own imperatives. In order to achieve the task objective, the **individual people** in the task group must be dealt with effectively. Finally, if these individuals are to function effectively as a group, there are needs related to group processes and functioning that must be satisfied. These three sets of needs must be integrated and satisfied in the light of the **whole situation**, which dictates the relative priority that must be given to each.

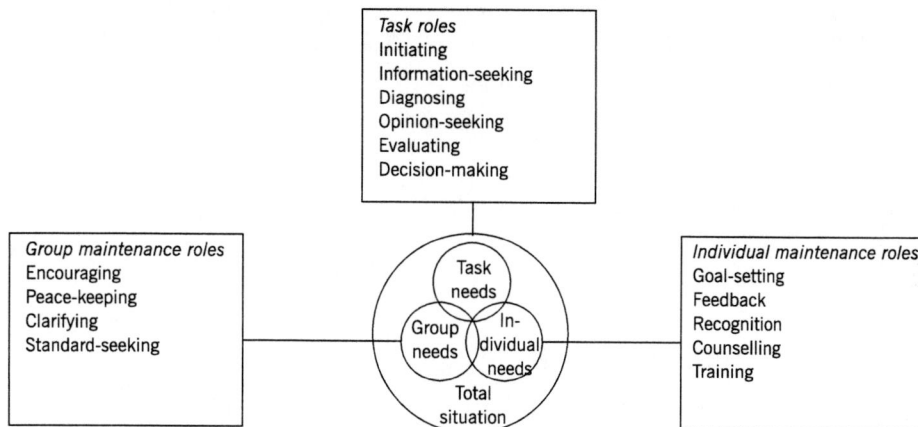

Figure 10.1: Three Needs of Functional Leadership

Official UK management standards, currently administered by the Management Standards Centre, are based on a functional analysis.

Adair's model can be related to McLelland's analysis of motivation in that managers with high nAch are firmly focussed on the task, possibly neglecting team and individual needs, while those who display high nAff behave in the opposite fashion.

4 Leadership behaviour

Leadership behaviour theories arose from studies in the USA upon the effect of leadership style on group performance. These theories are similar to the functional approach, though simpler, in that they analyse what leaders do into just two types of function. Mullins (2007) calls these **task functions** and **maintenance functions**, the latter encompassing action relating to both group and individual needs. Generally, the conclusion was that effective supervisors discharged both types of functions well and achieved a suitable balance between the two concerns. However, circumstances might make a change of emphasis appropriate.

(a)   Task functions are essentially those identified by Adair

(b)   Maintenance functions include establishing mutual trust and respect, showing warmth and concern for subordinates, delegating authority and encouraging participative problem-solving.

Mullins (2007) identifies McGregor's Theory X and Theory Y as being related to this dichotomy and gives the so-called Leadership Grid (originally the Managerial Grid, Blake and Mouton, 1985) as an example of an analysis using the concept of two major dimensions of managerial leadership.

LEADERSHIP BEHAVIOURS IN THE FORD MOTOR COMPANY

Integrity (Behaves with honour and dignity)

Demands the truth – holds self and others to highest standards

Does the right thing – takes the enterprise viewpoint

Drives diversity – respects and values each employee

Flawless execution (Passion for Excellence)

Business acumen – know-how that moves the Company forward

Innovation and technical excellence – discovers better ideas and applies expertise

Commitment to quality – applies a Six Sigma mindset

Courage – fights to turn dreams into realities

Drive for results – sticks with it to get the job done

Customer satisfaction – makes a difference for the customer

Relationship (Cares, develops, safeguards)

Develops employees and teams – fosters teamwork

Connects with customers – Customer is Job 1

Community commitment – acts to enhance the community

Blake and Mouton's Managerial Grid

Blake and Mouton carried out research as part of one of the studies mentioned above. They called the two basic dimensions **concern for production** (or task performance) and **concern for people.**

Along each of these two dimensions, managers could be located at any point on a continuum from very low to very high concern. Blake and Mouton observed that the two concerns did not seem to correlate, positively or negatively: a high concern in one dimension, for example, did not seem to imply a high or low concern in the other dimension. Individual managers could therefore reflect various combinations of task/people concern and these combinations can be plotted on a simple two axis grid.

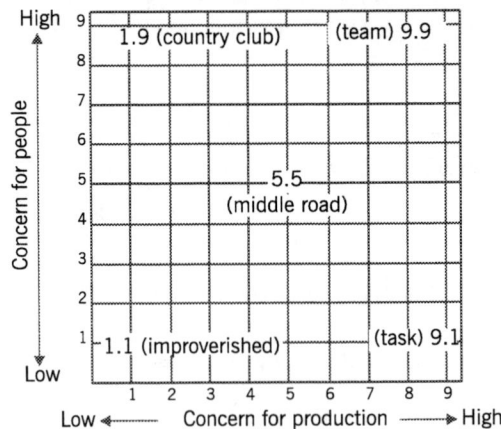

Figure 10.2: Managerial Grid

The extreme cases shown on the grid are:

(a) 1.1 **impoverished:** the manager is lazy, showing little interest in either staff or work.

(b) 1.9 **country club:** the manager is attentive to staff needs and has developed satisfying relationships. However, there is little attention paid to achieving results.

(c)   9.1 **task management:** almost total concentration on achieving results. People's needs are virtually ignored.

(d)   5.5 **middle of the road** or the **dampened pendulum:** adequate performance through balancing (or switching between) the necessity to get out work with team morale.

(e)   9.9 **team:** high work accomplishment through 'leading' committed people who identify themselves with the organisational aims.

ACTIVITY 1   10 mins

Here are some statements about a manager's approach to meetings. Which position on Blake's Grid do you think each might represent?

(a)   I attend because it is expected. I either go along with the majority position or avoid expressing my views.

(b)   I try to come up with good ideas and push for a decision as soon as I can get a majority behind me. I don't mind stepping on people if it helps a sound decision.

(c)   I like to be able to support what my boss wants and to recognise the merits of individual effort. When conflict rises, I do a good job of restoring harmony.

5   Leadership style

The theory of leadership styles is based on a rather different analysis from that used in the functions and behaviours approaches. The styles analysis is one dimensional, viewing task-focussed and people-focussed behaviour as the extreme points of a continuum or spectrum of styles.

5.1   A spectrum of leadership styles

Based on work going back to the 1950s, Tannenbaum and Schmidt (1973), cited in Mullins (2007), were the first to propose a continuum of styles that reflected the **balance of control** exercised in a situation by the leader and the team.

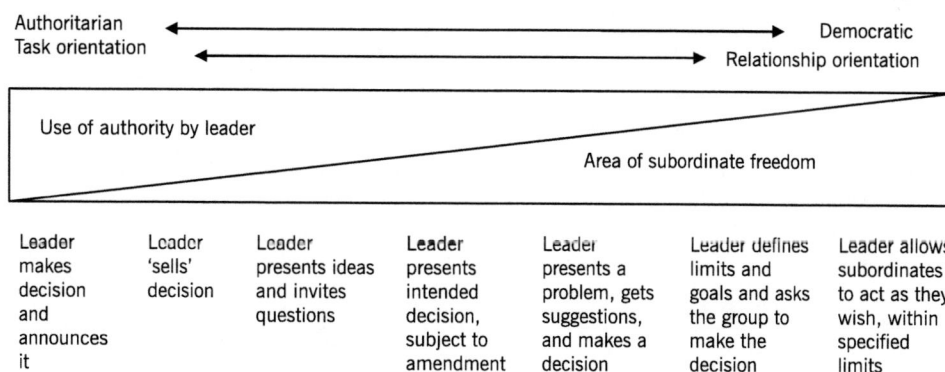

Figure 10.3: Spectrum of Leadership Styles. Adapted from Tannenbaum, R & Schmidt, WH (1973)

Tannenbaum and Schmidt suggested that a single style was unlikely to be satisfactory in all circumstances and pointed out three groups of forces that would affect the practicability and desirability of a given style.

(a)   Forces in the manager, such as personal value systems and degree of confidence in subordinates

(b)   Forces in the subordinates, such as the strength of the need for independence, identification with organisational goals and readiness to assume responsibility

(c)   Forces in the situation, such as the nature of the problem the extent of time pressure and the type of organisation concerned

As a whole, therefore, this is to some extent a contingency model. We will consider further contingency models after we have looked more closely at some more examples of the spectrum of styles approach.

Several studies have found it useful to focus on some specific points within the spectrum of styles. Two of the most noteworthy are those of Rensis Likert and the Ashridge Management College.

5.2   Likert

Likert (1961) reported on a number of studies in a variety of industries. The part of his work that deals with the spectrum of management styles was placed in the context of a complete organisation, rather than an individual work group. He described four 'systems of organisation':

(a)   System 1: **Exploitative authoritative**. Only senior managers identify with the organisation's goals. Dissatisfaction is widespread. There is little communication and what exists is largely downward. Leaders have no confidence or trust in their subordinates, impose decisions, never delegate, motivate by threat and do not encourage teamwork. Productivity is mediocre, scrap loss and labour absence and turnover are high.

(b)   System 2: **Benevolent authoritative.** The extreme case of the exploitative authoritative approach is modified by the use of reward as well as punishment – and by somewhat improved communication. Some decisions are delegated, but within clear boundaries. Productivity is fair to good, while scrap loss and labour absence and turnover are moderately high.

(c)   System 3: **Consultative**. Leaders has some confidence in subordinates, mostly use reward to motivate and will use the ideas and suggestions of subordinates constructively. Communication and co-operation are quite good. A substantial proportion of staff identify with the organisation's goals. Productivity is good, while scrap loss and labour absence and turnover are at a moderate level.

(d)   System 4: **Participative group**. The leader has complete confidence in subordinates who are allowed to make decisions for themselves. Motivation is by reward for achieving goals set by participation, and there is a substantial amount of sharing of ideas, opinions and co-operation. Communication is good, productivity is excellent and scrap loss and labour absence and turnover are minimal

Likert's research suggested that effective managers naturally use a System 3 or System 4 style. Both are seen as viable approaches, *balancing* the needs of the organisation and the individual.

5.3   Ashridge Management College model

The Research Unit at Ashridge Management College distinguished four different management styles. The researchers labelled their styles:

- **Tells**
- **Sells**
- **Consults**
- **Joins**

The Ashridge studies reached some interesting conclusions about management style.

(a)   In an ideal world, subordinates preferred the 'consults' style of leadership.

(b)   People led by a 'consults' manager had the most favourable attitude to their work.

(c)   Most subordinates feel they are being led by a 'tells' or 'sells' manager.

(d)   In practice, **consistency** was far more important to subordinates than any particular style. The least favourable attitudes were found amongst subordinates who were unable to perceive any consistent style of leadership in their superiors.

Style	Characteristics	Strengths	Weaknesses
Tells	The leader makes all the decisions, and issues instructions which must be obeyed without question.	(1) Quick decisions can be made when speed is required. (2) It is the most efficient type of leadership for highly–programmed routine work.	(1) It does not encourage subordinates to give their opinions when these might be useful. (2) Communication between leader and subordinates will be one-way and the leader will not know until afterwards whether the orders have been properly understood. (3) It does not encourage initiative and commitment from subordinates.
Sells	The leader still makes all the decisions, but believes that subordinates have to be motivated to accept them and carry them out properly.	(1) Employees are made aware of the reasons for decisions. (2) Selling decisions to staff might make them more committed. (3) Staff will have a better idea of what to do when unforeseen events arise in their work because the leader will have explained his intentions.	(1) Communications are still largely one-way. Subordinates might not accept the decisions. (2) It does not encourage initiative and commitment from subordinates.

BPP LEARNING MEDIA

Style	Characteristics	Strengths	Weaknesses
Consults	The leader confers with subordinates and takes their views into account, but retains the final say.	(1) Employees are involved in decisions before they are made. This encourages motivation through greater interest and involvement. (2) An agreed consensus of opinion can be reached and, for some decisions, this can be an advantage (eg increasing ownership). (3) Employees can contribute their knowledge and experience to help solve more complex problems.	(1) It might take much longer to reach decisions. (2) Subordinates might be too inexperienced to formulate mature opinions and give practical advice. (3) Consultation can too easily turn into a façade, concealing a 'sells' style.
Joins	Leader and followers make the decision on the basis of consensus.	(1) It can provide high motivation and commitment from employees. (2) It shares the other advantages of the consultative style (especially where subordinates have expert power).	(1) The authority of the leader might be undermined. (2) Decision making might become a very long process, and clear decisions might become difficult to reach. (3) Subordinates might lack experience.

ACTIVITY 2   15 mins

Suggest an appropriate style of leadership for each of the following situations. Think about your reasons for choosing each style in terms of the results you are trying to achieve, the need to secure commitment from others, and potential difficulties with both.

(a) Due to outside factors, the personnel budget has been reduced for your department and 25% of your staff must be made redundant. Records of each employee's performance are available.

(b) There is a recurring administrative problem which is minor, but irritating to every one in your department. Several solutions have been tried in the past, but without success. You think you have a remedy which will work, but unknown problems may arise, depending on the decisions made.

ADAPTATION IN STYLE

Brian Atkins was General Manager of a group of BUPA hospitals that were undergoing extensive and important changes when he arrived in post. During the initial, critical phase of his tenure, he consciously used an authoritative management style. Later, when the new direction was firmly set and progress was being steadily made, he adopted a more collaborative and facilitating style .

Hilary Walmsley, A suitable play, *People Management*, April 1999

6 Contingency approaches

In general terms, the leadership style approach recommends a single style for managerial success: managers should exhibit a high degree of concern both for their subordinates and for the tasks they are concerned with. The weakness is this is that circumstances inevitably alter cases and a single style may not always be appropriate to the prevailing conditions, as Tannenbaum and Schmidt indicated.

Contingency theory addresses this problem by defining effective leadership as being dependent on a number of variable or contingent factors. There is no one right way to lead that will fit all situations. Leaders need to adapt their style to the needs of the team and situation.

6.1 Fiedler

Fiedler suggested that the effectiveness of a work group depends on the **situation**, which is made up of three key variables.

(a) The relationship **between the leader and the group** (trust, respect and so on)
(b) The extent to which the **task** is defined and structured
(c) The **power** of the leader in relation to the group (authority, and power to reward and punish)

A situation is **favourable** to the leader when:

(a) The leader is liked and trusted by the group
(b) The tasks of the group are clearly defined
(c) The legitimate power of the leader to reward and punish is high.

Fiedler suggested that:

(a) A structured (or psychologically distant) style works best when the situation is either very favourable, or very unfavourable to the leader
(b) A supportive (or psychologically close) style works best when the situation is moderately favourable to the leader.

This is summed up in the diagram below.

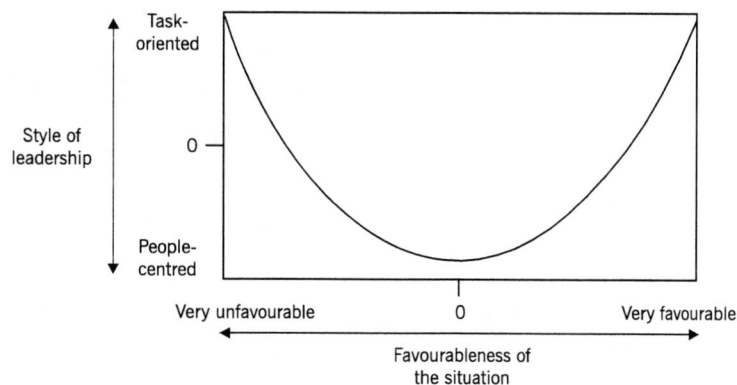

Figure 10.4: Fiedler's contingency theory

6.2 Hersey and Blanchard: situational leadership

In their influential **situational leadership** model, **Hersey and Blanchard** focus on the **readiness** of the team members to perform a given task, in terms of their task ability (experience, knowledge and skills) and willingness (whether they have the confidence, commitment and motivation) to complete the task successfully.

(a) *High-readiness* (R4) teams are able and willing. They do not need directive or supportive leadership: the most appropriate leadership style may be a joins or 'delegating' (S4) style.

(b) *High-moderate readiness* (R3) teams are able, but unwilling or insecure. They are competent, but require supportive behaviour to build morale: the most appropriate leadership style may be a consults or 'participating' (S3) style.

(c) *Low-moderate readiness* (R2) teams are willing and confident, but lacking ability. They require both directive and supportive behaviour to improve their task performance without damaging morale: the most appropriate leadership style may be a 'selling' (S2) style.

(d) *Low-readiness* (R1) teams are lacking ability and motivation/confidence. They require more directive behaviours in order to secure an adequate level of task performance: the most appropriate leadership style may be a 'telling' (S1) style.

This can be summed up as follows (Hersey and Blanchard, 1988).

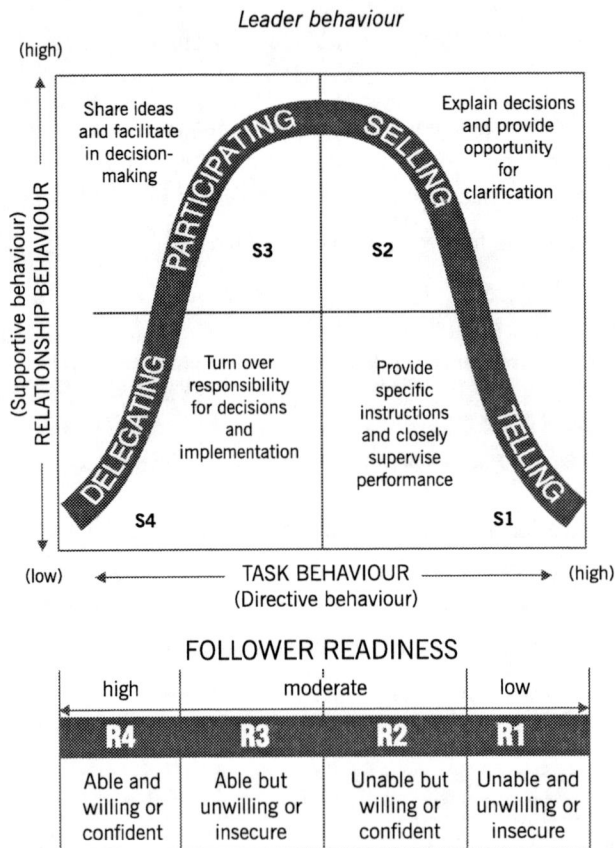

Figure 10.5: Hersey and Blanchard's situational leadership model. Adapted from Hersey, P & Blanchard, KH (1988)

This model can also be linked to McLelland's analysis of motivation. Achievement-motivated people tend to favour the styles of the first and second modes ('telling' and 'selling'); affiliation-motivated people tend to favour the third mode ('participating'); and the authority-motivated people tend to favour the style of mode four ('delegating').

ACTIVITY 3   15 mins

Diagnose the 'readiness' of a work or study group of which you are a member. What sort of leadership is likely to be most effective, according to Hersey and Blanchard's model? What sort of leadership does the team leader actually exercise?

Christy (2010) discusses research into leadership at the strategic level. This indicates that the organisation's stage of development creates a context that influences the suitability of various styles of management.

Company stage of growth	Appropriate management style
Start up	'Champion' – fights for the organisation, deploying a wide variety of technical skills
Expansion	'Tank commander' – develops teams that take the business forward
Maturity	'Housekeeper' – less entrepreneurial but plans, organises and controls
Decline	'Lemon squeezer' – takes tough and difficult measures to turn the business around

MANAGEMENT AT DIFFERENT STAGES

Stelios Haji-Ioannu is an example of the entrepreneurial champion style and has concentrated on starting up new businesses within his easyGroup. Sir Stuart Rose, who turned round Marks & Spencer between 2004 and 2006 is an example of the lemon squeezer approach.

7 Recent thinking

Recent thinking considers the functions, behaviour, style and contingency models as being no more than different approaches to the same thing, which has been dubbed **transactional leadership**. Transactional leadership is based on position power and an economic exchange between leader and led; essentially, good performance leads to reward, poor performance to punishment.

Recent writing has emphasised a variety of different but linked aspects of leadership that fall outside this simple transactional relationship. There is no single agreed model that summarises this thinking, nor agreement on what collective name to give to the ideas concerned. The terms transformational, inspirational, visionary and charismatic have all been used, not interchangeably, but when discussing different elements of the topic.

We will attempt to present the important aspects of this school of thought by considering some pervasive themes and threads of argument.

(a)   **Vision** and a **sense of mission** are very important aspects. Transformational leadership is closely associated with the introduction of major change into large organisations (hence the label) and the senior leaders involved must possess a clear vision of where they are going.

(b)   Creation of a high degree of **motivation** and **commitment** among staff is typical of the new leadership. It depends in part on communicating the vision and sense of mission referred to above, but also on developing a sense of justice, fairness and trust among staff. Nurturing a feeling of inclusiveness and belonging has also been referred to as typical of successful female managers; male managers tend to emphasise a separate, autonomous commitment.

(c)   To some extent, achieving these desirable ends depends on personal qualities, including **enthusiasm**, **empathy** and the **ability to inspire**. This analysis of leadership is thus related to the **traits** approach, since it seems to depend on the manager's possession of specific desirable personal characteristics.

(d)   There are disadvantages to leadership on this basis, particularly where **charisma** is concerned, in that the leader may be arrogant and egotistical and may rise by trampling on rivals. Staff may become emotionally dependent on such a leader and subject to manipulation. There is also the possibility that the organisation will be severely dislocated if the charismatic leader leaves.

8   The benefits and dangers of charismatic leadership

The dictionary defines 'charisma' as 'a special personal quality or power of the individual making him (or her) capable of influencing or inspiring large numbers of people', and 'charismatic leadership' is a widespread phenomenon in today's world – not merely for organisations but also for nation-states.

Typically, the charismatic leader will engage in the following behaviours – which help to reinforce and consolidate the leader's position:

- Articulating a vision which is appealing and optimistic;
- Using strong, expressive forms of communication when talking about the vision;
- Taking personal risks and making self-sacrifices in order to attain the vision;
- Communicating high expectations from others;
- Expressing optimism and confidence in the capabilities of followers;
- Role-modelling behaviours that are consistent with the vision;
- Managing follower perceptions of himself or herself as leader;
- Building identification with the group or organisation; and
- Empowering followers – provided they act in accordance with the vision.

Charismatic leaders can be impressive so long as they keep making decisions which turn out to be successful in taking the organisation forward. However, there are dangers:

- **Excessive confidence and optimism can blind the charismatic leaders to very real dangers either inside the organisation or outside it.**

- **Dependence on the charismatic leader inhibits the emergence and development of competent successors.**

- **Failure to produce a successor creates an eventual leadership crisis.** As John Larrere (from the management consultancy the Hay Group) has said, 'In some sense, with the charismatic person, it's difficult to prepare a successor, because they are bigger than life.'

- **Denial of problems and failures reduces organisational learning.**

It is not unusual for charismatic leaders ultimately to become 'toxic'. The US Army defines toxic leaders as commanders who put their own needs first, micro-manage subordinates, behave in a mean-spirited manner or display poor decision-making. Toxic leaders are people who manage by fear, who deliberately seek out as subordinates only those people who share their views, and create a 'blame culture' in which scapegoats are claimed to be the sources of all organisational failures and weaknesses.

In her book *Bad Leadership: What It Is, How It Happens, Why It Matters* (2004), Barbara Kellerman identifies seven different types of toxic leadership:

(1) *Incompetent* – the leader and at least some followers lack the will or the skill (or both) to sustain effective action.

(2) *Rigid* – the leaders are inflexible, unable to adapt to new ideas, new information or changing times.

(3) *Intemperate* – the leader lacks self-control.

(4) *Callous* – the leader and at least some of the followers are caring and unkind, ignoring, denigrating or discounting the views of organisational members who express disagreement or any kind of dissent.

(5) *Corrupt* – the leader and at least some followers lie, cheat or steal.

(6) *Insular* – the leader and at least some followers minimise or disregard the health and welfare of those for whom they are responsible.

(7) *Evil* – the leader and at least some followers commit atrocities, and rule by fear.

↳ Early theories suggested that there are certain traits or **personality characteristics** that are common to successful leaders. However, a single agreed list of such characteristics continues to be elusive.

↳ Leadership can be analysed in terms of the **functions** leaders must perform. Adair examines these in terms of the needs leaders must satisfy in order to be effective. He divides these into three groups: task needs, individual needs and group needs. UK management standards are based on a functional analysis.

↳ Work on **leadership behaviour** describes managers as having two main areas of concern for managers: concern for production and concern for people. These concerns are supported by the discharge of **task functions** and **maintenance functions**. Effective supervisors do both well, though the balance of emphasis will vary with circumstances. Blake and Mouton's **Managerial Grid** analyses managerial performance on these two dimensions.

↳ The **leadership style** analysis is one dimensional, viewing task-focussed and people-focussed behaviour as the extreme points of a continuous spectrum of styles. Rensis Likert and the Ashridge Management College offer similar analyses based on a range of four significant styles, varying from the task-focussed autocratic end of the range to the opposite, people-focussed, democratic end.

↳ **Contingency** theories emphasise that a single managerial approach will not be effective in all circumstances. Fiedler suggests that crucial variables are the leader-group relationship, the task and the power of the leader. Hersey and Blanchard focus on the **readiness** of the team members to perform a given task. Differing styles of strategic leadership may be required at different stages of a company's life cycle.

↳ Recent writing emphasises **vision**, **inspiration** and **charisma**, echoing the traits approach. These qualities can inspire commitment and motivation but charismatic leaders may be egotistical and manipulative.

Quick Quiz

1   What are the three groups of needs that Adair's functional analysis is based on?

2   What are the two kinds of functions that leadership behaviour research identified?

3   Who first described leadership styles as forming a continuum or spectrum?

4   What are the four management styles described in the Ashridge College model?

5   Who suggested that the effectiveness of the work group depends on three key situational variables?

6   What form of leadership behaviour do Hersey and Blanchard recommend for dealing with a low readiness (R1) work group?

7   What are the disadvantages of having a charismatic leader?

abe Association of Business Executives

BPP LEARNING MEDIA

Answers to Quick Quiz

1 Individual, group and task

2 Task and maintenance or concern for production and concern for people

3 Tannenbaum and Schmidt

4 Tells, sells, consults, joins

5 Fiedler

6 Telling

7 The leader may be arrogant and egotistical and may rise by trampling on rivals. Staff may become emotionally dependent on such a leader and subject to manipulation. There is also the possibility that the organisation will be severely dislocated if the charismatic leader leaves.

Answers to Activities

Activity 1

(a) 1.1: low task, low people

(b) 9.1: high task, low people

(c) 1.9: high people, low task

Activity 2

(a) You may have to 'tell' here: nobody is going to like the idea and, since each person will have his or her own interests at heart, you are unlikely to reach consensus. You could attempt to 'sell', if you can see a positive side to the change in particular cases: opportunities for retraining, say.

(b) You could 'consult' here: explain your remedy to staff and see whether they can suggest potential problems. They may be in a position to offer solutions – and since the problem affects them too, they should be committed to solving it.

Activity 3

There is no debrief for this activity.

Chapter 11

Employee engagement

Many practising managers and leaders have known for a long time that willing participation in work on the part of staff is extremely valuable to the organisation and they have expended much effort to achieve it. The value of this approach has been confirmed by research into what has become known as employee engagement. This chapter sets out to define employee engagement, describe its benefits and explain the factors that seem particularly likely to bring it about.

1   Employee engagement

Employee engagement is an aspect of the relationship existing between employees and their work. Some elements of this relationship are more or less formal in nature, such as the contract of employment, while others are informal; employee engagement falls into the latter category. Employee engagement exists when employees are motivated to connect closely with their work and want to do it well.

Employee engagement should be distinguished from **job satisfaction** and from **organisational commitment**. As far as job satisfaction is concerned, the distinction is simple: it is possible to be happy in one's work without making any positive contribution to the organisation. Organisational commitment reflects the employee's attitude towards the **organisation**, while employee engagement is, in general terms, about employees' attitudes toward the **work** they do.

Organisational commitment

People who are committed to their organisations do not intend to seek work elsewhere. There are three 'mind sets' leading to this condition.

(a)   **Affective commitment** exists when there is emotional attachment to the organisation. The employee identifies with the organisation's goals. This may be linked with job satisfaction.

(b)   **Normative commitment** exists when the employee feels a moral obligation to the employer. This may arise for a variety of reasons, such as having received favourable treatment in the past, such as high quality training, or perhaps simply from personal feelings about loyalty to one's employer.

(c)   **Continuance commitment** arises from a consideration of the costs and benefits involved in staying or leaving; here costs and benefits are not restricted to financial implications, but include social and psychological matters as well, for example.

Employee engagement

Alfes *et al* (2010) speak of three core facets to employee engagement.

(a)   **Intellectual engagement** leads to thoughtful consideration of the job and how work practices might be improved.

(b)   **Affective engagement** exists when the employee has positive feelings about the job.

(c)   **Social engagement** leads the employee to seek out opportunities to discuss issues related to the job.

The first two of these dimensions may also be referred to as cognitive and emotional engagement respectively.

As we said in Chapter 8 when discussing differentiator factors, engaged employees are loyal and productive. They undertake what is known as **discretionary behaviour**, that is, behaviour that goes beyond normally accepted minimum standards of performance. They put in extra effort, co-operate well and help others and they take the initiative in providing customer satisfaction, in solving problems and in developing systems of work. This kind of behaviour constitutes 'organisational citizenship'.

Organisations should take steps to enhance employee engagement, since it promotes four important outcomes (Alfes *et al*, 2010), p2.

- Improved **performance**
- Enhanced rate of **innovation**
- Reduced **staff turnover**
- Greater levels of **personal well-being** among employees

However, excessively high levels of engagement may lead to ill-health and burnout.

More specifically, a CIPD discussion paper, *An HR director's guide to employee engagement*, quotes research that indicates that high levels of employ engagement correlate well with higher operating margins (up to 19%), net profit, revenue growth and earnings per share (up to 28%).

The same paper remarks that employees benefit from engagement as well as employers. Job satisfaction is likely to be higher and sickness rates lower.

2 The extent of employee engagement

Unfortunately, the extent of employee engagement in numerical terms is, generally, not very high. The discussion paper quoted above remarks in passing that CIPD research in 2006 found that only about a third of workers in the UK are engaged with their work while similar research in the USA gave a figure of 29%. Alfes *et al* (2010) say that 'overall, 8% of respondents in our sample are strongly engaged with their work, with the majority falling into an intermediate category' (p2). They go on to say:

'comparisons across employee groups reveal a variety of interesting differences with respect to demographics and job types.

- Women are more engaged than men.
- Younger workers are less engaged than older workers.
- Those on flexible contracts are more engaged.
- Managers are more engaged than non-managers'

However, a 2001 report in *People Management*, the CIPD newspaper, by Marcus Buckingham, global practice leader at the Gallup Organization, reached slightly different conclusions.

(a) Only 17% of UK employees were engaged, while 20% were actively disengaged, psychologically absent and prone to complain to colleagues about their employers.

(b) The longer employees stay with an organisation, the less engaged they become.

(c) Corporate culture, which should support employee engagement, tends to be fragmented, varying from place to place, shift to shift and department to department.

The implication of point (b) is that promoting employee engagement is not a once and for all thing: it requires constant attention. The implications of point (c) are more complex, but certainly include clear notice that middle managers must send consistent messages to their staff; this probably implies that improved management training is widely desirable.

A simple way to ascertain the extent to which individual employees or even whole workforces are 'engaged' or not is to administer a test like the Gallup Q12 diagnostic tool [**though you should be careful not to copy the following statements, or use them in any way other than for your personal learning, without the express permission of the Gallup Organisation**]. The test consists of 12 statements to which respondents are required to indicate whether they 'Strongly Agree', 'Agree', 'Don't Know', 'Disagree' or 'Strongly Disagree'. Employee 'engagement' can be measured by the proportion of 'Strongly Agree' and 'Agree' answers.

1   Do I know what is expected of me at work?
2   Do I have the materials and equipment I need to do my work right?
3   At work, do I have the opportunity to do what I do best every day?
4   In the last 7 days, have I received recognition or praise for good work?
5   Does my supervisor, or someone at work, seem to care about me as a person?
6   Is there someone at work who encourages my development?
7   At work, do my opinions seem to count?
8   Does the mission/purpose of my company make me feel like my work is important?

9   Are my co-workers committed to doing quality work?

10   Do I have a best friend at work?

11   In the last 6 months, have I talked with someone about my progress?

12   At work, have I had opportunities to learn and grow?

[Marcus Buckingham and Curt Coffman, *First, Break All The Rules*, Simon & Schuster, 1999]

From the scores we can establish into which of the following groups the workforce (or a given individual employee) can be classified:

- **THE ENGAGED** – loyal, committed, motivated and enthusiastic; an ambassador for the employer and an advocate, promoting the organisation to potential employees and customers

- **THE NON-ENGAGED** – physically present but psychologically absent; doing just enough to 'get by' and reluctant to exceed the specific tasks and duties enshrined in the job description; instrumentally motivated (i.e., responds to financial incentives but not much else); sticks to the rules about hours of work, etc

- **THE DISENGAGED** – hostile, cynical, disruptive (though often cleverly so); will obey or enforce the rules even when doing so will make the situation worse (e.g., by upsetting a long-term loyal customer); denigrates the organisation to others, even to customers.

B&Q'S ATTEMPTS TO CREATE A HIGH 'ENGAGEMENT' CULTURE IN 2005

B&Q is a large UK-based retailer of do-it-yourself products and services like paint, garden equipment, self-assembly furniture and so forth. In 2005 the company experienced another very bad year of losses and, in the words of its HR Director, 'The business had hit a brick wall ... we needed everyone pulling in the right direction.'

Employee engagement was seen as essential to the company's recovery and so, with the aid of the Gallup Organisation, all employees were asked to complete the Gallup Q12 questionnaire. The results were startling and showed that 26% - over a quarter – of the workforce were actively disengaged. To quote the HR Director again, 'We must be a charity ... out of a £450 million wage bill, we're spending £120 million on people who don't want to be here. We're paying them to destroy our organisation and make life miserable for all the good, engaged employees.'

As a result the company embarked on a massive turnaround programme which, among other things, saw the departure of several managers who could not accommodate themselves to the new 'engagement' culture at B&Q.

---

3   Promoting employee engagement

Employee engagement is about a mutual relationship to which both employer and employee must contribute. It cannot be created by a top-down or command-and-control style of management.

Alfes *et al* identify six drivers of engagement.

(a)   **Meaningfulness of work.** Employees perceive their work as meaningful when they feel it to be significant in a wider context. You will remember that in Chapter 5 we discussed the three critical psychological states described by Hackman and Oldham (1980), one of which was **experienced meaningfulness**. We said that this depended on whether or not the work involved was regarded as inherently valuable and worthwhile.

ACTIVITY   10 mins

Revise the three critical psychological states and the five job dimensions.

(b) **Employee voice**. Employees like to make an input into decisions that affect their work. This is an issue of management style. It does not necessarily require a participative style of management, in which employees contribute to decision-making, but it is important that employees feel that their views are heard. The danger for managers here is that a failure to give genuine consideration to employee views is likely to be detected and create a cynical response. This will undermine engagement.

(c) **Senior management communication and vision**. It is part of the role of senior management to create and communicate a vision of what the organisation is for. Every organisation has a purpose and it is necessary to communicate that purpose to the organisation's members. (The apocryphal story about the cleaner working for NASA who told a visitor that he was helping to put a man on the moon is relevant here.) Senior managers must also be open, transparent and approachable.

(d) **Person-job fit**. People and jobs must be carefully matched. There are two aspects to this. First, job design must be effective. Second, selection processes must match individual skills to the job.

HOW TO IDENTIFY 'ENGAGEMENT POTENTIAL' IN JOB APPLICANTS

A recent article in *People Management* has reported some techniques which employers can use during the selection process in order to make it more likely that the people they recruit will subsequently become 'engaged'. The advice from the researchers is that interviewers should:

- Screen applicants for the six personal characteristics that predict the likelihood of 'engagement':

    – Adaptability
    – Passion (enthusiasm)
    – Emotional maturity
    – A positive ('can do') disposition
    – Self-efficacy and self-reliance
    – Achievement orientation

- Check for 'job fit' by asking candidates to describe their ideal job

- Explore the candidate's past experiences by seeking concrete evidence about significant past experiences and what the candidate learned from them – in this way hypothetical questions are avoided

[Source: Feature about Development Dimensions International (DDI), *People Management*, 27 July 2006]

(e) **Supportive work environment**. It is important that employees do not feel isolated at work. They appreciate an environment in which they feel they have support from others to help them do their jobs, where there is a feeling of teamwork and they can safely express themselves.

(f) **Effectiveness of middle managers**. Middle managers provide the necessary immediate link between the organisation and its staff. Collectively, they have a variety of important roles, though, naturally, necessary specialisation means that not all managers will be able to make a leading contribution to all of them.

(i) They make an important contribution to person-job fit through their input to selection and by the provision of training.

(ii) They are responsible for much communication with staff, both up and down the hierarchy.

ENGAGEMENT EXCELLENCE

Wychavon is a district in the Southeast of Worcestershire. The Wychavon District Council is a high-performing organisation in the public sector, with a reputation for outstanding service to the residents of the district. In 2007, the Council won the *Local Government Chronicle* 'Council of the Year' award for excellence in service provision. The senior management of the Council believe that employee engagement is the key to operational excellence and point to a range of specific policies that encourage this:

- Open leadership and employee involvement in decisions and innovation
- Teamworking throughout the workforce
- A culture of fun and shared values that listens to and supports staff
- Clear goals focussed on customers
- Positive, clear performance management

The council carries out regular staff surveys which show that staff are proud to work for the Council, enjoy their work, and are motivated by a sense of personal achievement. A good work-life balance is very important to many staff and is achieved through team-managed flexible working hours.

4 Engagement, motivation and differentiation

If you have been paying attention as you work through this Study Manual, you should be feeling a sense of *déja vu* about now. You might ask, with some justice, what is the distinction between employee engagement and employee motivation? How do Alfes *et al's* six drivers of engagement differ from the differentiator factors we discussed in Chapter 8?

These are both difficult questions to answer convincingly, because the various ideas involved are very similar and closely related. The only real answer that can be given is that the similarities and differences we observe in the theories we have discussed appear because there is, as yet, no fully integrated, grand unified theory of people management. Individual workplace situations, individual workers and groups of workers all have different characteristics and individual researchers and teams of researchers theorise in slightly different ways, so it is not surprising that we find similarities and divergences in the literature.

This is probably of little comfort to you, but an awareness of this problem will enable you to structure your learning so as to avoid confusion. You will also find that a familiarity with the various ideas presented and a knowledge of their similarities and differences will help you to make up your own mind about the real-life problems you will inevitably encounter.

THE ASDA 'WAY OF WORKING'

ASDA is a large UK supermarket business, once privately owned (by Associated Dairies – hence the name 'ASDA', made up of the first two letters from each of these words) but now part of the American WalMart business.

The ASDA 'Way of Working' is strongly derived from a book entitled *Gung Ho!* Written by Ken Blanchard and Sheldon Bowles, the book features such inspiring tales as 'The spirit of the squirrel', 'The way of the beaver' and 'The gift of the goose'. The company has several 'Core Success Factors', of which these are examples:

Will to win – focus on results

Team working with impact – visible integration

Knowing and satisfying your customers – exceeding expectations

Clarity of thinking – make sense of what's happening

Brilliant delivery – right first time, every time

New ideas and approaches – embracing change

Passion for learning- enthusiasm for new skills

ASDA's mission is to be 'Britain's best value retailer exceeding local customer needs ... always' and to bring this about it has embraced three 'Core Values' (not to be confused with the 'Core Success Factors' outlined above): respect for the individual, service to the customer, and striving for excellence. Here are some of the behaviours that underpin each of these Core Values:

Respect for the Individual

- 'Our objective is to have an environment that fully taps the potential of all colleagues'
- 'We treat others with respect and offer to help our colleagues out'
- 'Ask for help if you need it. Own problems, don't leave them for someone else.'

Service to the Customer

- 'The customer is the person who pays everyone's wages and who decides whether a business is going to succeed or not'
- 'Think like the customer'
- 'Respond to all requests quickly and exceed customers' expectations in everything you do"

Striving for Excellence

- 'Excellence means going beyond the normal job'
- 'Each day we should strive to be better than the last'
- 'Be successful: listen, learn, put forward your ideas and grow as an individual'

Chapter Roundup

↳ Employee engagement exists when staff have strong positive feelings about their work situation and, as a result, are loyal and productive and undertake desirable discretionary behaviour.

↳ Job satisfaction and organisational commitment are linked concepts but are not the same thing as employee engagement.

↳ There are three core facets to employee engagement.

- **Intellectual engagement** leads to thoughtful consideration of the job and how work practices might be improved.

- **Affective engagement** exists when the employee has positive feelings about the job.

- **Social engagement** leads the employee to seek out opportunities to discuss issues related to the job.

↳ Employee engagement leads to four important outcomes: improved performance, enhanced innovation, reduced staff turnover and improved staff well-being.

↳ Rates of positive employee engagement are low in the UK and the USA, at about 30% and possibly as low as 17%.

↳ Six drivers of engagement have been identified by Alfes *et al*.

- Meaningfulness of work
- Employee voice
- Senior management communication and vision
- Person-job fit
- Supportive work environment
- Effectiveness of middle managers

Quick Quiz

1 What is employee engagement?

2 What are the three core facets of employee engagement?

3 What is discretionary behaviour in the context of employee engagement?

4 What advantages does employee engagement bring?

5 Are there any disadvantages to employee engagement?

6 What are the six drivers of employee engagement?

Answers to Quick Quiz

1   Employee engagement exists when employees are motivated to connect closely with their work and want to do it well.

2   (a)   **Intellectual engagement** leads to thoughtful consideration of the job and how work practices might be improved.

    (b)   **Affective engagement** exists when the employee has positive feelings about the job.

    (c)   **Social engagement** leads the employee to seek out opportunities to discuss issues related to the job.

3   Behaviour that goes beyond normally accepted minimum standards of performance.

4   •   Improved **performance**
    •   Enhanced rate of **innovation**
    •   Reduced **staff turnover**
    •   Greater levels of **personal well-being** among employees

5   Excessively high levels of engagement may lead to ill-health and burnout.

6   •   Meaningfulness of work
    •   Employee voice
    •   Senior management communication and vision
    •   Person-job fit
    •   Supportive work environment
    •   Effectiveness of middle managers

Answers to Activity

Activity

Hackman and Oldham (1980) suggest that high motivation, performance and satisfaction occur when workers experience three **critical psychological states**.

(a)   **Experienced meaningfulness** depends on the extent to which the work is regarded as inherently valuable and worthwhile.

(b)   **Experienced responsibility** depends on the extent to which workers feels accountable for their work performance.

(c)   **Knowledge of results** exists when workers understand how well they are performing.

These critical psychological states are stimulated and enhanced by improvements along five core **job dimensions**.

(a)   **Skill variety** exists when a job involves the use of several different skills and talents.

(b)   **Task identity** exists when a job involves completing an entire, meaningful piece of work from beginning to end.

(c)   **Task significance** exists when the job is believed to have an impact on other people, whether inside or outside of the organisation.

(d)   **Autonomy** exists when the worker feels freedom and discretion in areas such as job planning, target setting and work methods.

(e)   **Feedback** exists when workers are provided with information on the effectiveness of their performance and the results of their work.

The extent to which enhancements to the five core job dimensions stimulate the critical psychological states and thus promote the desirable outcomes of high motivation, performance and satisfaction depends on three further **moderating factors**.

(a)   **Context satisfaction** is, essentially, the same thing as Herzberg's concept of hygiene factors.

(b)   Workers must perceive that their **knowledge and skill** are adequate to enable them to perform satisfactorily.

(c)   Workers may place a low value on personal growth and development in the job and take an instrumental approach to work. A person in whom the strength of the need for growth is low is said to exhibit low **growth-need strength**. Such people are unlikely to respond well to job enrichment: they may become anxious about expanded responsibility or even demand increased pay to compensate for it.

Chapter 12

High performance working

Throughout this book you will have learned that 'efficient' people-management strategies and processes do not necessarily yield high-performance outcomes. What they generate, at best, are people who are instrumentally motivated, who will fulfil the frequently passive, task-oriented obligations of their job descriptions but who will function mechanically rather than with commitment, and will have no interest in adding value or making the differences that can separate the world-class enterprise from its merely mundane counterpart.

Yet we must be increasingly interested in High Performance Working because, as we have seen, we live in a world which is characterised by vigorous (sometimes ruthless) competition, accelerating customer expectations, and no let-up in the pace of technological change. For an organisation to say that its performance is "good enough" is no longer good enough, because such an attitude reflects complacency and a performance level which probably exposes the business to predatory interventions.

High Performance Working has to be the way forward for all economies. Writing for the UK's *People Management* journal in 2004, Patricia Hewitt (then the Secretary of State for Trade and Industry) advanced the bold claim that 'High Performance Working should no longer be regarded as optional', and this is reflected in Gary Hamel's view that nowadays all employees must be expected to become 'strategic activists', playing a full part in taking their organisations forward. Perhaps the idea of employees as 'strategic activists' can be understood more straightforwardly if we suggest that employees should be 'thinking performers':

- Performing – undertaking their operational tasks efficiently and effectively; but also
- Thinking – reflecting and developing improvements and changes to make themselves and their organisations even more efficient and effective.

Undoubtedly organisations which seek the accolade of 'High Performance Working' must also recruit, select, train, develop, motivate and retain employees as 'thinking performers', and that is what this Chapter is fundamentally about.

1 What is High Performance Working (HPW)?

According to the CIPD, 'HPW can be characterised as everything that "Taylorist employment practices" are not.' This may be an unfair comment so far as F.W. Taylor is concerned (especially as his brainchild, 'scientific management' is still practised successfully in some quarters), but what the CIPD is trying to say is that HPW is the 'diametrical opposite of employment strategies based on short cycle times, skill minimisation and "one right way".' Such an approach may still be successful for industries which produce identical goods in very large volumes and which rely on market saturation as the source of their profit margins, but that is a model which is increasingly inappropriate. Gone are the days when Henry Ford could say about the Model T car, 'You can have any colour you like, provided it's black', because all automotive assembly lines today are geared up for the idiosyncratic requirements of each individual customer and therefore have to cope with different colours, different transmission systems, different upholsteries, different engine sizes and different degrees of personal customisation.

So this tells us the first thing we need to know about High Performance Working, namely, that it is more suited to product and service sectors that are interested (whether they like it or not) in meeting the needs of their individual customers, often located in different parts of the world where different values, priorities and expectations are held.

HPW places great emphasis on effective people management. Unlike simple repetitive work, which is subject to high levels of control and close supervision, product/service quality in a HPW business is delegated to those who deal directly with customers. Thus a HPW enterprise is characterised by empowerment – decision-making being pushed down to the lowest possible level, and generally this means to the individual job-holder. It then follows that a HPW enterprise has relatively little use for supervisors, foremen, chargehands, team leaders or middle-level managers, because much of the work previously undertaken by these people is now performed by operators themselves.

It follows that if a business is thinking about trying to become a HPW organisation, the strategic, cultural, organisational, developmental and relational implications are likely to be impressively profound. Not all managers are ready to believe that their subordinates can ever be trusted to make sensible choices if allowed to make decisions (e.g., when seeking to resolve customer complaints), and not all managers believe that low-level employees could indeed be sufficiently capable to exercise 'discretionary behaviour' options in a way that could balance the interests of the business with the interests of the customer.

LANDS END CLOTHING

One American company, Lands End Clothing, has operated a policy of total empowerment since its foundation and indeed attributes its long-term success and its growth largely to that reputation – apart, of course, from the quality of its products.

Lands End specialises in leisure wear. Its founder was Gary Comer, and if you were a newly-recruited member of staff Gary would appear in front of you during your induction course and would tell you that the company has eight principles for doing business with its customers. 'However,', he would say, 'you can't be expected to remember all eight of these principles, so just remember one of them. Whenever you're facing a customer problem and you have to make a decision about it, make sure that your decision is consistent with this crucial principle: **Don't worry about what's good for the company: Worry about what's good for the customer.**'

Think about this. What it means is that if a customer complains because they bought a pair of trousers and the colour's begun to fade, you agree to replace the trousers instantly, free of charge. There will be a small minority of customers (and believe me, it is never more than a very small minority) who will take advantage of the company's open-ended promise, but for the vast majority the Lands End Promise is an enormous source of psychological security and comfort – which means that their customer base continues to grow (often by personal recommendations) and the existing customers keep coming back for more.

Even better: the employees of Lands End Clothing feel good about themselves and the business they represent. They are proud of the company and so they stay there.

An OECD (Organisation for Economic Co-operation and Development) definition of High Performance Working refers to flatter, non-hierarchical structures, moving away from reliance on management control towards team-working, autonomous job design based on high levels of trust, communication and involvement. Workers are seen as more highly skilled, or as being capable of becoming more highly skilled, and are required to have the intellectual resources to engage in lifelong learning, so that they can continually master new skills and behaviours.

2 Why is HPW important?

In 2003 the (UK) Work Foundation interviewed 1000 Chief Executive Officers. This survey learned that high performing firms are those that adopt a joined-up approach to managing across five performance categories:

- Customers and markets
- Shareholders
- Stakeholders
- Employees
- Creativity and innovation

This analysis emerged from the Work Foundation's 'High Performance Index', constructed from performance in each and all of the five dimensions above. **Firms scoring highest on the Index were over 40% more productive than those at the bottom,** with the average UK business around 25% less productive than those at the top. Also, a particularly significant discovery in the report was that **a 1% increase in the High Performance Index score stimulates 2.5% extra sales per employee and gives a 1% boost to the profitability of the business**.

Among the other benefits from High Performance Working is the fact that a larger proportion of the company's customers become 'Advocates' for the business. This means that they not only give favourable feedback to the company itself, but they also say good things about the company to their friends, work colleagues, relatives, and indeed anybody whom they happen to meet. As a result, the HPW company acquires new customers without the need for any strenuous advertising.

Broadly speaking, a company's customers can be divided into three groups:

(1)   **The Positive Advocates** – the customers who are delighted with the service they receive and/or the products they buy, and are enthusiastic about telling others, via the Internet, dinner conversations, and so forth;

(2)   **The Passively Satisfied** – who feel quite pleased but who don't have any special loyalty to the company and who could therefore be persuaded to defect if offered a better deal; and

(3)   **The Detractors** – who devote a lot of their time to criticism of the company, its products and the service it delivers. You may wonder why such people remain customers, but it may be that they don't think that things would be any better if they went somewhere else, or perhaps they can't go somewhere else even if they wanted to, because the company is a monopoly.

Customer research can reveal the proportions of customers in each of these three categories, and it is important for the proportion of Positive Advocates to be larger than the numbers of the Passively Satisfied and the Detractors combined. This is indeed the case for a company called First Direct, an Internet and telephone bank, which has some very unusual characteristics which set it apart from other more conventional banks like HSBC. For example, First Direct will never recruit someone who has previously been employed in one of these conventional banks, because it believes that such applicants will not be unconventional enough for First Direct (see page 12)!

A report by Marc Thompson for the Society of British Aerospace Companies found that the proportion of aerospace establishments using HPW work practices increased between 1997 and 2002. However, his report identified a close link between HPW and financial performance. Companies with a high HPW index in 1999 recorded sales per employee in 2002 of £162,000 compared with £62,000 for those positioned much lower on the HPW scale. In terms of 'value-added' per employee, the corresponding figures were £68,000 and £42,000.

ACTIVITY 1   1 hour

Identify an organisation known to you that you would consider to be a HPW business. If you can't think of any relevant organisation with which you are already familiar, then select any one from the following: Tesco, Lands End Clothing, the John Lewis Partnership, Virgin Atlantic, Singapore Airlines, Shangri-La Hotels, or the Ritz-Carlton Hotel Group.

Find out all you can about your chosen organisation in an attempt to explain why it is so special as a HPW enterprise. If you have access to a computer, begin with a Google search.

3   What are the ingredients for HPW?

The CIPD says that the component parts of HPW are these (source: CIPD FactSheet, 2004):

- A vision based on increasing customer value through differentiating an organisation's products or services and moving towards the customisation of its offering to the needs of individual customers. Note that this 'offering' embraces not just the products and services themselves but also all the organisation's customer-facing processes and systems.

- To be meaningful, says Professor John Purcell, the organisation's vision, or 'Big Idea', must be:

    - **Embedded** – solidly rooted in corporate practice;

    - **Connected** – mutually reinforcing, both internally and externally;

    - **Enduring** – consistent over time;

    - **Collective** – binding the organisation together; and

    - **Measured and managed** – taken seriously, revisited from time to time to test its continued relevance, and not simply viewed as part of some corporate rhetoric.

- Leadership from the top initially and then cascading down through the organisation as necessary in order to create and sustain the HPW momentum, to ensure that the vision – the 'Big Idea' – is realised and driven forward.

- A decentralised, devolved decision-making philosophy in which most operational decisions are made by those closest to the customer.

- The development of people capabilities through learning at all levels, with particular emphasis on self-directed learning, self-management, team capabilities and project-based activities (with cross-functional project teams examining issues where remedial action is necessary, or looking for ways to improve and change.

- Performance, operational and people management processes aligned to organisational objectives – to build trust, enthusiasm and commitment to the direction taken by the business.

- Fair treatment for those leaving the organisation, and engagement with the community outside the organisation. This may not seem so essential for a HPW enterprise, but in practice it is vital as a mechanism for building trust and mutual confidence inside the organisations in the relationships between its directors, its managers and its workforce.

To this list we should add the obligation for strategic people resourcing based on the mantra 'select for attitude, train for skill'. In other words, a HPW business needs people whose motivational patterns go beyond the instrumental, who are willing to exercise initiative and make decisions, who are ready to undertake lifelong learning so that they develop and grow with the business instead of staying still while their employer goes forward.

If you find it difficult to remember all the ingredients linked to High Performance Working, you might find it easier to distinguish between three separate but inter-related groups of HPW practices:

(1)   **High involvement work practices** – e.g. semi-autonomous or autonomous group/team working, job rotation, information sharing, collective problem solving and continuous-improvement programmes.

(2)   **Human resource practices** – e.g. appraisal, performance management, high levels of training off-the-job, and so forth.

(3)   **Employee relations practices** – e.g. harmonised terms and conditions, joint consultative committees, regular social gatherings for employees, communications, team meetings.

4   How can we recognise HPW when we see it?

It is relatively rare to come across organisations which are totally and completely HPW enterprises, though in a minute we shall look at one or two. What we more commonly find are businesses which are moving towards HPW status – perhaps hesitantly and uncertainly, but nonetheless making moves which can appear to indicate commitment to the HPW goal. There are hotels which have introduced multi-skilling, key 'soft' skills and discretionary decision-making for staff; there is a bank which uses project work to move the business forward and looks for employees who have 'unconventional ideas' with a willingness to undertake 'prudent risk-taking'; in the UK a driving school has equipped its instructors with the capacity to use computers extensively in driver training and have scooped a larger slice of the national market for driver instruction as a result.

The best thing to do, if you want to find out whether a business is actually a High Performance Working company or not, is to follow this sequence:

1   **Look at its performance**. No company can genuinely claim to be a High Performance Working operation unless it delivers results which are measurably superior than those of its competitors – and even better than those typically found among organisations anywhere. Although the phrase 'High Performance Working' might suggest a focus on processes, procedures and operations, i.e., *inputs*, there's no point in introducing these HPW processes, procedures and operations unless the company's *outputs* and performance measures then become better than everybody else's. So ask yourself these questions:

   •   Does the organisation register better profits than its competitors?

   •   Has it registered better profits over a period of time, i.e. at least three years in a row?

   •   Does it have a lower-than-average level of labour turnover, especially among its higher-level employees?

   •   Does it enjoy a very positive reputation among its customers?

   •   Is there any evidence to suggest that its workforce is 'engaged'?

   •   Is the organisation thought to be 'ethical' in its dealings with customers, suppliers, employees, sub-contractors and others?

   •   Does the organisation have a highly-publicised 'Big Idea'?

2   **Look at its processes**. Of course, with many organisations this is easier said than done, because companies don't necessarily advertise every detail about the way they do business with their employees, their suppliers and so forth. However, by reviewing the organisation's recruitment literature, its annual reports, and the fluctuations in its share price (assuming it's a publicly-quoted company), it should be possible to learn a good deal. This can be supplemented by undertaking a Google search [simply enter the name of the organisation, press the 'Search' button and see what comes up], or by watching and reading the media to monitor what is being said.

According to Patterson and his colleagues [*The Impact of People Management Practices on Business Performance*, CIPD, 1997], there are 13 processes that you should expect to find in any organisation that aspires to be a truly High Performance Working operation:

(1)   'Appropriate' recruitment and selection systems, going beyond mere legalistic compliance.

(2)   Comprehensive induction programmes, socialising new entrants into the organisation's core values (which in any case would have featured prominently in the recruitment literature).

(3)   Sophisticated and wide provision for 'learning' (previously known as 'training').

(4)   Coherence, 'bundled' performance management with customer-derived achievement measures – 'bundled' in the sense that the entire performance management system operates to the same criteria.

(5)   Skills development within the workforce which is based on flexibility, multiskilling and 'employability', i.e., equipping employees with the knowledge and skills they will need to fill any vacancy requires in the future.

(6)   Jobs characterised by intrinsic variety and individual responsibility for outcomes, with expectations about 'discretionary behaviour'.

(7)   Teamwork, collaboration within and between corporate departments and functions – no evidence of a 'silo' mentality.

(8)   Frequent and comprehensive communications to and with employees.

(9)   Permanent use of quality-improvement programmes with cross-functional co-operation to ensure that strategic alignment and 'bundling' are not damaged or undermined.

(10)   Harmonised terms and conditions throughout.

(11)   Market-competitive levels of pay and overall remuneration (including benefits) plus non-cash recognition by managers who practise 'management by appreciation'.

(12)   Incentives related to individual and group progress, success and achievement.

(13)   Policies and practices intended to enhance work-life balance.

5   What are the arguments against HPW?

In 2003, the CIPD and the Engineering Employers Federation published a joint report [*Maximising Employee Potential and Business Performance: The Role of High Performance Working*] which, among other things, assessed the typical barriers to High Performance Working, especially among manufacturing firms.

The report found that companies wishing to introduce HPW must successfully win the trust of their employees, be prepared to let them be more directly involved in decision-making, provide extensive training for managers and employees, and introduce sophisticated recruitment and selection procedures to ensure that future managers and members of the workforce can support a HPW culture.

Furthermore, the success of HPW depends on a strong, continuous and active commitment from senior management, commitment from employees to the organisation's objectives, the opportunity for both managers and employees to apply discretion to their work, and the pursuit of continuous learning.

Unfortunately, when organisations are evaluated against these obligations and 'boxes' have to be ticked or otherwise, many manufacturing businesses fail to measure up.

The specific causes of obstacles to the take-up of High Performance Working are likely to involve any or all of the following:

- Straightforward resistance to change.

- The belief that 'we're doing all right as we are', so there is no momentum for radical change.

- Ignorance about the benefits to be gained from High Performance Working.

- A reluctance to believe the evidence about these benefits even when it is presented, perhaps based on the declared assumption that 'our organisation is different' (i.e. unique) and that, therefore, evidence acquired from businesses elsewhere is inappropriate and irrelevant.

- Defeatist attitudes among the management – the amount of change required would be so enormously intimidating, and the probability of success so ultimately problematic, that HPW must remain unattainable.

- An assumption that the 'costs' of change (principally the financial costs, but also the other 'costs') could outweigh the benefits, even if any benefits were realised.

In reality, some of the organisations which have moved consciously towards High Performance Working have done so because in a way they have had no choice. It has become apparent to them that they are failing and that nothing less than a radical 'operation' will ensure their survival.

ACTIVITY 2 10 mins

Think of an organisation known to you which is performing badly (in your view) and has been performing badly for some time (at least two years).

What are the causes of its poor performance? List at least five possibilities.

6 How can HPW be made to happen?

Undoubtedly the presence of a unifying '**Big Idea**' is a crucial starting point, preferably a 'Big Idea' which embraces all the key dimensions of corporate achievement: profitability, customers, employees and change (rather like the Tesco 'wheel'). This 'Big Idea' commonly has four features:

(1) It is transformationally aspirational rather than merely incremental. In other words, it propose a whole new world for the business rather than mere extrapolation of existing products, customers and profitabilities.

(2) It is based on such benchmarks as 'world-class' status and 'differentiation'. The term 'world-class' doesn't have any precise meaning, but it's similar to being in love: you may not be able to define it, but you know it when you see it. The 'world-class' enterprise is one which accepted as exhibiting superior performance to virtually every other organisation, either in its own sector or even for any sector. Examples include Tesco, Singapore Airlines, the John Lewis Partnership and the Ritz-Carlton hotel group.

(3) Its achievement depends on conscious effort, because attainment of the 'Big Idea' will not happen naturally.

(4) The contribution of people will be particularly critical, through problem-solving, creativity, 'added-value' activities and so forth.

The **organisation structure** has to be moved away from a traditional, command-and-control hierarchy with many levels and towards a more devolved pattern characterised by the centralised management of the only things which genuinely need to be managed centrally (i.e. the corporate strategy) and the delegated accountabilities for everything else – to separate units, factories, offices and even individual employees.

For the organisation structure to move in these directions and therefore place additional responsibilities on employees (at all levels), there have to be associated developments on the HR front, with **HR planning, recruitment and selection, learning and performance management.**

(1)   **HR planning** must set out the framework of new expectations around employee attitudes, beliefs and value-systems.

(2)   **Recruitment and selection** must be conducted within output-based accountability profiles rather than task-based job descriptions, and using company-wide competency frameworks rather than job-specific person specifications. Selection processes must heavily emphasise the need for a 'fit' between the would-be employee and the organisation's emergent culture, because the enterprise mustn't find itself hamstrung by people in the workforce who are hostile to change, cynical about employee involvement, and 'disengaged' from the high-level direction of the 'Big Idea'.

(3)   **Learning** must embrace a range of activities from competence testing and 'hard' skill acquisition to a focus on teamworking, collaboration and self-directed learning. In a HPW culture, virtually all employees must be multi-skilled (there is no room for those who claim that anything outside their narrowly vocational training is nothing to do with them), and the skills model covers not just lateral skills – job enlargement – but also upward-facing skills, i.e. the skills normally practised by managers and supervisors (job enrichment).

(4)   **Learning rather than 'training'.** As we have seen already in this book, 'training' is something that one person (the 'trainer') does to another (the 'trainee'). In the HPW business, the need to learn comes from within the 'learner', and the trainer's role becomes one of facilitation rather than remaining one of instruction. The beauty of this transition is that 'learners' actually want to learn, whereas 'trainees' often don't.

(5)   **Performance management** in the HPW culture must instil a balance between operational achievement (i.e. performing the essential duties associated with the job as defined in the accountability profile) and organisational contribution (i.e. taking part in project teams, team-working to construct continuous-improvement or remedial action programmes, advancing ideas to take the business forward). The HPW business will not make the mistake of concentrating on too few performance parameters and thereby silently encouraging employees to ignore others.

At the core of the HPW enterprise is the emergence, nurturing and enhancement of **trust**, and especially trust between those at the top of the organisation and those much further down the corporate tree. Only if there is a high level trust in the workforce will those at the top be prepared to delegate decision-making down to customer-facing staff; and only if there is trust in top management will those at the lowest level of the business be prepared to take the risks that are inevitably taken whenever one makes a decision. In other words, trust is a two-way street. It is especially crucial that the organisation's people feel able to use their initiative without fear that if they make a mistake they will be punished. Instead, they have to feel that if they do make a mistake (and they will – for every so often anyone who makes decisions will make poor decisions, or won't make a decision at all, which can be just as bad), then their mistakes will be viewed as 'learning opportunities' from which lessons for future decision-making can be taken.

The precise mechanisms for establishing 'trust' throughout a business can be notoriously difficult to pin down. Clearly employees need to have faith in each other, and this is dependent on their experiences of working together. As Charles Handy once wrote, a trusting relationship is as fragile as a pane of glass: it takes a long time to make, but can be destroyed in an instant. Thus employees may trust their managers, but can cease to do so if only one manager acts cynically or selfishly, or is judged to have done so.

The key issue for creating a climate of trust is the belief among employees that they are partners in a worthwhile **psychological contract** involving reciprocal obligations between managers and the workforce.

Perhaps surprisingly, too, satisfaction with the psychological contract partially depends on the extent to which the employer demonstrates positive attributes as a 'corporate citizen', e.g., by opening up the organisation's learning centres to local people and the families of employees. The CIPD reports one case where local unemployed workers were given opportunities for pre-employment training and were given preference when opportunities for employment arose.

MODELS FOR HIGH PERFORMANCE WORKING

You should know enough about Managing People now to understand that there is no 'one best way' which is absolutely the only way to manage people. That's true, too, about High Performance Working: there is no single 'recipe' for success.

However, there is also a good deal of agreement among various writers and researchers about the elements that should go into a High Performance Working 'package'. In the vignettes which follow, we've set out the views of some of these writers/researchers, and you'll see they have a lot in common. For example, they all emphasise the importance of leadership, team-working and training (in one form or another).

In effect, too, they all would acknowledge the absolute requirement to create a sound collection of infrastructure factors and a particularly imaginative set of competitive differentiators so far as the management and leadership of people are concerned.

PROFESSOR ROBERT JOHNSTON

1   Employment Security
2   Careful Recruitment
3   Teamwork and Decentralisation
4   High Pay with an Incentive Element
5   Extensive Training
6   Narrow Status Differentials
7   Lots of Communication

PROFESSOR JOHN PURCELL

1   Opportunities for Career Growth
2   Challenging Work
3   Influence Over How the Job is Done
4   Training
5   Working in Teams
6   Sensitivity to Work-Life Balance
7   Bosses Who Show Respect
8   Managers Who Lead

PROFESSOR DAVE ULRICH

1   Talent
2   A Shared Mindset
3   Speed
4   Learning and Knowledge Management
5   Accountability
6   Collaboration
7   Leadership

BPP LEARNING MEDIA

ROGER MAITLAND (ISR)

1 Leaders Who Lead
2 Leaders Who Know How to Follow
3 Innovation
4 Putting Customers First
5 A Healthy Culture
6 Investment in People

These lists may differ on points of detail but they all agree about the fundamentals for High Performance Working:

- Strong, continuous and consistent top-down leadership based on a meaningful 'Big Idea'

- Management practices and managers that place a high value on people

- A strong orientation towards customers

- Support systems which promote people performance through appraisal, coaching and continuous development

- Employee 'voice' through involvement and engagement at all levels and in all parts of the organisation

- Strong HR systems, especially concentrating on recruitment, selection, learning, development and total reward

- Job design that encourages team-working.

Chapter Roundup

↳ High Performance Working (HPW) is a term which embraces a range of strategic, leadership, operational and employee-management methods that together can be 'bundled' into a mix that yields superior performance over a sustained period of time.

↳ The presence of HPW methods typically leads to above-average levels of profitability and corporate reputation.

↳ HPW places great emphasis on effective people management and leadership, with lots of empowerment and encouragement of 'discretionary behaviour' at the customer interface.

↳ HPW organisations tend to have relatively few hierarchical levels and therefore relatively few managers, supervisors, team leaders and other roles in which legitimised authority is exercised over individuals or teams of people.

↳ HPW enterprises are more productive, more profitable, and have a majority of customers who are 'advocates', i.e., they 'sell' the organisation and its products/services to others.

↳ HPW organisations are characterised by a strong customer orientation, a single 'Big Idea' which governs everything that happens in the organisation, a focus on self-directed learning, and leadership practices that promote high levels of employee 'engagement'.

↳ In reality there are relatively few thorough-going HPW organisations, but there are many which appear to be moving towards HPW status – through multi-skilling, a high value placed on 'soft' skills, and a welcome for mechanisms which encourage 'employee voice'.

↳ There are systematic ways in which an organisation's commitment to HPW can be evaluated, through a review of the organisation's performance and its processes.

↳ Poor-performing organisations are inclined to be cynical or dismissive about HPW.

↳ HPW initiatives require high-level initiatives consistently displayed, plus a programme of 'bundled' HRM strategies concerned with people resourcing, learning/development and performance management.

↳ At the core of HPW is the nurturing of high levels of trust within the organisation and in the organisation's relation-ships with its external stakeholders.

Quick Quiz

1   Why is High Performance Working (HPW) important in today's business climate?

2   It is claimed that high performing organisations typically adopt a joined-up approach to managing across five performance categories. What are they?

3   Sometimes an organisation has a proportion of customers who are 'Detractors'. What does this mean?

4   Why do 'Detractors' remain as customers?

5   What are the five features for a worthwhile 'Big Idea'?

6   How can you tell whether an organisation is a High Performance Working enterprise?

7   Name three reasons why some organisations have resisted the take-up of HPW.

8   Why are recruitment and selection practices so crucial to the development of a HPW culture in an organisation?

9   When employees are empowered to make decisions, they will sometimes make decisions which turn out to be mistaken or inappropriate. What should be the reaction of a manager when one of his staff is guilty of making a poor decision – or even hasn't made a decision at all?

10   Summarise seven principal features of High Performance Working.

Answers to Quick Quiz

1   High Performance Working is important because today's world is characterised by highly intensive levels of competition, technological change, escalating customer aspirations and rising employee ambitions about work.

2   The five performance categories are: customers and markets; shareholders; stakeholders; employees; and creativity and innovation.

3   'Detractors' are customers who spend a lot of their time in criticising the organisation and its products. They may be especially caustic about the levels of customer service provided, the way the organisation handles complaints, and the lack of leadership which the organisation displays.

4   'Detractor' customers may stay with an organisation because they believe that they will receive no better treatment anywhere else or with an alternative supplier; perhaps they can't go elsewhere, even if they wanted to, because there is no available competitor or because the organisation is a monopolistic supplier; sometimes the amount of business they transact with the organisation is very small and so it is not thought worthwhile to change. *This list of reasons is not exhaustive, and students may be able to think of other reasons – perhaps from their own personal experiences – why someone may remain as a customer for an organisation which is not meeting their needs or expectations.*

5   A 'good' Big Idea should be embedded, connected, enduring, collective, and measured/managed.

6   It would be necessary to scrutinise the organisation's **performance** (outputs) and also its **processes** (inputs), evaluating both against the HPW template.

7   Among the reasons why some organisations appear to resist HPW programmes are these:

  • Resistance to change

  • The belief that 'we're doing all right as we are' – sometimes reflected in the assertion that 'if it ain't broke, don't fix it'

  • Ignorance about HPW and its benefits

  • Reluctance to believe the evidence when it is presented

  • Defeatist attitudes among the organisation's senior managers

  • A refusal to accept that the ultimate 'benefits' from HPW, even if realised, would justify the 'investment' in time, effort and resources

  • Hostility towards the 'soft skills' which HPW emphasises.

8   Recruitment and selection are important because it is vital to staff the organisation with people who have positive beliefs about HPW. This is often reflected in the axiom, 'recruit for attitude, train for skill', i.e. that it is preferable for organisations to recruit employees with supportive attitudes about change and continuous improvement; it is much easier to train them in the specific skills they will need to undertake their jobs than to try to undertake radical attitude changes.

9   The proper reaction of the manager is to regard the mistake as a learning opportunity. Blaming or punishing the employee will simply ensure that mistakes are never made in the future, by the employee or anyone else, because all decision-making will be scrupulously avoided.

10 Briefly stated, the seven common features in HPW enterprises are: top-down leadership; people-centred management practices; a strong orientation towards customers; support systems that promote people performance; an employee 'voice' through involvement and engagement; strong HRM systems; and encouragement for team-working.

Answers to Activities

Activity 1

Clearly we cannot provide precise answers for this task, because much depends on the nature of the organisation which you have chosen to investigate. However, you should expect to find that a HPW organisation exhibits at least some of these features:

- A strong, universally-recognised 'Big Idea'.

- An equally strong orientation towards customers – not just satisfying their needs, but also trying to anticipate what customers are going to want next (Amazon).

- A very disciplined approach to recruitment and selection, seeking only to accept applicants who are exhibiting positive attitudes towards their own development, their teams, and their customers.

- Lots of communication – downwards, sideways and upwards, including regular feedback from customers.

- Requirements for self-directed learning and an enormous investment in training.

- A continuous-improvement and transformational-change philosophy, derived from a permanent state of dissatisfaction with current performance, no matter how good, so that questions like 'Why do we ...?' and 'Why don't we ...?' are constantly being asked.

- An eagerness to learn from external sources, including the competition and leading-edge organisations in other sectors.

- Rewards, recognition and celebrations for evidence of progress, achievement and success – by both individuals and teams.

- Managers who encourage and motivate their staff, and who treat mistakes as learning experiences rather than opportunities for recriminations and scape-goating.

- A culture of 'discretionary behaviour' and 'organisational citizenship'.

Activity 2

The range of possible causes is very large, of course. The first thing to do is to ensure that the factors you have produced are genuine causes and not merely symptoms of poor performance. For example, 'poor profitability' is a consequence of poor performance, not a cause of it.

That said, here are some likely ingredients that can generate poor performance:

- Lack of competition – which encourages complacency and indifference towards customers.

- Lack of leadership – and perhaps the presence of leaders who are more interested in themselves than in the organisations they lead.

- Lack of focus – the organisation is trying to do too much, and therefore fails to make progress.

- Lack of 'engagement' among the employees – coupled with an employee relations climate which assumes that conflict is the normal way in which organisations operate.

- Lack of proper concern for recruiting the right people – so individuals are selected solely for their technical capabilities without any attention being paid to their interpersonal competencies and collaborative skills.

- Lack of interest in the external environment – and so a failure to pay attention to competitor initiatives.

- Lack of concern for continuous improvement – coupled with a belief that 'if it ain't broke, don't fix it', i.e. if things are currently going well, we can safely assume they will continue to go well into the indefinite future.

- Lack of teamwork and singularity of purpose among the top management group – so energies are dissipated through 'political' infighting.

- Lack of any strategic vision – with the result that the organisation drifts along without any clear goals.

- Lack of concern for the organisation's people – so labour turnover is treated as an unavoidable 'fact of life', and no attempts are made to 'engage' the workforce.

Bibliography

Alfes, K., Truss, C., Soane, EC., Rees, C. & Gatenby, M. (2010) *Creating an engaged workforce: findings from the Kingston employee engagement consortium project*. London, CIPD

Armstrong, M., & Brown, D. (2006) *Strategic reward: making it happen*. London, Kogan Page

Blake, RR. & Mouton JS (1985) *The managerial grid III*. Houston: Gulf Publishing Company

Bond, S. (2003) 'How to effect changes in working hours', *People Management*, 10 July

Buckingham, M. & Coffman, C. (1991) *First Break all the Rules*. New York: Simon & Schuster

Burns, T. & Stalker GM. (1961) *The Management of Innovation*. London: Tavistock

Chowdry, H., Crawford, C., Dearden, L., Goodman, A. & Vignoles, A (2010) *Widening Participation in Higher Education: Analysis using Linked Administrative Data, Institute for Fiscal Studies W10/04*. Available at <http://www.ifs.org.uk/wps/wp1004.pdf> [accessed 24 April 2011]

Christy, G. (2010) Leadership. In G, Rees & R, French (Eds) *Leading, managing and developing people*. 3rd ed. London: CIPD

Connolly, S. & Gregory, M. (2005) *Women and work*. Available at <http://www.economics.ox.ac.uk/members/mary.gregory/Crafts.pdf> [accessed 5 April 2011]

Cutcher-Gershenfield, J. (2006) *Introduction to The Human Side of Enterprise: annotated edition*. New York: McGraw-Hill

Drucker, PF. (1988) *Management: tasks, responsibilities, practices*. Oxford: Butterworth-Heinemann

Fayol, H. (1961) *General and industrial management*. London: Pitman

Field, S., Martin, J., Miller, R., Ward, M. & Wehmeyer, M. (1998) *A practical guide for teaching self-determination. Reston, VA: Council for Exceptional Children*. Referenced at <http://smhp.psych.ucla.edu/netexchange.aspx?tag=67> [accessed 24 April 2011]

French, JRP. & Raven, BH. (1958) The bases of social power. In D, Cartwright (Ed), *Studies in social power* (pp150-167). Ann Arbor: Institute for Social Research, University of Michigan Press

Goldthorpe, JH., Lockwood, D., Bechhofer, F. & Platt, J. (1968) *The affluent worker: industrial attitudes and behaviour*. Cambridge: Cambridge University Press

Guest, D. (2006) *Smarter ways of working*. Sector Skills Development Agency. Available at <http://www.thesmartworkcompany.com/pdf/DGHPW.pdf> [accessed 3 May 2011]

Hackman, JR. & Oldham, GR. (1980) *Work redesign*. Boston: Addison-Wesley Publishing Company

Harris, HR. (2000) Britain's Demographic Changes: 1971-2031, *Contemporary Review*. Available at <http://findarticles.com/p/articles/mi_m2242/is_1613_276/ai_63668439/> [accessed 3 April 2011]

Hersey, P. & Blanchard, KH. (1988) *Management of organisational behaviour: utilizing human resources*, Englewood Cliffs: Prentice-Hall

Higgs, M. (2006) *The emerging significance of total reward management as a strategy for building employee engagement*, Henley Research Note HRN 2006 04. Henley-on-Thames: Henley Management College

Huczynski, AA. & Buchanan, DA. (2007) *Organizational behaviour*. Harlow: Pearson Education Limited

Johnson, G., Scholes, K. & Whittington, R. (2008), *Exploring corporate strategy*. 8th ed. Harlow: Pearson Education Limited

Johnston, R. & Clark, G. (2008) *Service operations management: improving service delivery*. 3rd ed. Harlow: Pearson Education Limited

Kempner, T. (1987) *Penguin Management Handbook*. Harmondworth: Penguin Books

Likert, R. (1961) *New patterns of management*. New York: McGraw-Hill

Maslow, AH. (1943) A theory of human motivation. *Psychological Review*. 50,4, pp 370-396,

McGregor D. (1957) The human side of enterprise. In *Adventure in Thought and Action*, Proceedings of the Fifth Anniversary Convocation of the School of Industrial Management, Massachusetts Institute of Technology, Cambridge. Cambridge, MA: MIT School of Industrial Management

McGregor, D. (1960) *The Human Side of Enterprise*. New York: McGraw-Hill

Mullins, LJ. (2007) *Management and organisational behaviour*. 8th ed. Harlow: Pearson Education Limited

Paton, G. (2008) Failure to teach three Rs 'damaging economy'. *The Telegraph*, 18 Jan

Peters, TJ. & Waterman, RH. (2004) *In Search of Excellence*. London: Profile Books Limited

Purcell, J., Kinnie, N. & Hutchinson, S. (2003) Inside the black box. *People Management,* 15 May

Rayner, C. & Adam-Smith, D. (2009) *Managing and leading people*. 2nd ed. London: CIPD

Rees, G. & French, R. (Eds) (2010) *Leading, managing and developing people*. 3rd ed. London: CIPD

Roethlisberger, FJ. & Dickson, WJ. (1939) *Management and the worker*. Cambridge MA: Harvard University Press

Schein, E. (2006) Foreword. In D. McGregor, *The Human Side of Enterprise: annotated edition*. New York: McGraw-Hill

Sung, J. & Ashton, D. (2005) *High performance work practices: linking strategy and skills to performance outcomes.* London: Department of Trade and Industry

Tannenbaum, R. & Schmidt, WH. (1973) How to choose a leadership pattern. *Harvard Business Review*. May-June 1973

Taylor, FW. (1911) *Shop management*. Available at Project Gutenberg <http://www.gutenberg.org/cache/epub/6464/pg6464.html> [accessed 22 April 2011]

Torrington, D., Hall, L., Taylor, S. & Atkinson, C. (2009) *Fundamentals of Human Resource Management*. Harlow: Prentice Hall/FT

Tymon, A. & Mackay, M. (2010) Developing employees. In G, Rees & R, French (Eds), *Leading, managing and developing people*. 3rd ed. London: CIPD

Worthington, I. (2009a) The political environment. In: I, Worthington and C, Britton (Eds), *The Business Environment*. 6th ed. Harlow: Pearson Education Limited

Worthington, I. (2009b) The macroeconomic environment. In: I, Worthington and C, Britton (Eds), *The Business Environment*. 6th ed. Harlow: Pearson Education Limited

Index